JUST
ENOUGH
ROPE

JUST ENOUGH ROPE

AN INTIMATE MEMOIR

Joan Braden

VILLARD BOOKS

NEW YORK

1989

Grateful acknowledgment is made to Marie Brown Associates,
as agent for the NAACP, for permission to
reprint excerpts from "Little Old Lady in Lavender Silk" by Dorothy Parker and
for permission to use the title
from Enough Rope by Dorothy Parker.
Copyright © Estate of Dorothy Parker/The National Association
for the Advancement of Colored People (NAACP)

LIBRARY OF CONGRESS CATALOGING-IN-PUBLICATION DATA
Braden, Joan.
Just enough rope : an intimate memoir / by Joan Braden.
p.   cm.
ISBN 0-394-57458-3
1. Braden, Joan.   2. Public relations consultants—Washington
(D.C.)—Biography.   3. Washington (D.C.)—Biography.   4. Washington
(D.C.)—Social life and customs—1951–   5. United States–Politics
and government—1945–   I. Title.
F199.B77   1989   89-5757
973.92'092—dc20

Designed by Beth Tondreau Design/Gabrielle Hamberg
Manufactured in the United States of America
9   8   7   6   5   4   3   2
First Edition

For Tom Braden,
and for David, Mary, Joannie,
Susan, Nancy, Elizabeth, Tommy, and Nicholas,
our children, whom we have brought up,
fed, educated, fought with, and loved.

ACKNOWLEDGMENTS

———◆———

To be at once enthusiastic yet critical, imaginative yet meticulous, encouraging yet exacting is difficult. My editor, Diane Reverand, performed the difficult and in the course of performing it became my friend. Without her, *Just Enough Rope* would never have been completed.

And without my great friend Robert Bernstein, I would never have met Diane and the book would never have had the title. Without his intimate knowledge of Dorothy Parker's work, I would not have known that she had entitled a series of poems *Enough Rope,* nor would I have read her anthology, from which I have borrowed excerpts from her poem "Little Old Lady in Lavender Silk."

This book is mostly about men for reasons that I hope will be clear, but I want to thank my friends Irena Kirkland, Mollie Parnis, Susan Brinkley, Joanne Bross, Danielle Gardner, Lesley Stahl, Jean Smith, Patricia Bradshaw, Nancy Dickerson, my secretary, Jean Oh, and the late Beatrice Watkins for being patient and encouraging, and for standing by.

I also express my thanks to June Reid for typing and retyping and re-retyping my manuscript.

CONTENTS

———•———

——•——

The Great Green Glob

I decided to write a book about myself and what I've seen in a number of years of living because whenever I tell a new friend or acquaintance a story about what I've seen or done, the new friend or acquaintance expresses astonishment.

Why astonishment? Because, I suppose, I'm so average. Average looks, average intelligence, average background, average education, average ambition. And yet I've seen and done things and known people the average person does not get to see or know, and have gone places where the average person does not get to go.

And it occurred to me that quite apart from the usefulness of sorting out experience for my own education, and quite apart from such elucidation as my children might derive from the story of their average mother, other women who think of themselves as average—and most of us do—might learn from me that they too can go places, see things, and be a close witness to the times they live in, if they really want to.

It's a difficult balancing act that we women perform, balancing our jobs, our lives with our husbands, our lives with our children, our lives with our friends, and not most difficult but peculiarly difficult, our lives with friends who are men. Tom Braden, who is my husband, tried to describe his own balancing act in his book and in the television series *Eight Is Enough*, but I don't think he ever stated in so many words the real secret of the balancing act.

Which is that you really have to want to make it work, want to make it balance and try to make it balance. I was going to try to do that, and I was just about ready to get to work on the project when something happened that made me stop. I had talked to an agent because people told me that if you want to publish a book, it is wise to have an agent sell it to publishers. I had hired someone to write what is called a book proposal because the agent said that the book proposal, if it is sufficiently promotional, is what sells the book to publishers.

Then something happened. What happened was that excerpts from the book proposal were published in the *Washington Post,* and not only in the *Washington Post* but also in newspapers in Los Angeles, Chicago, New York, and London. Yes, London.

And that the excerpts were sufficiently tasteless as to border on vulgarity. They were embarrassing, deeply embarrassing.

Jackie Onassis called me. She was upset. She didn't want to read about Dallas again.

I got a handwritten note from the former chairman of New

York's Republican party: "You have disgraced the memory of Nelson Rockefeller."

People I had long regarded as friends suddenly appeared in the guise of guardians of the public morality. When I greeted them at gatherings, public and private, they bared their front teeth in an obligatory smile as they passed on. The *Washington Post* headlined its article, KISS AND SELL?

So what was I to do? Go to bed for a month? Hide in another place? Try to pretend I had never proposed to write this book?

But I had proposed to write this book. True, I had not realized that the proposal for the book would be circulated to so many publishers in Manhattan. And I failed to take account of copying machines. I had not realized that everybody in every publisher's office could, if they chose, make copies of the proposal and distribute them to their friends on weekends at the beach. Or that so many of them would so choose.

I had been naïve. I had not thought that a mere proposal for a book was very important. The book was important. But the proposal for the book? I had talked into a tape recorder, remembering a whole lot of things, and the writer had put some of this into the proposal. Stupidly, I hadn't even read it carefully. After all, the proposal was only a suggestion: Here are some of the things I remember. Would they make a book?

But now the proposal had turned into a monster. And I had turned into a courtesan—a brainless courtesan at that—who lived for the sole purpose of making herself attractive to men.

"Well," I said to myself, "you've been through this once before." The memory of "once before" drifted slowly into consciousness—a nauseating haze, a great green glob with bright green tentacles reaching out from a dark green center, the center hiding something darker, a dark green turning to black at the core, black at the depth, pulsing out headlines. As I recalled them, they leered at me anew: SEX SYMBOL GETS STATE DEPARTMENT PLUM. TOP APPOINTMENT GOES TO ROCKEFELLER, KISSINGER "FRIEND." DID HENRY KNOW?

"Yes," I said to myself, "I've been through all this before and I came out all right, and this time I'm not going to get sick about it. I'm going to take the advice of my husband. He's not always right, but he told me the great green glob would dissipate. I remembered his amused smile as he quoted Winston Churchill: "Leave it to time, that healer of all." Anyhow, he had been right. The great green glob was nothing now, an old memory. So I said to him when the book proposal hit the headlines, "What do you think I ought to do?"

And he said, "Joannie, you haven't written a book. You've just talked about writing a book. And the talk hit the newspapers, and it didn't come out the way you wanted it to come out or the way, in fact, it was. But that's because it was only talk. If you want to tell what really happened, and what really was, you have to write the book. *You.*"

So I did.

JUST ENOUGH ROPE

Just Enough Rope

Nancy is in a tree. Not under it, in it. It is a maple tree, and it is the fall of the year, so the maple is golden and red with just a faint touch of summer's green. People drive hundreds of miles to see such trees in splendor, but I have a picture of one of them with Nancy in it, clad in blue jeans. She has blond hair, oval face, blue eyes. She is laughing.

Nancy is my fourth daughter. She arrived as a baby too soon for her sister Susan to have much time to be a baby—ten months apart. If you think it hurt Susan not to have much time to be a baby, you ought to see Susan. I have a picture of her, too, in a green sweater from Dartmouth with a varsity *D*. She was on the tennis team at Dartmouth. She still looks as though she were on the tennis team.

I wanted eight children and I got them. I wanted to go to the Black and White Ball. That was Truman Capote's famous party for Katharine Graham in New York's Plaza Hotel ballroom. People who weren't invited to the Black and White Ball were badly hurt. Once I met a woman who said to me, "Why do you think I went to Acapulco? I had to get out of New York. I wasn't invited to the Black and White Ball."

But I got to go. Tom didn't want to go. He'd just come home from Vietnam as a reporter for the small daily newspaper we owned in California, and he'd never heard of the Black and White Ball.

"I won't fly all the way across the country to go to a dance." That's what he said.

But I showed him the letter from Mrs. Longworth, saying, "I do not think it advisable to wear a dress with pink in it to a Black and White Ball."

And the telegram from Joseph Alsop: DARLING, NO PINK.

I hid the pink with a black velvet sash, and I scorched the dress trying to press it, so I hid the scorch too.

We did fly all the way across the country, bucking winds and hail, and I nearly cried when the pilot announced we might have to spend the night in Pittsburgh. That plane was four hours late and the party was almost over when we arrived. Even so we had a wonderful time. I got there. I got to go.

I have a picture of Joannie. That's my second daughter. The one Tom is reminded of whenever he hears the overture to *The Barber of Seville*. He puts on the record in the morning, and once I said, "Why are you playing the overture to the *Barber of Seville* again?"

He replied, "It reminds me of Joannie. There's a repeated phrase that skips along like Joannie does."

Anyhow, my picture is not a real picture but a mental one. It is Joannie on the telephone from Middlebury, Vermont, where she is taking a graduate course in Spanish. She is failing, so she told Tom a week ago. She was in tears and said, "I can't do it, Dad, I just can't. I try and try and I can't."

Tom was talking to a world-renowned psychiatrist at dinner later that night at Joseph Alsop's house and he asked the psychiatrist what he should do.

The psychiatrist told him plainly. "It is wrong for a parent to force a child, and your daughter is still a child, into certain failure. She was asking for help. Call her and tell her not to take the final examination. She can do that some other time."

So Tom called her and told her what the psychiatrist had said, and added as his own opinion that it was nearly always better to try. So here she was on the telephone, a joyous proud voice bubbling. "You know what, Mom, I got an *A*. Can you *believe* it, I got an *A*."

I also got to go to the White House for the dinner for Pablo Casals, the one where President Kennedy rose and faced the guests seated before him in black ties and lovely gowns and said, as he looked out at the throng, that there hadn't been so much intellectual power in one room at the White House "since Thomas Jefferson dined alone."

Tom didn't want to go to the White House either. Can you imagine not wanting to go to the Pablo Casals dinner?

"Look, Joannie, it's a small newspaper and it's barely in the black. I can't afford to fly across the country to go to a dinner." But he was excited and charmed nevertheless and glad we had done it.

There were tables of ten for the Casals dinner at the White House. I think it was the first time anybody at the White House had broken up a dinner party in this way since, well, maybe ever. But Jackie did. She made it intimate and friendly and, though formal, informal.

I have a picture of Tom with Mary, my oldest daughter, who was born with her right foot turned outward. Tom is sitting on the back porch of a house in Washington, D.C., rubbing Mary's foot inward. I don't have a real picture of that scene because I got to go with Nelson Rockefeller to Venezuela, but I have a mental picture. Tom came home every noon to rub Mary's foot. The foot turned out fine; it's a straight foot.

I have a picture of Elizabeth, my youngest daughter, the one with red hair. I'd been attending meetings at the National Institutes of Health in Bethesda, Maryland, because I'd been appointed to the advisory board by the secretary of health, education, and welfare, and I learned about cerebral palsy. A child with cerebral palsy can't hold its head up straight. That's a danger sign, so the doctors told the advisory board at a lecture. And here I was back in Oceanside, California, holding Elizabeth's head. She was a tiny baby in a white nightgown who I held out at arm's length while I stood in the hall outside our bedroom, and Elizabeth's head fell forward. I did it again and again. Her head fell forward again and again. I got into bed and, crying softly, told Tom I thought Elizabeth had cerebral palsy. His response was terse, probably to calm me. "Okay, Joannie, if she has cerebral palsy there's nothing we can do about it. We'll take her to Dr. Harvey in the morning," and he turned over. With that I moved far over to my side of the bed and cried the rest of the night.

So we went to see Dr. Harvey early the next morning, and he held Elizabeth out at arm's length and said, "Of course her head falls forward; she's a tiny baby. She doesn't have enough strength in her neck to keep her head from falling forward. You've been attending too many lectures. I'm going to give you some sleeping pills." Elizabeth is grown up now. She learned to speak fluent Italian because she liked the sound of Italian. She holds her head straight up, and with all that flaming red hair she should.

I got to go to Africa when I worked for the Save the Children Federation, and I got to go to Japan and to China and to India with Jackie Kennedy, and I haven't even mentioned the boys. I have three boys, one of them a fisherman, who can whip a line high in the air so fast that it makes a sound and then drops a fly silently in a distant, quiet pool. That's David, who was my first child; and then there's Tommy, who was my seventh. I have a real picture of myself (Tom took it) getting into a car outside our house in California on my way to the hospital to have a baby. And there are six children, one in the arms of a baby sitter, lined up to say good-bye, and all of them have their arms in the air and all of them are holding up crossed fingers. That's because after David I had five girls, and even Tom, when Elizabeth was born, said she looked just like the last one. So the crossed fingers were for a boy; and when a boy was born, Tom didn't wait to discuss a name. "I know what we'll name him. We'll name him after me." Tommy is a reporter on a newspaper now.

And I had Nicholas, my youngest child. I carry in my head a picture of Nicholas being dressed by his sisters for his first day at school. They put on his socks and his trousers and his shirt and they tied his shoe laces, and Nicholas never complained. He went right through the whole procedure without a murmur. Tom and I said to each other that evening that Nicholas had matured faster than any of the other children.

But the next morning when it was time to get Nicholas dressed for school, I thought there was a bobcat loose in the house. Nicholas was screaming in anger and his face was bright red and he fought off one sister after another sister, lying on his back on his bed, kicking his legs in the air so that they couldn't possibly put his socks on. When I had quieted him Tom explained to him about going to school, and Nicholas began to sob again and through the sobs we got the message. "I went to school. I've already been to school. And now you want me to do it again?"

Nicholas finished college last year.

I'm proud of my eight children and proud of myself for having them. I wanted every one of them, and in between having them I've worked at a lot of jobs and seen a good deal of the world. I've worked for Nelson Rockefeller. I've worked for Oveta Culp Hobby. I've worked for Robert Kennedy. I've worked for Henry Kissinger. I've worked for the American Petroleum Institute and Charles Di Bona. I've worked for Save the Children Federation. I've worked as a reporter on television, and I've worked as hostess on a television talk show. In the course of work I've learned a whole lot about people and what's important about people.

The most important thing about them is that they're there. I always want to know them. I always want to meet them. I always find something interesting in them. I'm what the psychologists call "outer directed." I can't do anything without showing some person what I've done, without being able to seek his or her approval or criticism, without the fun and excitement of doing something or going somewhere with somebody.

So I've had Nelson Rockefeller as a friend as well as a boss and Henry Kissinger as a friend as well as a boss and Kirk and Anne Douglas as friends, Robert McNamara as a friend, and George Shultz, Stewart Alsop and his wife, Tish, and Nancy Kissinger, Joseph Alsop, John and Robert Kennedy, Mrs. Longworth, and Oveta Hobby, and I've learned something from all of them: taste and wisdom and humor and bearing and gracefulness. And if I haven't emulated them well, at least I tried to emulate them and know they are worth emulating.

When I feel sick or even when I am sick, if somebody says, You're invited to dinner, then suddenly I don't feel sick, even when I am sick. I always want to go. I might meet somebody. I might learn something. So I nearly always do go. Mrs. Longworth used to say, "Joannie, we're just alike. Like old war-horses, we feel we should stay at home, but once there our spirits rise and we enter into the party with all the zest of a teenager."

I was thinking about all these things I have had—the children, the friends, the jobs, the pictures, the getting to go—I was thinking about them because I wanted my book to say that other women could have all these things too. Then it occurred to me that some women couldn't because they don't have enough rope. That is to say their husbands hold them back, or they hold themselves back. If staying at home makes their husbands happy and makes them happy, they deserve equal stature with those women who choose to work. The important thing is that it be a joint decision and that each person bring an equal share to marriage.

My husband, Tom Braden, has given me a lot of rope. Sometimes he thinks it's been too much rope and he's refused to let the line out any further. Sometimes I've complained and sometimes when I've complained, he's let it out a little further. But sometimes he has not yielded at all and has pulled the rope tight, so I can't go any further without breaking a rope I don't want to break. You pay a price, obviously, if the rope is too tight because with a tight rope you don't get to go. You pay a price if you get too much rope because then you feel guilty. But then, no life is perfect. On the whole, I've always had just enough rope.

"*Time to Prepare a Face*"

My daughter Susan went off on a long bicycle trip last summer and found herself overnight in the town of Anderson, Indiana. Reflecting that her mother had grown up in that town and remembering scraps of family history she had heard at dinner table conversations, she went to the Anderson Banking Company, walked up to the lady at the desk marked by the sign "New Accounts," and asked whether that lady had ever heard of a man named Jesse L. Vermillion.

The lady answered, "He was the founder of our bank." Then having overcome her shyness, Susan explained that she was the great-granddaughter of the bank's founder. Whereupon, she was ushered upstairs to shake hands with officers of the bank, none of whom was old enough to remember Jesse L. Vermillion. "But," as she told me later with pride in her voice that made me feel proud too, "they all knew who he was."

I wish I remembered more about my grandfather than who he was. I know what he looked like because there is an oil painting of him somewhere about the house: a big man, slightly rotund, with full cheeks, a short, neatly clipped moustache, and slightly narrowed, sharp eyes.

It was "who he was" that counted for me when I was a little girl in Anderson, Indiana; and for my mother and father, this affected their lives in ways which he did not intend. Jesse L. Vermillion was power. He was affluence. He was rectitude. And for me, his name still conjures up a twinge of shame.

Jesse L. Vermillion owned the bank. He had a street named after him. He also owned the big house on the corner, and often sent my grandmother and my mother and me on the long train ride to Carlsbad, California, for a "winter vacation."

When the Depression came and other banks folded, Jesse L. Vermillion's bank kept its doors open, paying cash to the long lines of customers who wanted their money, paying every day during banking hours until the lines of customers who wanted their money faded away.

In the town of Anderson, Indiana, that was reason enough to earn a reputation for power, affluence, and rectitude. But in the smaller circle of the Vermillion family, there was another reason why grandfather stood on a pedestal, right-minded, upstanding, free of sin: Grandfather was not a drunk. And my father was.

"Now, Ed, we're almost there now. That's it. Home free. Get him a little over to the right, Charlie. Now, Ed, we'll lay you right down on the bed and you sleep it off. Evening, Mary. Evening, little girl. Your father's had just one too many. Just one, eh, Ed? And Ed's gonna be all right in the morning. Aren't you, Ed?"

I don't know who the speaker was. I remember big men holding my father upright, steering him toward the bedroom or sometimes big men holding him prone, one man at the shoulders and one man on each leg, walking backward toward the bedroom and placing him faceup on the bed while Mother stood in the middle of the living room and said thank you and cried.

My father was a big man, too, and good-looking, with thick black curly hair which turned white when he was still quite young. He had huge eyes, that, as I recall, were mischievous and lively early on but later turned placid, accepting, almost bovine. A farm boy from New Albany, Indiana, who came from a family of preacher-farmers, he had worked his way through college and law school by pitching on weekends, using an alias, for Louisville's triple A baseball team, but he wasn't good enough to make a career of it. When he got out of law school and married my mother, he made the mistake of his life. He went to work for his father-in-law at the Anderson Banking Company.

For generations, Americans have known that this is a mistake. The knowledge that it is a mistake gets passed down from grandparents to parent to child. And yet we continue to make the mistake, watching as feelings of inferiority, weakness, and jealousy take hold upon the one who got the job and feelings of suspicion, misplaced trust, and disappointment take hold upon the one who gave it.

We know, in short, that it almost never works. Sometimes a man can work for his father, though not without more pain than is usual in relations between an employee and a boss. But with a son-in-law, "never" is the right word. And yet we go right on doing it. We ought to stop.

Long after Grandfather died and we had moved from Anderson and my father had gone back to being a lawyer and stopped being a drunk, it was possible to discern that he had once been a drunk by a certain softness in him, a lack of conviction, a too easy tendency to say, "Well, that's all right with me," when he should have said the opposite. He lacked forcefulness. He felt defeated.

That's another thing we Americans have ignored. We talk about the dangers of alcoholism and we say to alcholics, "just stop." We are right to do so. But what we don't tell them is that even after they've stopped, they'll be scarred. I never knew a man who had stopped being a drunk who didn't have scars for a long time.

Some of my father's, I suppose, came from his having had to declare bankruptcy. Some scars must have come from his having had to move out of his own house—the white house he had just built and which had been pictured, to the admiration of everybody in Anderson, in *Better Homes and Gardens.* He had moved from that house into Grandfather's big house, installing his family on the top floor of what was big enough to be a mansion, though it lacked the finery associated with that name. There were scars from other causes. My mother bore him a second child, a son who lived just long enough to be named after him.

Maybe, for all I knew, some of the scars came from the crushing realization after Grandfather's death that although Jesse L. Vermillion was a rich man by Anderson standards, he was not all that rich—not rich enough to endow four children, including my mother, for the rest of their lives.

Perhaps I do my father an injustice. He was a poor boy who went off to school and married a banker's daughter and never came home again. Not once, as far as I know, did he ever take me or my mother to visit his own family back in New Albany. Maybe he was ashamed that he was ashamed.

Nor do I know of all the everyday things, the jealousies, suspicions, the failures to satisfy which may have marked the relations between himself and my grandfather and the years between marrying the banker's daughter and becoming a bankrupt drunk.

I do know that I loved my father very much. Whenever I went anywhere outside Anderson—to California with Mother and Grandmother or later to college—my father always took me to the train and always I cried. Always, he would buy a return ticket, and put it in my purse or my pocket and always say, "Now, if you don't like it, you just go right to the train station and here's your ticket, and you can come home to me." I loved my father very much, and he loved me.

But what happened to him during those years in Anderson must be the reason why I put Anderson out of my mind and out of my life, why I don't remember anything about Anderson. I mean the kind of things that other people remember about the towns and the people where they grew up. I don't remember teachers or school friends or play places.

And yet I learned a very important thing from Anderson, Indiana. I learned to pretend. Now pretending is a useful skill. To pretend that things are all right when you can't do anything about them anyhow is something many children must learn to do. I learned it well, and my grandfather and grandmother, my mother and father, my aunt and uncle all helped me. In order to pretend, you have to not notice and you have to forget. I pretended and didn't notice and forgot that my father was a drunk, that my mother had told me once in the security of the bathroom that she was going to divorce him, that we had had to move out of our new house and that other kids had come to watch us move.

And in order to pretend that everything is fine, you have to smile and say hello. I mean that quite literally. I learned to smile at strangers when I passed them on the street and to say hello to them when I met them in the candy store. I learned to compliment people on the sweaters they were wearing if I thought the sweater was a good-looking sweater. I learned to say good morning to elevator operators, to the man or woman behind the counter, to the porters at hotels, to the school janitor (a huge man in overalls who was standing in the hall armed with a large wrench), to the teacher when I entered the classroom, and to the girl or boy in the next seat.

I say I "learned" it. I don't remember anybody teaching me. But it was part of pretending, and I've done it ever since until now; it's second nature. And it's surprising what smiling and saying hello will do for you. People like it. Sometimes they are startled but they soon recover and they smile and say hello right back. Sometimes I've made good friends. Sometimes I've learned things I would otherwise not have learned. Sometimes it leads to getting to know people I soon found I didn't want to know.

But it was a good thing to have learned. I recommend it. I think now that I smile and say hello because I'm a person and the person I pass on the street or sit next to on the airplane is a person, and we inhabit for a moment an adjoining space in the same world and we might as well smile and say hello.

The real reason goes back to Anderson, Indiana, where I made up my mind that everything was going to be all right—that I was just fine and my family was just fine, and that my father would get home that night and he would be just fine, and that I was going to get away from Anderson where everything had the aura of defeat about it and I was going to succeed at something and that if I didn't succeed, I was going to pretend to succeed.

It didn't work out that way. The Briargate College (let us say Briargate) of my day was a finishing school which pretended not to be. I don't know why my family chose it for me. Because it was "nice," I suppose, and in the country and good for little girls. I suppose my grandfather paid for it, though I went there about the time that he died, and that may have been the reason that I didn't have a horse.

The important thing at Briargate was to have a horse. There were classes, of course, and a degree to be earned, but if you didn't have a horse, you didn't count for much. That may have been why Anne Johnson, who also didn't have a horse, chose my room in which to sit upon the radiator.

There she was, after the first class in the morning, sitting on the radiator in my room and crying, an oval-faced seventeen-year-old with breasts too large, even for her chubby face, and big thick legs. I said, "Anne, what's wrong?"

I said that to her several times because, apart from the fact that she didn't have a horse, I couldn't see any reason for crying. I didn't have a horse and I wasn't crying.

So finally she told me, amid sobs, that she wanted to menstruate and that she hadn't menstruated for more than two months and that her roommate had told her to sit on radiators. So here she was in my room, sitting on the radiator with a guilty knowledge and praying that the knowledge was not important and that the fear was an unfounded fear.

Horrible things can happen inside well-tailored, neatly clipped places. Briargate was well tailored and neatly clipped. Anne looked out the window at the rolling countryside—green grass sweeping away down to the trees beyond—and I thought that she might as well have been in an alleyway off a city street and in the dark of night because all that mattered to her was inside, and what was inside that really mattered was fear.

Briargate got rid of chubby, big-breasted Anne Johnson and did it properly, according to the tradition of the institution: with candles.

The entire school was assembled at one end of what was called the quad, an area of grass surrounded by buildings with a graveled walkway all around the grass and with a graveled walkway also through the center so that you could split a procession to march on each side of the quad, join at the far end, and then march in double file up the middle and stand in front of the assembly.

Which is what twenty-four black-robed members of the senior council did on that evening in the dim twilight, while the student body stood in silence, waiting.

They had met and heard the evidence presented by the dean, confronted poor Anne Johnson, and now the ceremony was carried out and the sentence imposed.

The twenty-four council members stood before us, and an appointed member made a long ceremony of lighting the candle which each council member held in her hand. Then they separated into two groups—one going to the left and one to the right—and then marched slowly in single file down the paths at each side of the quad until they came together at the gravel walk in the distance. There they formed a double line and came slowly toward us down the middle path and were at length standing again before us, a single line of faces, each lit by a candle. It was solemn and still and portentous.

When the line was straight, the president of the council stepped forward and broke the stillness. The senior council had met. The conduct of Anne Johnson was unbecoming a Briargate girl. The penalty: expulsion.

Awful, in the exact sense of the word. Scary, frightening, and doomlike. I never saw Anne Johnson again. I made up my mind that night that as soon as possible, I would never see Briargate again. And I never have.

THREE

•

The Renunciation of the Halo

I'm almost ashamed to admit this. It makes me feel a little guilty, a little out of it, a little as if I were standing before a judge and heard the words distinctly pronounced: "The defendant failed to assert her rights."

I suppose we all failed to assert our rights, at least most of my generation—the ones who graduated from college or went to work during the mid-forties.

But you see—and this is the thing I'm almost ashamed to admit—I never wanted to be a CEO. It never occurred to me to fight my way to the top in business or industry, to push and please, to carve, claw, and connive, to get on top, to command legions, plan futures, chart new courses, decide on new products and policies. Not that I thought I was incapable. Far from it. The reason that I went to Northwestern, aside from the fact that I wanted to get away from Briargate, the reason I majored in economics and got high grades and worked hard for them was that I knew I was capable.

Then why am I a little ashamed to admit that I never aspired to be a CEO? Because I now live in the world of 1989, and in 1989 women do so aspire and some of them make it. Everyone among us, except perhaps those who qualify for the status of genius, is a product of his or her times. In 1944, a female graduate of Northwestern did not aspire to be a CEO.

You can look it up. In 1944, there were no women among corporate America's executive officers. In all the United States, then populated with 150 million people, there were 2500 women lawyers, 8100 women doctors, 15 women architects, and 9 women engineers. There were, in that year, no women in the building trade unions and few women in police forces. There is no record of any women on the bench.

It was a man's world. I accepted the fact. I didn't protest, think it wrong, organize, or parade. So, to correct myself, it wasn't so much that I never wanted to be a CEO as that it simply never occurred to me. On the other hand, I also graduated into a world where women were just beginning to revolt against sainthood. Maybe I can say that in this respect, I was at least in the forefront of my generation. Because I knew, in 1944, that I did not wish to become a saint.

In the world into which I graduated all women were candidates for sainthood. Our grandmothers had been saints, and we had watched our mothers become saints. They were so pronounced by their husbands, and when they died the pronouncement was solemnly agreed to by all the bereaved.

That was the moment, among others, when husbands

paused to reflect upon their own struggles and careers, when it occurred to them that their wives had taken it all in good spirit, had not complained very much, and sometimes had actually helped in the struggle, and perhaps deserved a share of the laurels of victory.

Therefore, these wives and mothers could justly be characterized as saints. They had taken the moves from one town to another; they had accepted the household drudgery, the dishes, the diapers, the poker games at the Elks' Lodge, the drunken bouts with old friends, the affairs with the office secretary. They had taken it for years, had seldom complained, and had asked over the years only the most polite and discreet of questions. "You know, when I think sometimes of what I put that woman through, well, there you are, she's a saint."

My own mother was a saint. Tested, tried, and sanctified. But she got to wear the halo my father fixed around her memory and the incense with which he mentally anointed her only after she was dead. I was witness to many years of my mother's trial for the status of sainthood. In Anderson, Indiana, I saw all the other women trying out for the halo, and I knew very early that I did not ever wish to wear it.

Although I don't actually remember framing the situation in my mind when I graduated from college, the situation was framed for all the women of my generation. They did not aspire to be CEOs. But they did not want to be saints. That was the frame.

There followed an inevitable question. You could pretend to ignore the question, but you knew it was there. You knew when you decided after college to go home and live with Mother and Dad or get a job or marry a man or not marry a man that you were answering the question. And the question was, how do I get along in a man's world without becoming a saint?

The answer to that question is that you joined it. You joined the man's world, not as a matter of right, which is what my daughters do, but by intruding upon it in a fashion my mother's generation would have regarded as unladylike and my grandmother would simply not have recoginzed at all. But for my generation, the only way to join the man's world was to intrude upon it, and I remember the day I did it.

It was long before I graduated in economics from Northwestern, and I think it came about because I had been queen of Washington and Lee's annual Spring Holiday, chosen by representatives of the all-male student body from among the girls who flocked into Lexington for the weekend to meet their dates and go to parties at fraternity houses and to the big senior class dance on Saturday night. All I can recall about my reign as queen is that I smiled a lot and had my picture taken with a crown on my head, looked bright-eyed at the members of the queen's court, and smiled some more.

I had a lot of curly brown hair and a perfectly respectable figure, which is to say that I looked fine in a sweater and skirt, and I had freckles and smiled. I think it was the smile that did it. But the real prize for the honor of queenship was my coming out party, my meeting with the world of men, of power, and what seemed to me riches. It took place in a private railroad car on the way to the Kentucky Derby.

My husband has often asked me who won the Kentucky Derby that year. "Was it Count Fleet? Was it Lawrin? Was it Whirlaway?" He asks me because he remembers the names of those horses and, if I could tell him who the winner was, he could look it up and determine the year in which I joined the world of men.

But I cannot remember the name of the horse, and it doesn't matter. So he says that I won the Kentucky Derby that year and won it against generational odds. My husband is a journalist and likes to make up what he calls "leads." He puts my story this way as he recites it in stentorian tones to the children at the dinner table.

"An obscure filly from a dirt farm sprang suddenly from the pack this gloriously sunny afternoon and was ahead by a length at the wire to win the Kentucky Derby in near record time. The name of the horse was Joan and the odds were nine to one."

Nine generations of women in America, as he figures it, who hadn't butted in on male conversations as I had, and so he makes up the odds and recites his "leads" before I am finished with the story and I say, "Stop it," and refuse to go on.

But the children know the story anyhow, and they know the moral of the story is to ask questions and participate in the conversation taking place around you.

I got to go in the private railroad car because I had been the queen and my date was a redheaded boy from Indianapolis, which was a big city, and his last name was Lilly. I don't know now, and I don't think I knew then, whether he was the son of Eli Lilly, who owned the largest pharmaceutical firm in the country or whether he was the nephew of Eli Lilly. At any rate, my mother and all the people of Anderson considered him to be a very important date. He was extremely kind and pleasant to me. There were a lot of older men in the car, and some of their wives were there too, but the women sat in silence and so did the redheaded boy. As we took our seats I began to listen to their conversation.

They were speaking of things I had never heard of, and they used phrases that I did not fully understand: "gross profit," "ex-dividend," "cost paring," "marginal account." Instead of keeping quiet, which the wives of the men and the redheaded boy did, and which I suppose a college freshman taking the trip for the honor might be expected to do, I asked what the words meant. I wanted to know; I wanted to participate in the conversation. I wanted to have an opinion, as they did.

And so I said, "Pardon me, but I couldn't help overhearing, what do you mean when you say, 'the danger of staring at the gross profit figure'?"

The man to whom I addressed the question did not seem to be offended, and the man to whom he had been talking was not offended either. They both put down their cigars and they looked at me in my plaid skirt and sweater and they explained. They seemed very glad to explain. They gave me instances and examples, and the examples reminded them of stories about people who didn't count their costs. They were real stories. Some of them were amusing and some were sad, all gave rise to more questions from me and pretty soon I was the center of attention in the private car, each man vying with the next to explain and illustrate.

I was not putting on a show. I really wanted to know and they really wanted to tell me, and the train ride became exciting and funny and informative and everybody had a good time, especially me. I don't think I was the only one who was surprised when the train got to the Kentucky Derby nor the only one who was a little sorry when we had to get off.

I learned to be bold enough to ask questions and to listen to the answers. I learned that people like to be asked questions and to tell the answers and that in a crowd of men, a simple question, if it's honestly intended and the questioner really wants to know, can start a flow of conversation which is virtually unceasing and people have a great time.

Once having learned this, I have never forgotten it. It has seen me through many unexpected occasions and many might-have-been-awkward times. Some people look around a crowded room to see who is there. I never do. I ask a question of whomever I happen to be standing near, and I always ask a question to which I want to know the answer. The person to whom I am speaking stops looking around the crowded room and talks to me. Others are attracted to what appears to be an interesting conversation, and pretty soon they are conversing too.

So what do you do in a man's world? First, you intrude upon it. Then you join it. That's what I did to the world of Nelson Rockefeller.

Nelson

*I*nstinct is stored experience, ready to be used when it's needed. I didn't need that experience from the private railroad car until much later, when I was looking out the window of my mother and father's apartment on East 70th Street in New York City where they had been living since I went to college. I remember one day I sat and looked out the window for a long, long time. I thought about what I was doing and I decided—maybe all twenty-three-year-old girls do so—that the moment had come to decide and that I wasn't doing anything I liked or was proud to be doing. Here I was, well dressed, well fed, a college education behind me, with nothing more on my mind than running up to New Haven for house parties at Yale, thinking of myself suddenly as a little old for the job.

Spring house parties at Yale, fall house parties at Yale. Letters from Pete and letters from Jim and fraternity pins in the mail that had to be taken to the post office, carefully rewrapped, and returned with a nice note. Bibles received in the mail from nice mothers who had heard how much I meant to their sons at Yale and letters to be written to nice mothers to tell them that yes, their sons meant a lot to me too.

Nothing definite. Just nice and indefinite. Why didn't I do something? So I looked out the window and I said to myself, "What do you want to do?" And the answer was, I want to go to work for Nelson Rockefeller.

Between my junior and senior years at Northwestern, I had gone to Mexico to take a summer course in Spanish. Part of the curriculum for us students from the United States included working in villages and helping poor people. The project had Peace Corps aspects long before there was a Peace Corps, though it was not as well organized as the Peace Corps, not so much work was done, and not all the students were as interested in helping poor peasants as they were in getting out of Spanish classes.

Nevertheless, I learned a lot digging latrines and telling Indians what latrines were for. I found a girl who was the natural leader of the project. Not an appointed leader, but she became one because she took the work seriously, pulling herself at five o'clock in the morning from the rough blankets we had been issued and getting at the job. Also, she seemed to know more about what we were doing and why we were doing it than anybody else did, and I soon found out why.

Her name was Jean Wallace and her father was Henry Agard Wallace, vice president of the United States. I liked Jean then and I still like her. When I see her from time to time, wherever she is and whatever she is wearing, I see her as she was then: long bare legs under a long tunic, long black hair hanging down over the tunic, deep-set black eyes measuring the work to be done in the fields about her, arms around a big basket of hybrid corn.

That was her father's gift to the world. Sometimes the world turns in such a way the gods would call fitting. There was Jean, multiplying Indian corn production to an astonishing degree by handing them her father's invention: handful by handful of golden seeds. Her father would have been proud.

So the word got around—I suppose it was already around—that the daughter of the vice president of the United States was planting hybrid corn and digging latrines in Tepotzlan. She was invited to go to Mexico City one evening for a reception given by President Aleman for the U.S. Coordinator of Inter-American Affairs, Nelson A. Rockefeller.

And Jean took me. So I met the man, next to my husband, whom I would love more than anyone else in my life.

It was a perfunctory meeting. We shook hands in the receiving line and so did about eighty other people who had been invited. I noticed his good looks, his wavy brown hair, his lively enthusiasm as he exchanged *abrazos* with Mexican officials whom he had met before, his ability to remember everybody's name, his friendliness and interest in the few words they had to say.

But I didn't know whether he remembered my name or was really interested in the few words I had to say. I thought about this as I was looking out the window on the afternoon two years later. What was I going to say to his secretary or the lady who answered his telephone? That I was a friend of Mr. Rockefeller? No, because I wasn't. That I had met Mr. Rockefeller? That was true, but how would she know? Or how would he?

But I did it. Or maybe the house parties at Yale did it. I got out the telephone book and I called "Rockefeller, Offices of the Messrs." I talked to a lady named Mary Mills, and the next thing I remembered was the brown uniforms and brown caps and smiling, businesslike faces of the starters drumming on the doors of elevators and saying, "Step in please."

The first ride up the elevator to the fifty-sixth floor of the RCA Building was a stomach test: Would the stomach stay on the first floor or would it come up with the rest of me? Those elevators were at the time the fastest in the world. I hope nobody has invented any others faster.

But I suppose my stomach was queasy, even when I got on. I had said to the lady on the telephone that I had met Mr. Rockefeller in Mexico, that I was interested in the work he had done as coordinator, that now that the war was over, was there anything I might do to help him?

In those days, the fifty-sixth floor of the RCA Building was entirely devoted to the "Offices of the Messrs. Rockefeller." That's what it said on the double door. An office for the patriarch, Mr. Junior. And offices for Mr. John, Mr. Nelson, Mr. Laurance, Mr. Winthrop, and Mr. David, although Mr. Winthrop was still in the Army and Mr. David was finishing his graduate work in economics at the University of Chicago.

It was scary. A kindly white-haired gentleman behind the desk asked me if I wanted tea or coffee. I said, "Coffee, thank you." A silver tray with a silver coffee pot soon appeared, and coffee was poured by a man in a white coat. The gentleman behind the desk explained with a polite chuckle that when Mr. Nelson was very young, he had spilled the entire coffee service along with the coffee on the rug and "My, you should have seen the expression on Mr. Junior's face."

So I sat there and drank my coffee. After a while, a young

lady came out, and I went back to her office and talked to her. She offered me a job as a file clerk. I never even saw Mr. Nelson, and I went home. Going down the elevator wasn't quite so bad.

Yale or no Yale, Bibles from mothers or no Bibles from mothers, I was not going to take a job as a file clerk. After all, I had a degree in economics. I spoke Spanish. I had worked with *campesinos.* I would never attend another house party at Yale. But neither would I sit in a tiny office with another girl and file papers. So I went home and looked out the window.

And so there came a day, I don't know why—some chance thought, some looking at a list, some half-remembered occasion—as I say I don't know why. But Mr. Nelson called me. He said he remembered me. He said there was some work to be done in his office, that he had brought a lot of files up from the Department of State during his time as assistant secretary for Latin American affairs and that if I would come and start on these, it wouldn't take me very long to get them in order and then there would be other things, more day-to-day things.

So there I was, with a desk right next to that of Louise Boyer, who was Mr. Nelson's secretary and confidante, and I was doing the files and helping Louise arrange luncheons and tickets and schedules. Every morning when Mr. Nelson passed through our office on the way to his own, he ruffled my hair.

Mr. Nelson liked to ruffle my hair. I suppose it was because my hair was short and curly and had never been to a beauty parlor, and maybe he liked to ruffle other women's hair, too, though I never saw him ruffle the hair of Louise. But I always looked up and pretended to be just a little bit annoyed, and he would stand by my desk and laugh. It happened every morning. It was the way to start the day. When Louise got married and took a month's vacation I took her place. A month after she got back I became his assistant for IBEC (the International Basic

Economy Corporation), which he had started in Venezuela and Brazil.

Sometime after that the race began. I got into the office one morning on time and found him already there. I resolved that this would not happen again. The next morning I got there earlier than he did, and the next morning, he got there earlier than I did; pretty soon I was getting up at seven and arriving at eight and then at six and arriving at seven and he was doing the same thing, beating me sometimes and not beating me other times. I was racing down Fifth Avenue at a dog trot and cutting across at 50th Street and into Rockefeller Plaza and breathlessly asking the brown uniformed starter at the banks of elevators if I could go up just as soon as the express touched the ground floor without having to wait for other passengers to assemble and for him to give the signal. Sometimes Mr. Nelson was there before me and sometimes he wasn't, but not a word was said about the race. No acknowledgment. No smile of victory. Just the race.

Finally one morning, out of exhaustion perhaps, he called it off. As I remember, it can't have been much after 7:00 A.M., I was there triumphant and opened the door of the office and there he was, standing by my desk, laughing. "What would you say," he asked, "if I met you outside your apartment at a respectable hour every morning and we walked to work together?"

The race had been exhausting and it had gone on for too long, and anyhow I was flattered and I said I thought it would be a splendid idea.

Two things about IBEC in those early days stand out in my memory. One was a defeat for Nelson (I stopped calling him "Mr. Nelson" about the time that he called off the morning race), a defeat which he turned into a victory and of which he was privately very proud. The other was a defeat for me, an amusing defeat, unless you happen to like chickens, but let us take Nelson's defeat first.

IBEC was Nelson's idea, combining two aims or principles basic to third-generation Rockefellers. IBEC was intended to make money. At the same time, IBEC was intended to do good. Old John D. the first had made money and made it in a fashion which his grandchildren, by the time they were in college, had been forced to confront. I remember Nelson's younger brother David saying in a tone of exasperation, "How would you like to go through college in the middle of the Depression and have your grandfather described by every one of your history and economics professors as 'chief of the robber barons'?" The third generation of Rockefellers had to cope with that. Nelson's father, Mr. Junior, had to cope too and had done so (I suspect religious persuasion as well as public relations counselors were at work) by devoting his life to philanthropy, giving away money to the most worthwhile cause he could find after painstaking and scholarly consideration, with all sorts of boards and advisors to help him.

IBEC was Nelson's way of coping. He would try to make money. That was a given. How could any scion of a family made great by making money not try to make money? But the Great Depression had taught him that the system by which people struggled to make money had certain flaws, among which was the flaw that a lot of people who were engaged in making money neglected their duty to serve humanity. Service to humanity was an absolute duty for the third generation of Rockefellers. No matter what muckrakers might say about service to mankind being an afterthought of a family who had acquired so much money that they didn't know what to do with it, the second and third generation of Rockefellers truly did believe in service to humanity. At least Nelson did. So how can you be sure that while you are making money, you are serving humanity? And how can you be sure that while you are serving humanity, you are making money?

What you do is start the International Basic Economy Corporation and put it to work in a part of the world you know best. Let's start with South America, and let's start in particular with Venezuela.

Venezuela's coast abounds with fish. Yet people who live inland don't have enough to eat. Why can't the private enterprise system provide these hungry inland people with fish? A project which serves mankind. A project which also makes money.

That was the basic idea of IBEC, and it's only one of the things (it happened to be the first thing) that Nelson tried to do. It was a big job. In order to haul the fish, you would need a railroad inland, and you would need refrigeration cars; you would need markets, and you would need to build all of these in a poor country that didn't have any of them.

All of which would cost money. Nelson started IBEC with a good deal of money, and a good deal of money ran out. There came a time, in short, that IBEC was about to go belly-up.

So Nelson went to his father. He went in a businesslike way. He asked for an appointment with his father and walked down the hall and entered the office of Mr. Junior and explained the situation. He took with him charts and profit-and-loss statements and prospects, and he gave his father a briefing, ending with a request. If his father would advance three and a half million dollars to the International Basic Economy Corporation, the corporation could do good and make money.

Now three and a half million dollars in 1944 was the equivalent of about twenty-one and a half million dollars today, so it was no little sum for which Nelson was asking. Nevertheless, he knew his father could advance it if his father wished to do so. Nelson was surprised and angered when his father, having listened carefully throughout an hour-and-a-half briefing with charts, at last opened his mouth and spoke quietly, as Mr. Junior always did.

"I will lend you three and a half million dollars," said Mr. Junior, "on one condition—that you use the money to liquidate the company."

Nelson told me this story many times and always with that little hardening of the eyes which revealed anger, but also with a steely sense of triumph. You could almost see him squaring his shoulders as he told it. "Thank you, Father," Nelson said, and then to me, "I walked out of his office and I raised the money and I saved the company and here we are now."

In those early days of IBEC, time wouldn't move fast enough for Nelson. Here he was, hardly fifteen years out of college, having held two important government jobs, but not yet a successful man of business, anxious to prove he could be a successful man of business, to prove that IBEC could work, that this strange venture in making a profit while doing good could be an enormous success.

Nothing moved fast enough. I think, for example, of the chickens which, looking back on it now, was a perfectly sound, logical, even brilliant idea. It was Nelson's idea. If you brought fresh fish from the coast to inland villages, you had to find a way for the villagers to pay for the fish. Nelson and Stacy May, an economics professor from Dartmouth College whom Nelson had lured from Hanover, New Hampshire, to help organize IBEC, had gone down to the inland villages and explored the ground and discovered that there was no way the villagers could pay for the fish. The villagers were scratching the ground with their pointed sticks and seeding it with their bare hands, hardly raising enough crops to feed themselves and their families, but not enough, nowhere near enough, to pay for the fish. Which, according to Nelson's plan, they would soon be getting by refrigerated railroad cars.

Now, how to deal with that? It was good to bring in fish from the sea. Healthy for the villages. Might do away with the goiters they tended to develop in middle age and which came from lack of iodine. But IBEC was a profit-making corporation, and it was not profitable to give away fish. Therefore the chickens. I don't know whether Nelson thought of the chickens when he and Stacy saw a few of them scratching the dirt around some poor village but anyhow, he thought of it. If the villagers could raise chickens on a large scale and ship the chickens to the coast, they could pay for the fish and IBEC could show a profit. It was all cost-accounted and profit-margined and in theory it worked.

So we transported a load of fine chickens over the rough back roads, we built housing for them and we brought in food and found caretakers in the village, and we waited. And cost-accounted some more. And waited some more. And then one day, there came a telegram.

ALL CHICKENS DEAD—COLDS AND OVERCROWDED CONDITIONS, the telegram read.

All the cost accounting on all the yellow tabs of paper was for naught; all the enthusiasm generated by the logical, sound why-didn't-somebody-think-of-this-before idea was deflated; and Nelson and Stacy and I and all the helpers in the office went around with sad faces for days, mourning the death of the chickens.

In the long run it worked. In the long run, Nelson was a great success. The sheds for the chickens were washed down and made ready to receive a new population; the villagers learned to take care of them; the rail line got built, the refrigeration cars imported the fish, and the chickens were hauled back in return and sold in the city markets. In the long run, IBEC did good and made a profit doing good.

But it was a very long run and many millions of dollars and the horrifying discovery that the villagers didn't like fish. They'd never seen fish. They wouldn't eat fish; they were taught to eat fish. They grew to like fish. In the long run everything worked out for the best. But as I have kept saying, it was a very long run; and by the time the run was finished, I had left IBEC and Stacy May had left IBEC, and Nelson, still in charge of IBEC, had turned his principal attention to other things. Years later I ran into Stacy May, plodding his way up Fifth Avenue, his Phi Beta Kappa key swinging from the chain at his plump waist, and I said, "Stacy, how are the chickens?" And he laughed in recollection and made a mournful face. "Alas," he said, "the poor chickens." And then we laughed again because we both knew that we had suffered during those early days and that time had brought success.

One thing I learned while working with Nelson on IBEC: Only a woman could ever know Nelson Rockefeller. That seems odd to say because Nelson knew a lot of men who thought of themselves as close friends and who thought they knew him well: college fraternity brothers, associates in business, congressmen, senators, government officials in Albany and Washington, artists and art connoisseurs, the landed rich in Latin America and the politicians they put in charge. All these men, variously embraced, arms squeezed, backs slapped, their names greeted with enthusiasm, were friends of Nelson Rockefeller.

With the exception of his brother Laurance, I don't think any man, not Jock Whitney in the early years nor Henry Kissinger in the later years, ever really knew him.

Only a woman could. Because Nelson was not suspicious of women. He was totally himself with women. Whereas he was very suspicious and not totally himself with men.

What Nelson wanted, more than anything else in life, was to succeed despite his name; to succeed as himself, because of who he was inside his skin, and not because of the name by which the skin was called. Everything he did, his mannerisms, his style, his countenance was intended to make people forget this name and to look upon him as himself. That's where "hiya, fella" came from and his insistence on sitting in the front seat with his chauffeur, when he had to have a chauffeur. That's why he always stopped in the kitchen when visiting a friend's house to thank the person who had prepared the meal. That's why he shook hands with the elevator operator; that's why he usually carried only ten dollars in his pocket and frequently borrowed change from startled companions. It was all intended to show the world that he was not just a very rich man, but a good joe, a nice guy, intelligent and able, a doer in the practical world who yet respected the intellectual world, and whose name happened to be Rockefeller.

Thus came the suspicion. In a man's world, those who met Nelson Rockefeller almost invariably had in mind that they were meeting several hundred million dollars. It wasn't their fault. They were not to be blamed for it. But that's what they thought, and what they thought showed on their faces or in their manner or in what they said. And Nelson's reaction was not at all that of a man with his hand on his wallet when he enters a crowded subway. It was rather, why doesn't this stranger take me for myself? why does he regard me only as a pile of money, to be respected as a pile of money or to be worshipped as a pile of money or to be admired as a pile of money?

Except for Wally Harrison, the architect; John Lockwood, the family lawyer; and Tom Gates, the banker who was to become secretary of defense, he had few friends; had none, except for his brother Laurance, to whom he could say, I'm beaten, or I'm desperate, or simply, what shall I do?

I remember crying on the telephone one night when he called, as he did most nights, and saying to him, "You don't have any friends to help, to understand." A silly thing to say, now that I look back upon it because it was so obvious, but it was so obvious because it was true.

Nelson didn't like to compete. He wanted to run whatever show he was in. Which, of course, is another reason he didn't have friends. And it is the reason why a woman could more easily know him. A woman wouldn't compete or ask questions he didn't want to answer or take time he didn't want to give. I remember going home with him one night in a cab and arguing gently and as a matter of courtesy about who would pay the fare. And suddenly, in exasperation, he looked at me and spoke as though he were making a pronouncement, "Joannie, money means nothing to me. My time does."

—•—

The Problem

Now all this time I was working hard and for long hours, and so was Nelson. He had the Museum of Modern Art to look after, a project he had inherited from his mother. His father called him in one day and told him to set about the secret purchase of the land on which the United Nations was eventually to be built. There were also various projects which he thought up for himself, such as trying to persuade Walter O'Malley to keep the Dodger baseball team right where it was in Brooklyn. And, in addition to all this, Nelson had the project of a wife and five children.

I stuck pretty much to Venezuela: to the chickens, the fish, the Venezuelan government's decision to make an investment in

IBEC, the refrigeration cars, and the markets. We went off to Venezuela several times to discuss, plan, and project.

And during this time I forgot that this man I was working with was Nelson Rockefeller. I mean I forgot that he was a very rich man who could do things other men couldn't do. I forgot that when you mentioned the name Rockefeller, people stopped and listened. I forgot that he was famous. I forgot that he knew he didn't have any right to be famous, that his fame was based on his money, and that he was driven by a desire to be known for something more. But I forgot all of this. He was Nelson to me, one of the handsomest and by far the most enthusiastic, life-loving, ebullient, and intuitive men I have ever known.

He loved beauty, and he knew a lot more about beauty than I did. For example, I thought that statues should be on the tops of hills, probably because I had never seen them anywhere else. But Nelson thought that a Henry Moore statue he had bought for the family home at Pocantico Hills should be placed halfway down a bank leading to a ravine, so that you came upon it, a surprise. He was right. He knew, instinctively, where trees should be planted. He knew the difference between a hall that was grand and a hall that was merely big, between the fine and the exquisite, between the plain and the simple. He cared desperately that things appealed to the eye. I never saw him enter a room of any quality without detecting in his glance a desire to rearrange the pictures, even if it was only that one of them was the tiniest bit out of line.

I don't know where Nelson got his sense of beauty, whether from his mother or from Alfred Barr and Dorothy Miller at the Museum of Modern Art. None of his brothers had it to the same degree. I suspect that it came from Abby Aldrich, his mother, whom he cared about more than he cared about his father and more than he cared about any other woman he ever met.

To anyone with any sensitivity, Nelson's enthusiasm for beauty, his desire to make life better for everybody, his joy in the discovery of public problems, and his almost insatiable desire to do something about them was catching.

I had the sense, and so did everyone who ever worked with him, that we could do anything if we got the right people and the right plans and worked hard at it. We could feed the poor, make the city more beautiful, settle the strikes, resettle the lands, literally, almost literally, move mountains.

Nelson didn't read much. He listened instead. And when I found out that he had dyslexia, I read books for him and submitted short précis, which he digested and which we talked about. Conversations gave him knowledge and ideas. We would be discussing the morning headlines that dealt with commuter problems of getting into New York and the inability of the railroads to handle the traffic, and he would say, "Joannie, I don't know enough about railroads, so let's have a meeting and find out about them."

And so we would, with all the best-known experts on railroads and commuter problems. Sometimes there would be two or three meetings, and when they were over Nelson knew something about railroads; perhaps more important he had come to know those who knew all about them.

That sort of meeting was the genesis of Critical Choices, a project he started about the time he first cast his eyes on the presidency and which critics in the press labeled a campaign stunt. It was not a campaign stunt. These gatherings of experts to discuss public problems were Nelson's substitute for getting a graduate degree. He really wanted to know and he really believed that if all the people who knew most about a problem were assembled to discuss it, the problem could be solved.

I became an enthusiast for Nelson's method of solving

problems, and I still am. I only wish he were here to get everybody to come to the meeting and to say, "Now, fellas."

I suppose it's inevitable that when two people are working together for a long time and one admires the other greatly, and when they are discussing everything from fish in Venezuela to railroads in New York City, and when they place statues together and hang pictures together and say, "Don't you think it should be a little lower?"—when in fact they become good friends and like each other a lot, there emerges from the relationship what is called in businesses and households all over America "the problem." And it seems to me logical to suppose that as more and more women work with men, what I thought of in my day as "the problem," will become *the problem*. I don't know of any other way to cope with it than the way I coped with it, and I don't want you to suppose for one minute that I knew exactly what to do when the problem first arose. But it is a problem, and it will be a greater problem; so I may as well tell you how it came about with me.

It began with the shredded wheat dinner. Nelson asked me one night when we had been working late whether he could come to dinner. He knew from an earlier conversation that my parents were out of town. He asked if he could come to dinner, and I said of course he could come to dinner. It wasn't until I had said yes, of course, that it occurred to me that as far as I knew there was nothing in the refrigerator.

Looking back now, it also occurs to me that being possessed of what people used to call a "social conscience" can't really make up for having a lot of money. In other words, I doubt that Nelson, despite his great interest in people who were poor and in doing what he could to help the problems of the poor, ever really faced the mundane middle-class fact that through chance or poor planning or people being out of town, there might be nothing to eat in the house. At his house, there were servants who saw that there was always something to eat in the house and who were ready at any hour to put it on the table.

I don't want to make too much of a sociological point of this. It was really nothing more than an accident, but I think he was surprised when we walked into the kitchen and I started going through the refrigerator and the shelves and discovered that the only thing there was to eat was toast and butter, and shredded wheat and milk.

And so I got down the dishes from the cupboard, and we set the table. I served it and he helped and we found the sugar for the shredded wheat and milk and laughed a lot. He said it was the best toast and butter and the best shredded wheat he had ever tasted and he went home.

Several days later, he asked me if he could return the favor. He said we'd have dinner at his father's house on 53rd Street, which was at the moment unoccupied, and I accepted. We had caviar and champagne. We had a fire. We had music. We had the caviar and the champagne served at a small table right in front of the fireplace. The caviar was all surrounded with ice and dishes of chopped eggs and chopped onions and chopped lemons and whatever kind of toast it is that you put the caviar on. It was all strange to me because I had never tasted caviar nor champagne and I didn't know where to put the chopped things or how thick to spread the caviar, but I learned fast. It was, as I look back on it, one of the best evenings I've ever had in all my life.

Nelson was amused, not so much that I liked the caviar and wanted more, but that I had never tasted it before. It went with my being from Anderson, Indiana—straight, untutored, virginal, not having been around.

I knew, because he mentioned it so often, that my lack of sophistication appealed to him, and I sensed that it made me

physically attractive. But I couldn't do anything about it. I was
what I was. One day in the office, he suddenly leaned over me
with a startling revelation. "Joannie, I want you to know that
Todd and I have an agreement that we will never get divorced
but will live our own separate lives."

"Why are you telling me this?"

"Because we're working together, and I think working
together and sleeping together are the same thing. They're part of
a whole."

"That's a ridiculous sentence."

One evening, when we had worked late at his father's
apartment and I had to go to a party, I asked him if I could take
a shower. He showed me where it was. I was busy showering
when suddenly, the curtain parted and he was in the shower too.
Furious, I jumped out, sputtering and spilling water and grabbing
for a towel. Nelson laughed, went on showering, and I got
dressed and went to the party.

Afterward I said to myself, "Well, it was perfectly natural.
We were working late and I had to go to the party and there
wasn't time to go home so why shouldn't I have taken a shower?"

But hindsight and experience tell me that alone with a man,
a woman who decides to take a shower is asking for trouble. She
is being suggestive. She wants him to respond. Nelson did.

But that is all hindsight. The fact is that on that particular
evening, taking a shower was as natural as saying may I use your
bathroom? I was innocent. I was not being suggestive. The
innocence was.

I tried to be honest about my innocence. We held long
conversations about the fact that he was married and I thought
that nice girls didn't sleep with men who were married to
somebody else and that married men shouldn't be trying to get
them to do so. In fact, I told him, even the phrase "sleeping

together" embarrassed me because I hadn't ever thought about "sleeping together." Nelson laughed.

I had squeezed enough time out of my life with Nelson to cast passing thoughts on a man named Tom Braden whom Nelson had brought down from a teaching post at Dartmouth College to be executive secretary at the Museum of Modern Art. In fact, Nelson had, in a way, introduced us. When Tom first came to Nelson's office, I was designated to go out and tell him, "Mr. Rockefeller will be with you in a minute." There had been a flurry among the women in the office about which of us was going to get this task. We had all been apprised of the appointment. Pictures had been sent down from Dartmouth and been passed from hand to hand. Also, a biographical sketch had been circulated. The young instructor in English had a war record in two armies. He had traversed the top of Africa with Montgomery's Eighth British Army and had joined the U.S. Army, where he had been a parachutist for the OSS in France and Italy. He and Stewart Alsop had written a best-selling book about it. He was single. We were all curious.

So I went out and spoke my lines to this object of curiosity who was sitting in the reception room reading a magazine. When I returned, everybody looked at me with the same unspoken question. "He's tall," I said, "and quite good-looking but he hardly looked up from his magazine. He said, 'Thank you.'"

It was a month before I heard from Tom Braden again and then only by indirection. A friend called and said she was having a party. I was sorry. I had another engagement.

"Oh, that's too bad. Tom Braden is coming and I thought he could pick you up."

"Oh, well, I think I can change the other engagement."

Happily, I mentioned it to Nelson. "I'm going out with a friend of yours tonight."

"Who? What friend?"

My remark had stopped him in his tracks. He had been pacing the room, explaining something to me about chickens or railroads, and now he turned suddenly and his eyes were narrow and hooded, the only expression I ever saw on Nelson that was unattractive and made him look evil.

"Tom Braden," I answered.

"I knew it. I knew it the minute I brought him in here. And goddamn it, you'll marry him. I know you will and I won't let you marry him. I'll send him to Mexico. I'll send him to Rome or I'll get rid of him and I'll see that he never gets another job. I won't let you marry him."

There was another blowup later on, and I called Tom at his office and told him. I was scared for him. Maybe Tom was scared too but he didn't show it. "Nelson's too big a guy for this sort of adolescence. I suggest we ignore it. He'll get a hold on himself."

I married Tom Braden. Nelson came to our wedding. Nelson was a friend to me and a friend to Tom throughout the rest of his life. When our first son, David, was born, Nelson was his godfather. When Tom wanted to buy a newspaper, Nelson lent him most of the money he needed to borrow. Whenever we had another child we heard from Nelson. Often, he simply came.

During all the years I knew him, working or playing or merely being friends, he taught me the most important thing I ever learned. He taught me that life goes on forever and is so full of challenges that you hardly have time to surmount them all, but that you always can surmount them; and that if you try, you always will.

I know that's not true. I know Nelson knew that it wasn't true. But Nelson lived his life as though it were true, and I learned from him that it's a good way to live.

—•—

SIX

Start with Snuggling

I wonder about the word "snuggle." The dictionary defines it as "to lie snug or close especially for warmth or comfort" and dates its use from 1687. There is a ring of childhood to the word. Perhaps Tom's mother used it with him when he was a baby in Dubuque, Iowa. Or perhaps my mother used it with me when I was a baby in Anderson. I can't remember whether Tom brought it to me or I brought it to him. My guess is that unlike "bundling," it was long ago transported from New England to the Middle West and its origins forgotten. At any rate, I've never heard it used by people whom I think of as Easterners.

But I can tell you how it's done, and I recommend it as a way to feel safe or at least protected, as a way to go to sleep, as a way to forget whatever you have been worrying about, as a way to make a marriage work, as a way to make a marriage last.

It's important that you do it right. You can't just flop into bed and snuggle. At least you can't just flop into bed and snuggle after you've been married awhile and lust has given way to comfort. You have to do certain things first before you snuggle. You have to talk for a while about a book or a movie or some incident of the day. The incident must not be one which lends the mind to worry. For example, you must not talk about children or money or another man or woman whose name will arouse jealousy or suspicion in the mind of the person with whom you are about to snuggle. You let the conversation drift until it becomes almost but not quite boring, and you must sense that the realization of this fact is mutual. Then you say, "I guess we ought to turn out the lights," and when you get either no response or a grunt in acknowledgment, you do so, or he does so, and it is only then that you snuggle.

I lie on my side and Tom lies on his side, and he puts one arm around me and draws me close. And then we go to sleep, "snug": "trim, compact, close fitting, comfortable, quiet or private," as the dictionary says.

And I suppose, childlike. But Tom and I have been snuggling for forty years in five homes and four cities; we are no longer children. I think snuggling has a lot to do with, as near as anything can be, a perfect marriage. Which is not to defy the common knowledge that no marriage is perfect. Tom has faults and so do I. Sometimes we point them out to each other; sometimes we get angry; sometimes we take the name of the Lord in vain and we shout at each other. He has a very low voice and shouts better than I, but through imitation, I have found that in a shouting match, I can take the name of the Lord in vain as frequently as he.

It doesn't happen very often. Our marriage is different from that of most people, and the difference is important. I won't say it's most important, because the most important thing about our marriage and most marriages is that we trust each other.

My friend Stewart Alsop used to say that when a husband and wife have a serious quarrel, it is for one of two reasons: money or a third person, man or woman.

If there's truth in that—and I think there is—then Tom and I have eliminated one of the causes for a quarrel. We don't interfere with each other's friendships. I mean that if I want to consort with another man, I do and if he wants to consort with another woman, he does. We trust each other. We have too much respect for each other's individuality to want to destroy it by fixing boundaries on friendships and the development of friendships. So we give each other total freedom—just enough rope—trusting in each other's honor, love, and sense of courtesy.

I don't see how, in a world of absolute equality between the sexes, marriage can have any other rules. I know it does have other rules, but that is because a world of absolute equality between the sexes does not yet exist. It will exist. It is coming fast. Look at the entering classes in the colleges. Look at the faculties. Look at the first breaks in the ranks of corporate executives. It is coming, but it is not here yet, and so the new rules and the old rules coexist for a while to everybody's embarrassment.

When a man says to me, "If my wife knew that I was having lunch with you, she'd have a fit," I put him down as unenlightened and something of a boor and I try not to have lunch with him again.

He's out-of-date. He hasn't come to terms with a world in which men and women coexist in equality. And his wife hasn't come to terms with that world. All I can say is he will and she will. And when they do, the once-common expressions "he is cheating on this wife" or "his wife is cheating on him" will no longer be common.

Tom and I don't have to cheat. We trust. And I don't recall that we ever sat down, thought it through, and enunciated it together. I think the trust was there from the start and the enunciation followed.

Enunciation began, I think, with Reinaldo Herrera, a tall, handsome Venezuelan who wore his black hair long, and before the sun went down was usually clad in a white suit. Nelson had introduced him to me on one of our trips to Venezuela and, as I was working for Nelson in New York, he frequently asked me for lunch at the 21 Club when he was in town. When I got married, he said he wanted to meet Tom and asked us to spend an evening with him at El Morroco, a popular and expensive club for dancing, drinks, and dinner. Tom and I went with him several times, and then Tom said he wouldn't go anymore because he didn't have enough money to pay and he didn't feel comfortable letting Reinaldo pay.

"So I don't want to go, Joannie," he said, when Reinaldo came to New York one day and asked us for dinner and dancing. "You go."

Now the fact is that Tom said he didn't have enough money to pay his share and I knew he didn't or rather that we didn't, but I also knew that Tom couldn't dance like Reinaldo Herrera, that he wasn't in the same league with Reinaldo, either in money or ability to dance. I love to dance and I knew Reinaldo was many times a millionaire and so I went. It wasn't Tom's league; it was Reinaldo's league, but I could play in it and why not?

I still remember that evening, and Reinaldo looking in the mirror over the bar, ordering a drink while he smoothed his jet-black hair. He was exciting to look at and exciting to dance with, and when we got home late and he took me to the door, there was Tom—waiting, reading *Sherlock Holmes*, and taking care of David. He was pleasant to Reinaldo and pleasant to me, but I sensed that he felt a little put upon and I sensed that I had been discourteous. I didn't go dancing with Reinaldo again.

Violations of courtesy can sometimes be explained away so that they are no longer violations of courtesy. I recall the gift of a watch encased in a gold bracelet that Nelson gave me the Christmas after Tom and I were married, which, for a reason I found inexplicable, sent Tom into a rage. It was a beautiful bracelet, of modern style, not at all gaudy or over-large but very much a bracelet and large enough to have a good watch encased right in its center. I say it was not large or gaudy, but it was noticeable. Instead of being excited as I was and admiring as I was and proud as I was, Tom complained.

He complained loudly and constantly, and finally one day as I was getting ready to go to work and he was getting ready to go to work, he said, "Take that goddamned thing off."

And I said, "I won't. It's my watch and I'm going to wear it." I think it was our first real quarrel, and it proved Stewart Alsop's point because it involved a third person. It wasn't the watch which angered Tom. It was the fact that Nelson had given it to me. I was as proud of it as he was jealous, and there was nothing to do but talk about it over dinner and get it straightened out.

Tom remembers that we went to a French restaurant and the meal cost twelve dollars, an insignificant amount of money now, but which was a lot of money for us in 1950; I remember that I said to him, "Ask yourself what you don't like about this watch. Is it the watch or is it Nelson?"

"It isn't the watch and it isn't Nelson. It's the fact that somebody besides me gave it to you."

And I said, "That's really silly. But if it makes that much difference to you I won't wear it."

And he said, "I suppose, Joannie, that what would be really silly is not wearing a good watch when you have a good watch to wear."

So that was the end of it. I don't know where the watch is now. I wore it until it ceased to be useful. I mentioned it to Tom the other day, and he said he'd forgotten about the watch and forgotten that I no longer wore it. After that dinner, it became no longer a symbol, just a watch.

In a marriage where two partners are equally free to preserve and develop their own individual selves, they must also consider courtesy to others, others besides the partners in marriage—third persons, even fourth persons. I had a problem with this about which I was unaware. Tom pointed it out to me.

He was standing along the sidelines at a private dance one evening. Now we didn't get to go to many private dances. Only the rich can afford them, and the rich tend to invite the rich. But once in a while we did get to go. Tom, as usual, was on the sidelines and I, as usual, was on the dance floor. I love to dance. I think I'm a good dancer. Literally, I could dance all night and often have.

Tom dances. He dances well enough. When we first got married and he discovered how much I liked to dance, he scrimped and saved quite privately and took lessons in dancing. But what he learned was how to take steps: Take this step and then take that step. As everybody knows—and so does Tom—a good dancer not only knows the steps, but also improvises when the music is really good or really fast; and sometimes you don't even bother with the steps—you just dance.

At least that's what I do, and when I find a man who can

really dance, I get the way some people get when they drink. I just go. Well, I did find such a man, and we danced all night, danced well. In fact, a small circle formed around us—we were that good. And in the mid-morning hours, Tom went home and went to bed, I suppose, just to show me, but he said he just couldn't stay awake any longer.

Well, so we had that chapter behind us. In the meantime, the Dancer, who was tall, blond, and rather well-known, had called me quite a lot and taken me to lunch quite a lot. And here we were at another dance, me dancing again with the Dancer, and Tom on the sidelines.

Tom said to me later, "A young lady came up to me; a rather petite lady, quite pleasant-looking in her white gown and introduced herself, and then she said, 'I understand we have a mutual problem. Do you want to name a time and place where we can discuss it?'"

Tom told me that he felt a little bit as though he had just been challenged to a duel, and he wished to remain uninformed about the cause.

But he could guess. And he said to me later when we got home, "Look, Joannie, I don't know this lady and I don't want to know this lady. The thought of taking her to lunch and discussing her relationship with the Dancer, and the Dancer's relationship with her, and the Dancer's many lunches with you, and whether or not the problem is mutual which is what she hopes, is something I just don't want to do.

"So I think you had better stop seeing the Dancer and stop hearing all about his work when he calls you on the telephone."

So I did. I had not been discourteous to Tom, except perhaps on that one night when he went home to bed and left me. Maybe I could argue he was discourteous to me in doing so, but I had been discourteous to the Dancer's wife. I apologize to her and, if it's any satisfaction, I will say to her that she taught me a lesson I needed to learn.

I honestly can't think of a single time when Tom has been discourteous to me. Now that doesn't mean that he may not have fallen in love with somebody over the forty years we have been married or that he may have thought he had fallen in love. It doesn't mean that he hasn't, in all the times he's been to Europe or Asia and not in my company, permitted himself to get swept up by an Italian princess or a British beauty of noble blood. And it's an unwritten rule of our marriage that I don't ask. All I know is that with the possible exception of that one time on the dance floor, he has never been discourteous.

So that makes two violations of the courtesy rule for me and none for him. Granted, he may have violated the rule by being discourteous to a fourth person, in the way that I was discourteous to the Dancer's wife. But I don't know. If I ask, it will spoil trust. If I spoil trust, it will spoil marriage. So I'll never ask.

—•—

SEVEN

Oveta

We moved to Washington in the spring of the year. Allen Dulles, whom Tom had known during the war, had asked Tom to join him as his assistant when he took up his duties in the new Central Intelligence Agency. Bill Donovan, who had been Tom's commanding officer in the OSS, was enlisted by Allen to call Nelson and persuade him that Tom ought to go. So we went, carrying David in our arms and a baby inside me.

The Korean War had broken out, but it seemed very far away from anything that had to do with me. The new baby, a sister for David named Mary, was born that fall and when I finished nursing her, there was Nelson on the telephone with new plans for me.

I was to run the small Washington office of a new venture called Hands Across the Sea. I wince when it occurs to me now—as it did not occur to me then—that the new venture may have been explicitly intended to give me something to do. But Hands Across the Sea didn't last very long. When Dwight Eisenhower came into office, Nelson was on the telephone from New York with new ideas. He was to become under secretary of a brand-new department of government to be called Health, Education, and Welfare, and I was to help him.

But that was just telephone talk. Tom and I had found a tiny house to live in—our first house—and the CIA was expanding and Tom was helping it expand. We made a lot of new friends through Stewart and Tish Alsop, who had been Tom's friends during the war. We went out to dinner most nights; I didn't think very much about Nelson's new department of government until a day in June 1953 when I woke up in a white hospital gown with no makeup on my face and there was Nelson standing at the foot of the hospital bed, exclaiming over the birth of my second daughter, Joannie. The enthusiastic exclamations were mixed with enthusiastic entreaties. He was running the new department on an interim basis. Oveta Culp Hobby was to be the secretary but she wasn't on the job yet, and he was going to organize it and get it ready for her. Health, Education, and Welfare (HEW), Nelson explained, had been formed from a number of bureaus and independent agencies which were not only unfamiliar with each other but, in some instances, were rivals. *"E pluribus unum,"* Nelson said with a laugh which was half serious. It was like the thirteen jealous states forming a union of states. It was a historic task. Nelson said so.

Just then Tom came in and began taking pictures of the new baby with a flash camera, and though Tom seemed genuinely glad to see Nelson, it seemed to me that he was a little annoyed at finding him in the room viewing the baby before he had. I noticed that he kept taking pictures with the flash after Nelson, having a care for the baby's eyes, said that he should stop. "All right, Joannie," Nelson said as he departed, "you'll want to nurse this new baby, so let's say you come to work the day after Labor Day."

Tom drove down the broad, busy avenue which fronted the new department and let me out at the curb. I was very nearly in tears. Tom said, as my father had once said, "Now, if you can't stand it, you can always come home. Just call me and I'll come and get you."

I was scared because I'd never worked at anything which seemed so vast and complicated. And Nelson, I shortly discovered, was a little scared too. He'd never worked for a woman before. Mrs. Hobby, formidable and forbidding, wore a hat, securely fixed upon her head as she grimly strode, aides rushing to keep up with her, through the halls.

As soon as I got to know her, I discovered that she was scared too. Though she'd been the highest-ranking woman officer in World War II (colonel-in-chief of the WACS) and was a power in Texas politics, she knew she'd been a power in Texas politics partly because her husband had been governor of Texas. She called him every night. To staff the new department, Nelson had brought down a lot of bright lawyers whom he knew and a lot of college professors whom he knew, and none of them had served in government before. We spent a lot of time telling each other that President Eisenhower really wanted this new department to work.

But what if it fell on its face? None of us knew what we were supposed to do or what we ought to do first. Maybe we should do nothing. The bureaucracy was at work, and just because it had been placed under a new name and had a cabinet position with a secretary and an under secretary and a lot of assistant secretaries and their assistants didn't mean that it would cease functioning just because we were there. Maybe we were in the way.

The thought occurred to some of us. And the thought occurred to me to get in touch professionally with the Dancer. He was working for Richard M. Nixon, vice president of the United States. The offices of the vice president and of the secretary of HEW were not far apart and so when the Dancer called from time to time, suggesting lunch, I found the proposal not inconvenient.

I also thought it might be profitable. The Dancer's boss knew Washington and government from the inside, knew the pathways to the Senate, the House, and the White House, knew the mores and the foibles of the big contributors, knew what to say and what not to say and when to say it and when not to say it. So the Dancer's proximity to knowledge and power far exceeded my own. I thought I might learn something.

Tom didn't like the Dancer. When I asked why, he answered, "I don't know, I don't like him."

I said, "Look, Tom, this man knows what's going on, or at least his boss does. And none of us have any idea what's going on. So leave me alone."

Mrs. Hobby called me in one day, and I stood before that enormous desk and listened. She had to give a speech, a political speech, before an audience of Republicans in New York City. This was a national meeting, celebrating the beginning of the Eisenhower era. It would be attended by governors, senators, congressmen, party officials, and big contributors. It had to be a good speech. Would I prepare it?

Now I had reason to be scared. I had never written a

political speech, nor had anyone else in the department. I worried all afternoon, and that night, I asked Tom. He said he didn't know enough to write it, but he had an old friend who was a speech writer and a Republican and was vice president of the Ford Motor Company for public relations. Tom put in a phone call to Charlie Moore and I got on the line.

Charlie was pleased, glad to be of help; he would come at once and bring the best speech writers the Ford Motor Company could provide. So they flew out from Detroit, and we went to the apartment Oveta had rented on Connecticut Avenue and Oveta fixed sandwiches and coffee. Charlie and his people asked questions and set to work. At 2:30 in the morning, Charlie had a first draft.

That noon I had lunch with the Dancer. It turned out that the Dancer was working on a speech for Mr. Nixon and that Mr. Nixon and Oveta were to speak from the same platform and on the same morning. In fact, Mr. Nixon was to speak at 11:00 and Oveta was to speak at 11:30. Here we were, the Dancer and I, engaged in a joint enterprise. What a happy coincidence.

Oveta and I went over the speech in the airplane. It was a pretty good speech. In fact, I thought, but didn't dare say, that she might bring the crowd to its feet with that speech. There were some applause lines about continuing the "crusade," this time not for Europe, but for health, for education, for welfare.

And maybe she would have brought the crowd to its feet. But Mr. Nixon was to speak first and the moment he began, I wished that I were elsewhere. I wished the floor would open and I could drop through. I couldn't look at Oveta, sitting up there on the stage in the hotel ballroom. I couldn't look at anybody. I sat there, staring at my hands, conscious that my face was growing bright red.

Almost word for word, paragraph for paragraph, Mr. Nixon

delivered Oveta's speech, Charlie Moore's speech, my speech. The applause lines rolled out one by one, and even the faintly humorous asides. For fifteen pages of a twenty-five-page speech, Mr. Nixon went on, and when he sat down a little more than half of Oveta's speech was ready for the record books, delivered, received, and applauded.

The world, it seemed to me, would never quite be the same again. I was embarrassed to be seen in it. I would crawl home and get into bed and draw the covers over my head and take a sleeping pill. But that would be later. Right now, I had to sit and watch poor forlorn Oveta Hobby, standing at the rostrum, smiling at the polite applause which greeted her name, with a speech in her hand that was as good as dead, and Mr. Nixon making his way out of the hall, shaking hands, on his way back to Washington. In the little entourage behind him, smiling as he paused behind his boss, waiting for the outstretched hands to recede for the little procession to move along the aisle was the personification of evil and betrayal. There was the Dancer become the devil, the devil with a photographic memory. By accident he looked at me as he smiled out at the crowd, and then quickly, he looked away.

My impression is that Oveta handled it not only as well as she could but very well. I have a vague impression of her telling two stories about women in the cabinet which drew polite laughter, and she congratulated the vice president. She agreed with him. She couldn't have put it better herself. She knew that she could look to Mr. Nixon for ideas and support. And then she went on with the rest of the speech, the part that Mr. Nixon had cast aside, which was statistical and therefore dull and boring. My impression is that she finished a little early but without the slightest indication of despair.

But that's my impression. I wanted her to be all right. I

wanted her not to wilt, as I was wilting. I wasn't really listening. My eyes, not my brain, told me that she made it. And when we had taken our seats in the airplane, she said, "Joannie, what happened?" I told her. "I see," said Oveta, and that's all she said. Never, during the ensuing years, did she mention the speech again.

And after that, nobody, not Nelson, not Tom, not even Dwight D. Eisenhower could have said anything to the detriment of Oveta Hobby without hearing a spirited defense from me.

It's odd that history has paid so little attention to Oveta Hobby. Only Madame Perkins, the secretary of labor in the Roosevelt administration, had preceded her as a woman in a cabinet post; and without disparaging Madame Perkins, it seems to me fair to say that Oveta was more of what the world thinks of as a woman. She was beautiful. She was attractive to men. She'd borne two children. She dressed simply but in great style. She cared a lot about how she looked and spent time at caring. (It infuriated her when Nelson looked in her appointment book and found "beauty parlor.") In that sense she fit the world's stereotype of a woman. Could men fall in love with her? They often did.

But in every other sense she did not fit the stereotype at all. A woman is supposed to be weak, needing a man to provide backbone. A woman is supposed to be indecisive, vacillating. A woman is supposed to be unable to see the big picture; she makes judgments about people on the basis of appearance. A woman is supposed to be garrulous. That's the stereotype. It fits weak people, men and women. It doesn't fit Oveta Hobby.

Oveta never let her strength show. It was, rather, revealed. She never raised her voice, never demonstrated anger, never said, "We'll get back at him" or "I'll take care of her." When she got word that her husband, Will, was dying in a Houston hospital, she put her coat on and was pausing to say good-bye to me at the office door when the surgeon general of the United States rushed up, literally wringing his hands. "Mrs. Hobby, I think you ought to know that the Salk polio vaccine was released two days ago and I've just had reports that several children have died after taking it."

Oveta made a half turn toward her desk, dropped her coat on the chair, and looked full in Dr. Sheele's anguished face. She said quietly, "Dr. Sheele, we have met regularly and at least thirty times since I took office, and thirty times I have asked you to report to me on the activities under your supervision. This is the first time you have mentioned that you intended to release the polio vaccine."

That was all. Oveta's husband was dying. She had to go. But as far as I know—and I think I do—she never mentioned to anyone, certainly not to the newspapers that Sheele had made a tragic mistake.

Oveta took the blame, and the blame was headline news for days. And she took the cartoons that portrayed her as someone who was making up her face while babies died, as someone who had fumbled her job while she was fumbling in her purse for her lipstick, as someone who was, well, you know, a woman.

Imperturbably, she took it. Imperturbably, she sat on top of this vast bureaucracy, hastily pulled together out of many separate bureaus and fiefdoms, over some of which she had no line of authority (the surgeon general, for example, was a presidential appointee). As she gradually pulled it together into a functioning unit with clear lines of authority, responsibility, and reporting functions so that she could know what was going on, she stuck to her maxim with a will of iron: "Never complain; never explain."

I don't know where Oveta got that line. But when the Social

Security Agency or the Children's Bureau or the Education Bureau or any other of the separate and distinct agencies of government which had been rolled into one department made a mistake and the mistake hit the newspapers, Oveta would recite it as though she were reminding herself. "Never complain; never explain." And she would set about making sure that the mistake didn't happen again because she would know in advance that a mistake was in the making and could step on it before it got made.

Nelson had suggested to Oveta that I become her assistant and had done so, I suspect, for very personal reasons. Tom wanted to buy a newspaper. Tom had known Nelson long before I had known him. In the long ago, Tom had gone to Nelson and asked him, "If I find a newspaper and I find other investors, will you help me?" Nelson had said he would, and Nelson did not intend to renege on his promise. But now Tom was making trouble for both of us, telling me—and more formally telling Nelson—that he was hot on the trail of a newspaper in California. Probably for different reasons, neither of us liked what we heard.

And so I suspect—though I'll never know for certain—that Tom's pursuit of a newspaper was one of the reasons why I ceased being the assistant to the under secretary of health, education, and welfare and suddenly became assistant to the secretary instead. What I know is that Nelson thought Tom was making a great mistake and harangued me about it at the office. Here I was, he pointed out, at the center of things in a brand-new department of a brand-new administration, learning a whole lot, which might lead to a whole lot more, and I was about to throw it all over and for what? To watch my husband run a newspaper while I played bridge with the wife of the police chief and the manager of the J.C. Penney store? And Tom, he was a division chief in the Central Intelligence Agency. Allen Dulles, the CIA's deputy director, had told Nelson that Tom was doing important work. Why did he want to do unimportant work?

And so, one morning, Nelson said to me, "Mrs. Hobby wants to see you." I started, wondering. "No," Nelson said, "it's all right. Just go in and see her."

She had an enormous office, and there she sat with her hat on. I walked up to the desk and said, as people do to start things, "Mrs. Hobby?"

Oveta has a lovely smile. It begins at the eyes and moves down, opposite of most smiles. She smiled as she told me that President Eisenhower had mentioned at the cabinet meeting that he had enjoyed reading in the newspapers about the meeting of the school teachers which the department had organized. (Which I had organized. The president of the United States. Mentioned at the Cabinet meeting. My conference. "Be ye not puffed up.")

So I said that the meeting had been very interesting, as though to disclaim any personal involvement. I had just finished this short declaration when Oveta leaned toward me, her face serious now but still benign. "Joan, I want you to work for me. I want you to be my personal assistant, help me organize, help me with public meetings, with private meetings, help me keep track of what's going on, help me with everything."

My mind whirled. What about Nelson? Did he know this? Would he be angry? What about Tom and the newspaper?

"Mrs. Hobby, I'm flattered. I want to do it. But my husband and I are leaving for California tonight to find out whether we can buy a newspaper." At that moment a grinning Nelson Rockefeller put his head through the connecting office door. "Well?"

As Tom and I were boarding the airplane that night, there was Oveta Hobby sitting in the passenger lounge, waiting. She rose and kissed me on both cheeks as we dropped our hand baggage in surprise. "Joannie, for Tom, I hope you get this newspaper, but for you and for me, I hope you don't."

Tom never got that newspaper, for which I was secretly glad, but I knew he would get one eventually because he was determined that he would. So I knew the argument would recur. In the meantime, I had a new, larger office with two secretaries and a White House telephone which made me feel very important, though I had uneasy moments wondering what would happen if it rang. Then I got so busy that I didn't have time to worry about it. It occurs to me only now that the telephone never did ring. The phone was one of those Washington status symbols, important to the holder, who will not realize the emptiness of the symbol until the symbol is no longer held.

Oveta began to take over the department, taking jobs away from Nelson. Nelson had run the staff meetings. Oveta decided that she would run the staff meetings. Nelson had presided over the early morning meetings with the bureau chiefs. Oveta decided that she would preside over these meetings. Nelson asked to bring his new assistant, Nancy Hanks, who had replaced me, to the meetings. Oveta said no.

Looking back now, it seems amazing to me that my friendship with Nelson survived these days. He had organized this department, brought the people in, and been the principal player, and now quite suddenly he had a new assertive boss, a woman, beautiful but without vanity, who didn't throw her weight around, but knew what she wanted people to do and got them to do it. Including Nelson.

For some reason—and it can't be the importance of the event itself—an event nevertheless stands out in my mind as the day when Nelson realized that he was the under secretary and Oveta was the secretary and the secretary ran the show. The event was Nelson's party for all the Cabinet, which took place at his home, a vast estate with giant trees and beautiful vistas, on Foxhall road. It was a summer evening, and we were to have dinner on a terrace overlooking a sweeping lawn, at the very tip of which stood the golf tee which Nelson had installed for Dwight Eisenhower. We looked past the tee down to the circular green far below—that had also been built in the hope that Eisenhower would want to use it. On a golf course, it would have been a par three. As I think of it now, it is sad—that long-gone monument to Nelson's ambition—because Eisenhower never swung a club on that tee, never even laid eyes on it. At the time, it represented a fresh promise of camaraderie to come. We looked out past the green and then up to dense trees and rolling country and the city of Washington. All the Cabinet was there.

I remember that I knew right away that something was wrong with that party but I didn't know what. We all stood there on that lovely spot like so many pasteboard cutouts. None of the Cabinet members knew one another well, and none of their wives knew one another at all. People were saying, "Well, we live in Detroit." I couldn't think of anything to say to the wife of Attorney General Brownell except, "Do you play golf?" And then I didn't know what to say when she answered that no, she didn't.

As I say, I couldn't figure out what was wrong with the party, but Oveta knew at once what was wrong. I found myself by the door where Nelson and his wife, Todd, were greeting guests. And Todd was saying how do you do to somebody to whom she had already said how do you do, when I saw, out of the corner of my eye, Oveta approaching at a fast clip. "Nelson," she said when she got to the door, "drinks." Whereupon Nelson turned to a waiter and said, "Madame Secretary would like a glass of wine."

"No," said Oveta, "I don't want a glass of wine, Nelson. I

want scotch, bourbon, gin, vodka, rye. I want it for everybody and I want it right now."

All the while she was smiling politely, but through her teeth was snapping out the names of alcoholic beverages. Nelson had a look of wonderment on his face, as though somebody had just told him that Cabinet officers were human beings and the correctness of the observation had struck him forcefully.

He ran off the terrace and into the house and Oveta turned to me. "Charlie Wilson, the secretary of defense," she said, "is about to die."

Nelson returned with Todd at his side, who said (I suppose by hastily decided prearrangement), "Mrs. Hobby, we're about to serve dinner," and Oveta responded this time to Mrs. Rockefeller: "Hold dinner. Hold it until everybody has had a drink and don't serve it until the secretary of defense has had two."

Dinner on the terrace in the spring was a little late. Dusk was falling by the time the secretary of defense rose at Oveta's request to give us a rendition of "The Face on the Barroom Floor." He sang lustily and to great applause. There was plenty of wine and everybody had a splendid time, except perhaps Nelson, who had a learning experience instead.

Texas stories were Oveta's specialty. She had been around men all her life, in the Texas legislature and at the *Houston Post*; and the men with whom she had been around were or had been farmers or oil riggers, plainspoken men who swapped stories that would not have been told in Park Avenue apartments. Some of them were sidesplitting but only if you had more than a glass of wine to go with them.

Oveta was a tougher boss than any man for whom I've ever worked. She had grown up in a man's world, competing against men and competing successfully. By which I mean that often enough she had won. The effort had required more self-discipline than most women of her generation ever had to demand of themselves. If she could discipline herself, other women could too. So though I don't reach the conclusion that women are tougher bosses than men are, I do think I get close to the truth when I say that women bosses appear to be tougher on women employees than men.

Once I parted with the Dancer, I had lunch with Oveta almost every working day for a full year. So I had a right to feel a friend and fellow worker as well as an employee. One day, a Saturday, which is very likely memorable on the charts of those who keep weather statistics in the nation's capital, Washington had a storm which is memorable to me: high wind, torrential rain. Power went out. Lines were down. Telephone poles snapped. I couldn't get anybody on the line at home. I couldn't reach Tom at his office, and I had three children, tiny children stranded in a forest high over the Potomac River at the end of a long dirt road.

Was it feminine of me to want to go home? Maybe. Mothers who think their children might be in danger at home want to go there. Anyhow, I did. I said to Oveta, "I'm scared. They're out there at the end of the line and the only adults in the house speak nothing but Spanish and I'm sure they're scared. I ought to go."

And to this day, I'm ashamed that I didn't go. But I didn't. Because Oveta, looking out her window at the rain-swept emptiness below, said, "I'll send the chauffeur out." Which she did, and he reported that the children and the housekeepers were huddled in the basement, safe from the danger of broken glass from those great windows overlooking the river, and that all was well.

Oveta relayed the message to me and went on about her work, presuming that I would go on about mine. Maybe she was right. The children were safely huddled. They would not have been any safer by my huddling too. Moreover, the roads were made dangerous by falling trees. The chauffeur was a professional and negotiated those dangerous roads better than I could have done. But in a time of danger to children, a mother wants to be there.

There was no question in my mind that Nelson would have said, "Yes, go. I'll have the chauffeur take you." Bobby Kennedy, who was to become my boss, would have said go. Both Charlie Di Bona and Henry Kissinger, who were to become my bosses later on, would have said go.

But they were men; Oveta was a woman. She said, "I'll send the chauffeur out."

It was a day, a scary day, but only a day; and neither that day nor the next day did I have time to reflect on the gender aspects of employment. We worked hard and we played hard, and Oveta had it about right when she said, "This town is like a merry-go-round. You're swung into the melee and then you're swung out, and before you know you're swung out, you've swung back in again."

It was exciting while it lasted. I thought it would last forever, if only it hadn't been for Tom and his fixation on buying a newspaper. I had brought him to the White House and he talked with Dwight Eisenhower. I reminded him of it. I said, "Would you meet Dwight Eisenhower in Oceanside, California?" (Oceanside was the new town in which Tom thought he might be able to buy a paper, and Oceanside was even smaller than the other town, the one where he hadn't been able to buy one.) Anyhow, I said, "Would you meet Dwight Eisenhower in Oceanside, California?"

And Tom said, "Joan, I appreciate very much your serving as a bridge between me and Dwight Eisenhower. Exchanging pleasantries with Dwight Eisenhower is probably something I shall always remember, but it is not a basis for a career and it will not serve to educate three children and neither will Bankruptcy Ball. I want to get out of here because I think we're getting over our heads."

Bankruptcy Ball was a symbol for both of us. For me, it was the most exciting, most glamorous, most fun party I'd ever attended—and indeed, as far as my world was concerned, given. To Tom, it was a reminder that he didn't belong. And Bankruptcy Ball was a catalyst, too, urging Tom toward his decision to get out of Washington and pulling me to the opposite conclusion so that Bankruptcy Ball was very nearly a catalyst for a parting of the ways.

We had rented a house, high over the Potomac, a lonely house standing at the very end of a dirt road. The house had three bedrooms upstairs and a small kitchen downstairs and the rest of it consisted of one enormous room with a huge fireplace. The house was that room. That room was the house. A hardwood floor, about one hundred feet long and thirty feet wide. I don't know who built that house or why. Somebody said it had been a gambler's hideout. We couldn't furnish that room properly and, looking back now, I think we were right not to try. You stood in that room and looked out at the river. If the gambler had wanted to give a party for his ladylove, it was a good room in which to give it.

And I don't know what the cost of our party was. We provided the room plus four hundred dollars. The other hosts—all friends—including Stewart and Tish Alsop, Joseph Alsop, Paul and Phyllis Nitze, Philip and Katharine Graham, John and Joanne Bross, Frank and Polly Wisner (there may have been others)—provided the money.

And it must have been a lot of money to have warranted the

jocular title, Bankruptcy Ball. But liquor arrived by the truckload, tables and chairs by the truckload. Chauffeurs made the drive for days before the event, and explained, "I'm driving for the president of the World Bank and I just wanted to be sure I knew the route." The caterers moved in and the orchestra moved in and the people moved in and there were secretaries and assistant secretaries and generals and admirals and ambassadors. Tom had been to Paris and bought me a dress, a beautiful dress, cut very low and giving the not altogether false impression of trans- parency, and I danced until three in the morning and I guess it's true that I thought I owned the town.

About 2:00 in the morning, Tom walked around the house outside on the pathway which led to the homemade swimming pool into which the brook flowed, and he reported to me the next day that he seriously thought the house might fall, that it was visibly shaking with the dancing and the music and in his mind, the bankruptcy.

"Now look, Joan, I was coming downstairs just when the first guests arrived and there were some people seated way over at the far end of the room and I heard somebody say, 'Who owns this place?' And someone who didn't know me—but I knew him, David Acheson, Dean Acheson's son answered: 'Some rich Republican. They come in here and make a splash and think they own the place. It happens with all Republican administrations. I hear this guy works for the CIA.'

"Now look, Joan, I love you and you looked sensational last night. I love our house and we're lucky to be able to rent it for three hundred a month because nobody wants to drive this far. You know what Nelson said to me last night? We were standing outside looking down at the river and he said, 'Why don't you buy this house?' I wouldn't borrow money from Nelson to buy a house because we don't really belong here. But more important, we shouldn't buy this house. I love what I'm doing and you love what you're doing, but do you want to be doing this in five years or ten? We have to get started, and we can't get started in a place where everybody we know has already arrived."

So it went on like that for days and weeks. Bankruptcy Ball was my coming out party in Washington. On the day after it was over, Tom had turned it into a sad and sometimes quarrelsome farewell.

●

EIGHT

Beached

There was a long pier with benches on which a few old men sat, holding their fishing poles, waiting. There was some not-in-use playground equipment, orange in color, sticking up out of the sand. The sand was gray and wet, a little dirty-looking on this November morning; and there was a cold wind coming in from the sea.

Tom and I stood near the lonesome playground equipment and looked eastward, up from the beach, up the slight rise toward the town, which consisted of a long street of small shops—some of them boarded up—the sidewalks almost deserted. Tom had explained that the nearby Marine Corps base at Camp Pendleton was very nearly empty, the Marines having gone to Korea and that a lot of Oceanside's business had consequently disappeared.

Beyond the main street, spotted with tall palm trees, were a few connecting streets, branching eastward. Beyond them there were brown hills, barren, unpopulated, stretching away as far as the eye could see.

"Well," said Tom, "this is it. Population, sixteen thousand. Circulation, two thousand. I think it's the smallest daily newspaper in the United States, and it's going to be a long pull to pay off five hundred thousand dollars. But we own it, Joannie, and this is our town."

I had taken off my shoes and stockings, and the sand was cold on my bare feet. I wondered what Oveta would think of Oceanside. I wondered what Nelson would think of Oceanside. I wondered what all the people who had danced at Bankruptcy Ball would think of Oceanside. I thought I knew.

And I looked at Tom: tall, lean, with a face faintly reminiscent of pictures of Indian braves; handsome, his hair blowing in the wind, his determined words sounding in my ears.

What a waste. What a terrible unconscionable waste—of time, of things that could be done, of people who could be known, of places that could be seen, of parts that could be played, of a life that could be lived. What a terrible, dreary, deadening waste.

No contrary argument came to my mind. No lift of hope or humor came to my spirits. I was dealing with a man who had a mission, and the mission was too small and he couldn't see that it was too small. I was married to him, had three children with him, and the fourth was on the way. He must have seen the expression on my face and sensed danger. He took my shoes, with the stockings rolled up inside the toes, out of my hand and put them under his arm. Then he kissed me and afterward our eyes met. He saw the challenge in mine and drew back, standing a little way apart.

"Look, Joannie, this will be ours. We've never owned anything. All the people that we know own things. Now we'll own something. We'll make it something to be proud of, the best small daily in the country. We won't make a lot of money. We don't make a lot of money now. But we'll be building something, something to be proud of, and someday maybe we'll want to go back to Washington or New York but we'll go from a base, something solid that's ours."

I didn't say anything. We stood there, looking at each other, two people alone on a beach on a gray day. Tom spoke again. "Look, I'm trying to build something for us. Do you want to help or don't you?"

The moment was over. We walked back up the dank cement steps, up onto the deserted street fronting the beach, got into the car, and drove back to the motel.

I went back to Washington, back to the department, back to Nelson and Oveta, back to friends, and back to the children. Tom stayed in Oceanside on the beach, and I never answered his question. At least not in so many words. He had no trouble in persuading my father, now retired from his law office, to come out and give him a hand in taking over the tiny newspaper. They both came back to Washington for Christmas, bringing tinselly presents bought in Oceanside, and I said, "Thank you."

In fact, as I look back on it now, I behaved about as badly as any woman could behave to a husband who is starting something and trying to make a career of something and wants her to be a partner.

On the other hand, why should the man be the one to decide what the partnership will do? I argued the question with myself. After all, I had always known that Tom wanted to buy a newspaper. I had heard all the stories about Charlie Moore and John Clark and Tom trying to buy the *Manchester Union Leader* in New Hampshire and about how Mrs. Knox had sold it to William Loeb instead. I knew Tom had worked for a year on this project and that he had worked on newspapers and knew all about William Allen White, linotype machines, printing presses and leads, and that it was, so he thought, in his blood.

So now he had found a newspaper. What did I propose that the partnership should do instead? Well, I didn't really have a proposal. Go on doing what we were doing in Washington, I suppose. Was Tom right in saying that this couldn't last, that we were getting in over our heads? What did he mean by that? Well, there's the future. And there were the children, three children and now there was to be one more. Maybe he was right that we couldn't go on doing what we were doing. But why would anybody choose a depressed beach town next to a half-deserted Marine base as a jumping-off place?

Suddenly, my office, two secretaries, and a White House telephone became a security blanket. I stayed right where I was and, at night on the telephone, I inquired after his health, after the health of my father, and after the health of my mother, who, still trying for sainthood, had followed my father to Oceanside. I asked how the newspaper was doing and would he send me a copy. This went on for all of six months. I made myself a hectic life in order to avoid being lonely. I wasn't alone. I had the help—the Mexican man and his wife in that strange house over the river. I had David, who was four, Mary, who was three, and Joannie, who was one. I had besides a baby inside me, and quite suddenly new friends—congressional friends—and, in particular, the young congressman from Ohio.

I don't want to get into this. It isn't important. It's only noteworthy. But it is a fact, contrary to public assumption, that a woman who is very pregnant, prominently pregnant, may nevertheless have trouble fending off attentions. I was surprised when I discovered that this was true. I told Tom over the telephone that perhaps the young congressman from Ohio was simply exhausted from making the long drive through town and over the bridge and up the hill and down the long wooded lane, and that was the reason I couldn't get him out of the house. Tom didn't think it was funny. "You'd better get out here, Joannie. The whole thing sounds like the dregs of too long a party."

The baby was due toward the end of May. Finally, about the first of May, I told Tom I was ready to go, and he came out and got me. Why did we drive to Canada on the way to Oceanside? Why did we visit Lake Louise? We drove about two thousand miles out of our way. I'd like to think it was because we were young and foolish, which in fact we were, but I know it was because I was fighting every step of the way. I didn't want to go to Oceanside. I didn't want to run a newspaper. Looking back now, I think I might have found a way out of it if it hadn't been for the baby.

I had never had any trouble having babies, and Oceanside, California, was a good place to have them. By the time I arrived, Tom had already made friends with a doctor named Stub Harvey, a man of roughly his own age who had just started practice in Oceanside and may have been the last doctor in the United States who started a practice with the intent of making house calls, and who stuck to the intent.

Dr. Harvey delivered five of my children over a period of eight years. In addition to delivering them, he saved them, cured them, fixed them, and knew them. How odd to reflect that doctors don't do that anymore.

I found a house on the beach and insisted that we buy it. Tom was reluctant because if you lived on the beach in

Oceanside, you were regarded as being upper income, and Tom, not being upper income, didn't think it safe to pretend. But it was one of the best major family arguments I ever won. A house on the beach is the best place in the world to bring up little children, and bringing up little children was how I spent nearly all my time in Oceanside and how Tom spent nearly half of his.

On a beach you can run, you can learn to swim, you can build a fire and have supper, you can fish, you can play touch football, you can put up a swing and swing, you can ride a horse. All these things our children did, and all the time they were doing it, there sounded in their ears the metronomic crash of the waves breaking on the beach. Always there was that running sound, running behind all other sounds, mounting gradually, then crashing in crescendo, and then behind the crescendo, the sound, running again.

We lived with that sound always, day and night, for so long that it is in my mind still. Wherever our children go and whatever they do and wherever they live, they will always carry in their minds that stirring, running, crashing sound; a reminder that the earth goes on repeating itself and that it triumphs over successes and failures, life and death, and other small problems, and is all we really know about eternity.

I don't know why I think that's a good thing for children to be reminded about; I suppose because it's true.

So we brought David to the beach at four, Mary at three, Joannie at one, and we had Susan almost as soon as we got there; and then came Nancy, Elizabeth, Tommy, and Nicholas, and these last were all homecoming celebrations.

Homecoming was the reason why I had so many children in Oceanside. Oveta had appointed me to a board at the National Institutes of Health, and after that President Kennedy appointed me as a member of the board of the National Cultural (Kennedy)

Center, so that I was taking the plane back to Washington at least ten times a year and staying on for a while each time I made the trip. When I got home, Tom was glad to see me, I was glad to see him, and we celebrated my homecoming. A lot of the celebrations were spontaneous, and some of the ones that were spontaneous resulted in babies. Tom and I would look at each other when I told him the news a little ruefully, a little scared, a little braced but nevertheless, glad.

I remember when I first noticed the presence of Nicholas —those first signs of feeling slightly sick and having a sudden craving for salt and lemons. Dr. Harvey said he could, if I wished, consult the county board of doctors and get approval for an abortion.

"Why, Stub, are you worried? Should I have an abortion?"

Stub had a way of answering questions by looking off to the side and saying "well," with a certain frowning perplexity, as if he were thinking his way through a problem, and then looking directly into my eyes with the answer "That weak back of yours carried seven babies, and I think it might be getting a little tired."

It was the first time I had ever thought of myself as a machine with parts which might reveal wear or which might fail. It was not a thought for happy homecomings.

I pulled the sheet around me and sat up on the examination table in Stub's office. "Now, Stub, is this baby going to be all right? Is there some danger? Tell me."

"I think the baby will be fine. But I think it's about time you and Tom knew that the chances of a fine baby diminish with each fine baby. You've had seven fine babies, and this will be eight. Don't you think eight is enough?"

So when Nicholas came, Tom and I both knew down deep that he would be the last. He arrived beaten to a pulp, black-eyed and bloody and as messy as though he'd been fighting his way through a swamp. Tom ran down the empty corridor shouting, "Is there a doctor anywhere in this hospital?" because Stub had suddenly left the room and gone somewhere, maybe to the men's room or to lie down for a while. It was late at night, and there seemed to be no one in the corridors. Nicholas came very fast, surprising even Stub with the speed of his passage and hurting hard. Tom got scared when I screamed, but Stub got back in time and Nicholas was fine.

When Bobby Kennedy learned of Nicholas's birth, he sent Tom a telegram quipping that if this was a competition, he and Ethel would bow out. Regardless of the telegram, he and Ethel went on to top us by three with their eleven children.

So they were all fine, all eight of them; and I'm glad I had every one of them, even now when one of them or two of them or even three of them at the same time make me sick with worry about what they are doing or not doing. I often think of a line which Tom quotes to me from Balzac's *Old Goriot*: "My son, do not have children. You bring them into the world; they send you out of it." I consider it a warning to myself, not to let them send me out of it, and I'm still glad they're here.

I am glad I got through them all, pretending they weren't there, lacing waist pinchers onto myself and going to Washington dances with them hiding inside the waist pinchers, wearing dresses which concealed them—or nearly so—and wearing them so successfully that it wasn't until the last month that I could no longer pretend. Joe Alsop said, "Joannie pops them like lima beans," and I was proud.

Mrs. Nicholas Longworth disapproved. Which is how Nicholas got his name. The name was a kind of retort to her disapproval. And Tom, having been a chief participant in the homecoming celebrations, refused to go into the delivery rooms, except for that one time with Nicholas. The reason he would never go into the delivery room was, he said, because he couldn't stand to hear me crying out in pain. He actually said, "I'm afraid of myself, Joannie. I would hit the doctor. I would do something horrible in order not to hear you cry."

And I guess I cried a lot. It's a peculiar thing God did for us when he gave us memories and then arranged our memories so that they don't remember pain. If God has a mind, mothers must have been on it when He devised this scheme. Because we don't remember. We remember that it hurt, but we can't remember exactly how it hurt and what the hurting was like. Thank God. When it's all over, and the baby is fine, that's what you do.

The other day, one of my daughters, now married and with a child of her own, told me that she would soon have another and that she was concerned about her job, not that she would lose it but that she would fall behind. She wants to be a CEO. She's in the competition to be the CEO. She thinks she has as much chance for the job as any of the men who are competing for it; in fact, she thinks she can win.

But to take two months off or three—two or three months out of the competition; add to that being in the competition when she feels sick in the mornings and tired in the night; add to that the one at home who needs a lot of attention and care and time. Her husband helps. He helps a lot. He can get dinner and wash the dishes and take care of the child. And he does. But he can't help carry the baby. And he can't keep her in the competition while she has the baby. So it's not fair. Here she is competing with a lot of men who don't carry babies and don't have to take time off from the competition to have them; and competing with some women too who, she says, are smart enough not to have babies because babies interfere with what they've got their minds on—the job and success in the job.

So we discussed all this, and I had in mind her strong

opinions about women being without question the equal to men, her strong conviction that men put women down, and her recent discovery that one way they put women down is by taking advantage of the "accident" that women are the ones who have to have the babies. I said to her at last, "What's the question?

"Is the question, Do you want this baby? or is the question, Do you want to stay in the competition?"

"They're both the question, and the answer is I want them both. But it's unfair."

"No," I said, "it's not unfair. Because the winner of that competition, if it's not you, will be someone who has never had a baby."

NINE

The Spectator

*A*ll my life, whether at home or abroad, through my childhood, through marriage, in jobs and between jobs, whether about to bear a child or not, whether duty called or duty didn't, I have had to cope with a singular problem: I always want to go.

Other people—not all but many—don't always want to go. Or if they do, reason takes hold, reason that says, "you don't have enough money to go" or "you just went" or "you have too much to do right here."

I don't receive these warning signals from the mind; I can't help myself. My first thought upon hearing of adventure afoot or of friends about to visit far-off or little-known places, whether starlit islands, unexplored rivers, unclimbed mountains, or restaurants pronounced to be four-star quality is "Do I get to go?"

Stewart Alsop used to tease me about this whenever he heard or read of any adventure which sounded in the slightest amusing or interesting. "An expedition is forming to conquer Mount Everest," he said, upon learning of the British effort which culminated in the triumph of Hillary and Tensing. "It is under the command of John Hunt, who was your husband's company commander in World War II. Do you get to go?"

Stewart mimicked my use of the word "get" because, he said, it suggested that I was being taken along. Leaders of expeditions could see at once that I looked upon their projects with such enthusiasm and sheer joy that a single question occurred to all of them: Would it be unkindness, bordering on cruelty, to leave me behind? Maybe, indeed, that's the way I got to go to all the places in my life to which I got to go.

It was without question the basis for my friendship with Alice Roosevelt Longworth, the daughter of Theodore Roosevelt. As I say, I got to go from Oceanside to Washington a lot. Washington was my oasis, my place to find out what was going on, my place to gather strength and interest and gossip against what sometimes seemed to me the dreary sands of Oceanside; and Mrs. Longworth, as Washington's reigning dowager, became the chief figure in my oasis.

She lived alone in an ancient mansion just off Washington's DuPont Circle, surrounded by other ancient mansions, now become headquarters for various charitable organizations where office secretaries kept mailing lists in what had once been the spectacular drawing rooms of the rich and powerful barons of Washington, for the most part senators or ambassadors of kings.

There she had ensconced herself when she married the speaker of the House, Nicholas Longworth of Ohio, in 1906; and here she remained, "an aging relic," as she called herself, surrounded by the objects of an era long gone. There along the wall on the many steps which led from the anteroom at the front door to the high-ceilinged, fireplaced drawing rooms and libraries on the second floor, hung the tattered remains of the tiger, one long claw hanging askew, which "Father shot in Africa."

There were the books stacked on the shelves and piled high in the corners of the library. Somebody had read them once, and there were the red leather upholstered chairs in which to read them again. Except, of course, that nobody did, and nobody had for forty years or more. There was the dining room, a-glitter with ancient crystal, and the small room off the library where Mrs. L. poured her afternoon tea, which was furnished with small, high-backed chairs of dark-stained wood where friends sat and visited while she poured. That was the room with the pillow with the embroidered motto, large enough to be clearly visible at a respectable distance: "If you can't think of anything nice to say, come sit by me."

That house was a lived-in museum, and Mrs. L. treated it as such. She guided my husband to the tiny bedroom on the third floor where we were to spend the night, and beckoned him to the small window from which she gazed out at the steep-slanted shingles of the roof next door. "You see," she said, "if you're agile, you can easily make the leap. Nick used to do it late at night when he visited the Belgian ambassador's daughter."

Tiny, quick as a bird, bony, and bright-eyed, fragile, strong willed, and sharp tongued, Mrs. Longworth lived on into a new world and treated it with the same amused contempt she had treated the old. It was in that red and gold dining room in which her butler and the waiters hired for the evening wore the white gloves of a time long past that she turned brightly on an evening in the mid-sixties to her guest of honor, Robert F. Kennedy. "Senator," she declared in a voice intended for the entire table, "we have *all* been breathless reading the news of your adventure with the mountain. Each morning, we awaited the bulletins of progress. Each night we wondered, will he make it? Then came the glorious news of your success. And now, the most brilliant stroke. To name the mountain after yourself. That was genius. May I offer my congratulations?"

And Bobby sat, dumb and red-faced, subsiding a little in his chair, but wary eyed, searching his mind for a riposte. And while he reflected, Mrs. Longworth asked her question: "Have you thought of anything you can do as an encore? What about running around Kennedy International Airport?"

I could see Bobby's jaw thrusting forward. He had thought of an answer, and it fell short. "What preparations are you making, Mrs. Longworth, for your funeral?"

As I say, I think Mrs. Longworth liked me because I wanted to get to go and she wanted to get to go too. She knew the feeling. She had "gone" all her life, and now that she was in her mid-seventies and couldn't get to go physically as she once had, she got to go vicariously by talking and being with the people who were planning expeditions and assaults on pinnacles of mind or matter and watching to see whether I got to go too.

The first time I met her was at tea (people served tea to Mrs. L. long after the fashion of having tea went out of style) at the home of Joseph Alsop, her cousin. Joe and Stewart Alsop called her "Cousin Alice" which put them on the top rung of courtiers. David Bruce, the tall handsome blond man who had served Harry Truman as under secretary of state and was ambassador to France under Eisenhower, ambassador to England and NATO under Kennedy, to the Vietnam peace talks under Nixon, and to China under Nixon and Ford, called her Alice. I suppose that privilege went to those who knew her when she was a girl or who might by virtue of age have assumed the status of equals. Felix

Frankfurter called her Alice, so did Averell Harriman and Dean Acheson. Friends who could not assume that status, called her Mrs. L., and to the rest of the world she was Mrs. Longworth.

It mattered to her what she was called and by whom. When Senator Joseph McCarthy of Wisconsin was riveting the attention of the nation on the question of who in the Army of the United States had promoted a Communist dentist to the rank of captain, Mrs. Longworth became an eager spectator at the Senate hearings. Each morning her aged limousine with her aged chauffeur, Turner, at the wheel delivered her to the little flight of stairs under the portico entrance to the Senate; each morning she sat attentively as McCarthy flailed. Often I went with her, and often I noticed that McCarthy looked her way. It seemed to me that he assumed her support.

At any rate, it was during these Army–McCarthy hearings that someone suggested that McCarthy attend her at one of those large parties in honor of somebody, which are really intended to raise money and to which Washington is necessarily addicted. He accepted the honor at once; a fact of which Mrs. Longworth, who intended, of course, to go to the party, was totally unaware.

To her surprise, McCarthy arrived at her house, bearing orchids. Perhaps it was the orchids, a flower Mrs. L. detested, that put her in a particularly caustic mood. When the senator greeted her from the foot of the long staircase with the words "Good evening, Alice," she raised herself to her full five feet one, and defined where she stood on the matter of her name. "Senator, only the garbage man calls me by my first name. To you, I shall be Mrs. Longworth."

I met her, as I said, at Joseph Alsop's house, and we conversed at length about my children and my life. And she said, "When you're in Washington next, you must come to stay with me."

And so I did, beginning a friendship which spanned some twenty years. But it was not until a night when David Bruce brought me home (that is to Mrs. L.'s house) and walked up the stairs to say hello to her before he left, that I realized what an honor she had paid me with that first invitation. "You know," she remarked to David as we sat in the little parlor, "this is the first time I've had an overnight guest in the house since 1912."

I amused her. From behind the curtains of her sitting room she listened while David Bruce and I chatted after an evening at dinner. From behind those same curtains, she listened as Nelson, after the death of Robert Kennedy in 1968, sought me out to come and work for him in his campaign for the Republican presidential nomination. I could tell from the questions she asked me when they had departed that she had been listening, and I could tell that she knew that I knew.

But that was part of her wickedness, accepted, I suspect, all her life by those who knew her well. Certainly her father, the president, knew she was wicked and appreciated it. "I remember," she once told me, "Father and I had to go to old Senator Fessendon's funeral."(I think it was Fessendon but Mrs. Longworth was always mentioning the name of long-forgotten senators as though they were household words.) "When the funeral ended, there was President Taft, huge and stalwart, marching down the aisle. And I said to Father, in a loud whisper, 'Father, look, he's preceding the casket.' And Father made a loud *ssh* and said, also quite loudly, 'It's all right Alice. Let the dead bury the dead.' "

Mrs. Longworth was at her most wicked on the subject of presidents, and I was always a little shocked by the manner in which she spoke of them. I mean, I only knew about presidents from history books, and I had an Anderson, Indiana, public school girl's respect for every one of them whose name I could recall.

But Mrs. Longworth had known them, known them all, and had reached the stage of "known them all already" as T. S. Eliot defined the surfeited mind, for as far back as Benjamin Harrison, and she spoke of them as you might speak of people we know, and we do not always speak of people we know with awe or even with respect. Without exception, the men who occupied the White House were men first and presidents later, an obvious truism, but one which points up the fact that most of us don't see the man because the president gets in the way.

She made great fun of Woodrow Wilson, who was president simply because "Father and Taft had a falling out." Having grown up in the White House, she regarded his occupancy of the house with natural animosity. She told me of how she and her friend Evelyn Walsh MacLean spent evenings making dolls in Woodrow Wilson's image, sticking pins in the dolls at the spot where the heart would be, and then "ordering up the carriage" late at night, driving to the White House, running out, tossing the dolls up on the White House lawn as far as they could throw them and dashing back and "galloping away." I had to down my innate distaste for the disrespect to the president and to remember that as a girl, I might have done something similar back in Anderson, Indiana, to the people who moved into our house when we had to leave it and move upstairs with my grandfather.

To Mrs. L., presidents were men and they had one thing in common: extraordinary ambition. She knew that the ambition was an essential to reach the job, but to see the ambition revealed amused her. She watched for it and chortled at discoveries. For example, she told me, "Here was Bill Knowland [the senator from California and majority leader under Eisenhower] lying on the sofa, tired after a long session, his eyes closed in repose. And then he suddenly awoke and said, with childlike seriousness, 'Alice, do you think I could be president?' " It may be that in order to please Mrs. Longworth, ambition had to reveal itself in boldness and vigor, which was the way she thought of her father. Bill Knowland had not revealed ambition by boldness and vigor. Neither for that matter had her husband, Nicholas Longworth, and I always suspected that Mrs. L. had despised him for the failure. "He'd rather be tight than president," she had once said of him. Wilson was not bold and vigorous and neither was Calvin Coolidge. "Dull, almost lifeless." she said of Coolidge and remembered that upon hearing the news of his death, she had remarked to a circle of friends at tea, "How could they tell?"

The Kennedys were vigorous and bold, and Mrs. L. admired them, though as a Republican, she supported "Dick." But of all the presidents whom she observed with amused and knowing eyes, the only one for whom she bore real contempt was Warren G. Harding.

I gathered that her contempt for Harding was well known among her friends and had been well known since the Harding administration. One of these friends, whose name she would not reveal, was a retired editor at a New York publishing house who had been called back to duty sometime in the early seventies for the purpose of editing a biography of Harding, then in preparation. There had been an enormous feud with the descendants of President Harding about this biography, and Mrs. Longworth's friend had been at pains to try to make the book acceptable and avoid a lawsuit.

Which he did by removing from the book the pornographic poetry which Harding had penned to a lady friend. Excerpted neatly in galley form and mailed in a plain envelope to Mrs. Longworth, they provided her with a source of almost unending pleasure.

With glee, she would produce them at tea whenever Tom and I dropped in on a Sunday afternoon. "Shall we have a reading?" she would say and go off to her room for her bundle. For fifteen minutes she would read out loud and when she had come to some particularly gauche inanity, she would fold them, and take them back to her room. "My," she would pronounce, "what a slob."

There was about Mrs. L. a certain cast of mind and character that made her a spectator. Sometimes an enthusiastic spectator, hardly ever a cheering spectator, more often a critical spectator who commented caustically on the scene before her eyes. Stewart Alsop used to lament the fact that "Cousin Alice had wasted her life being a spectator. She is bright; she is able; she could have done a great many things and done them well, and instead, she chose the role of spectator."

Stewart had a point. Mrs. L. did not participate. Asked to preside over Washington's annual horse show, she sent me in her place. The grand master, decked out splendidly in white tie, red sash, and highly polished black boots, had to ride smartly from the ring, dismount, salute, and usher me to the seat of honor rather than the grand guest Mrs. L. would have been. But being the grand guest or honorary president of a local event was too much participation for Mrs. Longworth. She didn't like to be touched physically, didn't want her arm held, even when descending a flight of icy stairs, didn't want me to help her adjust her shawl. In an era when everybody kissed everybody as they entered a private gathering for a gala evening, nobody would have dreamed of kissing Mrs. Longworth. I don't know what she would have done had anybody had the bad taste to try. But something about her, and it was a carefully cultivated something, forbade even the thought of it. Not even Dick or Jack, two presidents whom she called by their first names, or Mr. Ford, whom she did not know except as Mr. Ford, would have thought of kissing her when she greeted them in the little anteroom outside the parlor during the annual afternoon celebrations of her birthday.

I thought she was a fine judge of character. She could spot vanity at a glance and was cruel about it. "Never trust a man who parts his hair under his left armpit" was a cruel thing to say about General Douglas MacArthur, who must have worried a lot about losing his hair. "He looks exactly like the little man on the wedding cake" was an unkind thing to say about Thomas E. Dewey. But, alas for him, true.

She had her own vanities, which had to do with old family and old wealth. I went to Japan with her and with her granddaughter, Joanna Sturm, and was treated to a particularly icy display of this vanity when we stopped off at a Rockefeller-owned resort in Hawaii.

It wasn't I who made her go to a Rockefeller resort. She had asked me to arrange accommodations, and I had done it through the Rockefeller office in New York and wished I hadn't.

In her defense, I must say that the whole trip may have been a sad one for her. She had last gone to the Orient in 1905, Princess Alice Sails; Much Excitement and Merriment. President on Dock to Wave Good-bye; Speaker of the House on Board. So the newspapers of the day headlined the event. On this trip, though we had the best hotel rooms and Mrs. Longworth was escorted by a government-provided Japanese guide, she must have felt nevertheless something of a comedown. And when we reached Hawaii, there were no old families—no Doles, no Dillingworths, to greet her. The old families and the old estates had gone. Which is why she asked me about the Rockefeller resort. And we went. And from the moment that we got on the Rockefeller-provided tourist bus with its bullhorn pointing out places of interest, which drove us to the resort, and entered the various-colored Rockefeller-designed rooms, she taunted me. "Just like the Rockefellers," she said when she saw the bus; "just like the Rockefellers," when she saw the pink rooms; "just like the Rockefellers," when the tea was both weak and on the cold side.

Mrs. Longworth was accustomed to the solid, the quiet, the tasteful. She liked solid old wood, high ceilings, chairs meant to be sat in and not for "lounging." She liked big solid banisters on stairways; and she liked stairways, not sloped runways, built of solid wood, not cement disguised with paint and carpets. In fact, Mrs. Longworth didn't like carpets; particularly she didn't like wall-to-wall carpets as in this Rockefeller resort. She liked rugs old and thick, and there were none.

And so I heard "just like the Rockefellers" for the hundredth time; I heard "they're new and they don't have any taste" for about the fiftieth time; and I heard "you and your friends, the Rockefellers" for about the twenty-fifth time. Then one day she stepped into my room and I was on the balcony gazing out at the beach and I said, "Isn't it a beautiful beach?"

She replied, "It's a beach for the rich and indolent. Just like the Rockefellers." And I'd had enough. "Tomorrow," she said that night at dinner, "I've arranged for a car to take us to the volcano."

"I'll stay here, Mrs. L., with the rich and indolent." Next morning at seven she called me. "Joanna is here and we're ready to leave for the volcano."

I said, "No, Mrs. L., I prefer the rich and indolent." I went skin diving that day for the first time in my life.

But it was impossible to continue a quarrel with Mrs. L. I was traveling tourist, and she and Joanna were traveling first class; when Joanna, perhaps sensing that her grandmother was behaving testily, decided to join me in tourist for the trip home, Mrs. Longworth almost cried. I didn't say she cried. But almost, I could tell. Right then, I decided to cease attacking, and Joanna decided after all to go first class with her grandmother and the tiff was over. On that trip, we never mentioned the Rockefellers again.

The other day on Massachusetts Avenue I passed the tall narrow mansion which had been for some seventy years Mrs. Longworth's home. It has been partially destroyed now to make way for an apartment building, and I suppose the library and the staircase and the dining room and parlor are gone. I thought of all the people whom that house had entertained and all the Washington ways it had seen. In the era of the twist, Mrs. Longworth had remembered the era of the poker game. I thought of her, as she recalled for me how on a Sunday afternoon she had come down the long staircase and paused. Something was wrong; she didn't like the sound coming from the poker room. "At the foot of the stairs, two gentlemen from Ohio were leaving, and I could see at once that they were most disturbed. And then the senator from Kansas, Charlie Curtis, came down the stairs, and for a man of his bulk he was positively slinking. There was something wrong.

" 'So,' I said to Nick, 'the two gentlemen from Ohio seemed overwrought and Senator Curtis seemed embarrassed. What happened?'

"And Nick said, 'Charlie Curtis held five kings.'

"Well, I waited. That was a Sunday afternoon. I waited through Monday. On Tuesday I took my parasol and ordered up the car and I went to the Senate Office Building and I called upon Senator Curtis.

"He greeted me, rising from his desk, and offered me a chair, and then he returned to his desk and looked at me with those baleful Indian eyes [Senator Curtis, later Vice President Curtis, was part Cherokee], and there was silence. So I spoke. I said, 'Senator, the two gentlemen from Ohio were very much disturbed'—(because I wanted him to know that I knew)—'and I have determined that we shall not play poker at my house again.'

"And he said, 'Very well, Alice.' And I rose and took my parasol and left.

"And that," said Mrs. L., ending her story, "was the way the poker era ended in Washington."

As I say, I thought of all this when I passed the old mansion—or rather what remains of it—and I thought of the afternoons I had spent with Joanna watching Mrs. L. die. Not enough afternoons. Joanna spent all her afternoons and her mornings too. Mrs. Longworth was an interested spectator until almost the very end. She lay there wrapped in a shawl and wanted to know what was going on and who had said what to whom and where it was and who was there.

Stewart Alsop was right about her being a spectator and right to lament the fact that she could have been much more. But what a shrewd spectator. How knowing and how keen; and how she enjoyed it. Every single minute of every single hour.

Death for Mrs. Longworth was an expected and long-awaited visitor, not to be greeted eagerly to be sure, but not to be made a fuss about. I remember realizing that fact quite suddenly one evening a year later, when the lady seated next to me during after-dinner coffee at a Washington dinner party leaned toward me so that I could see almost all of the gold brocade on the back of her chair and whispered sternly, "Don't you think it's disgraceful that we don't even know where she is buried?"

I could see that she had given the matter a lot of thought and was about ready to take a public stand. "Is it not the responsibility of the family to state, at the least, whether the site is Oyster Bay or here in Washington? Are we not to know whether she was cremated and, if so, where the ashes were scattered?

"Yet, we get not a word. Not a notice in the papers. Nothing in private. Do you think it possible that there was no funeral at all?"

Suddenly before my eyes, intervening between me and the lady in the gold brocaded chair, there appeared the face of Mrs. Longworth. It was a beautiful face, lively with intelligence and wearing that wicked grin which appeared when she had spotted a weakness in somebody's armor. And suddenly I realized what Mrs. Longworth had done to that lady—and to a lot of other ladies—who had been waiting to go. Deciding what to wear. Possibly the black hat with silk brim, the matching gloves, and the single-strand of black pearls? There was her husband's schedule to rearrange (he occupied a decorative post in the Carter administration) and there was Tuesday's dinner party to think about. But Monday had come. And Tuesday. And no word.

Before my eyes, Mrs. Longworth was now chortling with glee. She had fooled them, fooled them all. Unwittingly, I smiled. It was an unexpected response and the lady sat back rather huffily upon the gold brocade.

I hadn't meant to hurt her feelings. But Mrs. Longworth had done precisely what Mrs. Longworth might have been expected to do and, being Mrs. Longworth, should have done. She was ninety-six. She hated pomp and demonstration of sentiment, and particularly she would have hated pomp and demonstration of sentiment about anything she had lived with on such intimate terms as her own death. So she had arranged not to have any pomp and demonstration of sentiment, and if that decision fooled and surprised those of her acquaintance who liked pomp and demonstration, so much the better. She went off stage laughing, but to herself.

TEN

·

Triumph

There must be thousands of people in Washington—and maybe hundreds of thousands in the United States—who pass the White House during the course of a year and reflect in passing on the time when it was "mine."

I don't mean to denigrate national property. The White House belongs to all of us. I am speaking of those who possessed for a time a special sense of pride in being of it, of those who knew its occupants, who had business there, who felt a sense of kinship, and were welcome at the door.

It doesn't last long. Four or eight years and that feeling of belonging is gone because there are new occupants, new faces,

new people with new business. Now it is "their" White House;
it is no longer "mine."

"My" White House was John Kennedy's White House, and
"my" president was John Kennedy. I suppose this feeling of
kinship is partly generational. I've often heard people say, "John
Kennedy was *our* president." And when I look at he or she who
says it, I find I'm right: They are of an age. Yet Richard Nixon
was not much older than Kennedy. Do we hear people say,
"Richard Nixon was *our* president"?

So there must have been something more to John Kennedy
than simply being of an age. And whatever it was, I was
fascinated, like a moth that flutters around a lamp and never
ceases fluttering until it dies from exhaustion or somebody turns
out the lamp. I know other women behaved in a similar fashion.
I saw them so behaving and recognized them as fluttering moths.
But I couldn't help it. I behaved so too.

My friendship with John and Jacqueline Kennedy began at
Joseph Alsop's house on a summer night in 1958. Joseph Alsop
had been, since the Franklin Roosevelt years, one of Washington's most influential columnists. Behind his horn-rimmed spectacles there lurked a mind of keen intelligence, remarkable
learning, and scathing wit, all cocked and ready to be fired at
unsuspecting politicians of a lower breed who had made the
mistake of crossing him. But when Joseph Alsop met that rare
politician whom he admired, the man was coddled, entertained,
and extolled both in private and in print. John Kennedy was one
of these men.

There were eight for dinner, and I think Isaiah Berlin and his
wife were there. The Kennedys were the last to arrive and they
made, as everyone of an age knows, a spectacular sight. Jackie
was wearing a low-cut pink dress and she glowed. The senator
had a handsome tan through which he glowed. We sat outdoors

in Joseph Alsop's meticulously correct English garden, and then moved into his dining room, where the portraits of his eighteenth and nineteenth century ancestors stare grimly at his guests. There is not a one among these gentlemen on the wall of the deep red lacquered dining room whose stern visage does not warn those seated at the table against the light and the frivolous. Duty, they remind you, is first to your country, second to the amassing of an estate for the benefit of your posterity. Seated, as I have often been, under their gaze, I half expected to hear a sepulchral voice: "Gentlemen, the Federal Union, it must and shall be preserved."

Joseph Alsop, at the head of the table, maintains the tradition, though not without humor. On this occasion, as is his wont, he remarked that we would have general conversation, whereupon he threw out several questions bearing upon the defense and well-being of the United States of America, accompanied by allusions to British and American history which served to answer his questions. After which, he cupped his lower jaw in both hands, eyed the senator over his spectacles, and waited for a response, in order to pounce upon it.

Senator Kennedy was not at all discomfited. He deplored President Eisenhower's defense posture, and in jocular fashion he fenced with Alsop's invitations to assess the chances of Hubert Humphrey, Stuart Symington, Lyndon Johnson, and Adlai Stevenson; but there was no talk at all of what everyone present sensed and what Joseph Alsop probably knew—that the handsome senator and his beautiful wife would soon be in the presidential campaign. It was a perfect dinner, and the conversation sparkled. Tom and I went back the next day to Oceanside.

The afterglow of that evening was to last for a long time: If those personable, lovely, intelligent two people wanted to go to the White House, they could. Not only that, they should. And they would. And I'd do anything I could to help them.

So I said to Tom on the way back to California on the airplane. We were seated side by side, and I told him what I thought. He was more appraising and then he said to me, "What about Nelson?"

Well, yes. What about Nelson? If Nelson Rockefeller ran, I certainly would not be doing anything I could to help John and Jacqueline Kennedy. It was one of those questions to which there is only one response: "hmmm."

And so it remained for a while until Paul Ziffren raised it again, in a different light. Ziffren was the tall, angular, intelligent, and fastidious leader of the Democratic party in California, and I met him in New York at a dinner at the home of Marietta Tree. By then it was clear that Kennedy was running, and I told Paul about my meeting him at Joe Alsop's house. Paul was not a Kennedy backer, at least not officially, but he would be in charge of the Democratic convention of 1960, which would be held in Los Angeles. And he asked me on the spot to come and work for him. *What about Nelson?* came into my head at once, and I told Paul that it did.

Ziffren was much more certain about the outcome of the Republican race than he was about who would be the Democratic nominee. "Nelson Rockefeller will not run," he said with the certainty of a man who holds the outcome in his hands, and then he made it clear how certain he really was.

"I'll tell you what, Joannie. You come to work for me, and if Nelson Rockefeller runs, I'll go to work for him."

We parted laughing, and I often thought later on of that night when Paul and I had laughed together and of how much work that laugh would be.

Because Paul Ziffren had already decided that when the Democratic convention was over and the nominee selected, he would cap his selection with an acceptance speech not from the convention rostrum, where acceptance speeches are customarily delivered, but from a different rostrum in a different place. The Democratic Convention of 1960 would go down in history, Paul thought, as the one where the nominee delivered his acceptance speech before the largest crowd ever assembled to hear any speech of any kind. He would give his acceptance speech in the Los Angeles Coliseum.

I had once been to the Los Angeles Coliseum. Tom had taken me there to see Early Wynn start the fourth game in the World Series of 1959. All I could remember about it was a sense of distance, vast distance. The ball players had looked like little midgets seen at a distance. The Los Angeles Coliseum had a seating capacity of one hundred thousand. Paul's idea was that those seats were to be filled. The job he had in mind for me was to fill them.

How Paul ever sold this idea to the Democratic National Committee I don't know. As chairman of the host delegation, I suppose he carried certain weight, but I should have thought there might have been doubts expressed by the managers of the various candidates, and as it turned out there were. I first heard about the doubts in a telephone conversation with one of them. Robert Kennedy was not only doubtful, but also rude. Paul had suggested that Bobby call me, since I was to be in charge of filling the place, and I suppose Paul thought that I might allay the Kennedy fears. I was young. I was reasonably bright. And I had the confidence of naïveté. My job was to fill the coliseum. I would fill the coliseum. And when Robert Kennedy called, I told him so.

"If," came the voice from the other end of the line, "my brother speaks to empty seats, I will shoot you." And he hung up. He hung up before I could remind him that perhaps his brother would not have to make that speech. Perhaps Stevenson would make it or Symington or Humphrey. But I never got to remind him. Robert Kennedy was in drive gear, and he was driving a steamroller. You don't get in the way of a steamroller, as Adlai Stevenson found out. And Stevenson must have known that Robert Kennedy was a steamroller long before I did.

Stevenson, at that convention, tried some steamroller tactics of his own, and Mrs. Franklin Roosevelt was breathless in her excitement about them. Stevenson supporters marched and circled and surrounded the convention hall, and they sent up a great noise; and Mrs. Roosevelt, arriving at a dinner given by her cousins Joseph and Stewart Alsop, and Tom and me, was moved almost to tears. She wore a floor-length white gown of satin with a great bodice, and the waiters at Perino's bowed. I have never seen waiters bow before or since, and I can only tell you that they did indeed bow and it seemed perfectly natural for them to do so. I don't suppose she noticed, rapt as she was in admiration of the Stevenson demonstration. "I called Herbert [Lehman]," she told us, "and I said, 'Herbert, you should have been here. It was so exciting.' " The long drawn "been" and the emphasis on the words "should" and "so" gave her speech a distinctive cast which has remained with me ever since. But I couldn't help feeling a little sorry for her because I knew by that time that Robert Kennedy was driving a steamroller.

By that time too, I had come to know Robert Kennedy, and I had, or so I thought, filled the coliseum for the ceremony which was to honor his brother and to inaugurate his brother's campaign.

I bussed in the people from nursing centers and old people's homes, state societies and regiments of schools, and I still didn't really fill the coliseum. The newspapers estimated the crowd at seventy thousand to eighty thousand, which means that there must have been at least twenty thousand vacant seats. But eighty thousand people—if that's how many there were—were sufficient to create the impression of size and bustle and noise and success. There was a desperate moment just before the nominee was to appear when it became clear that hundreds of seats we had reserved for dignitaries who had not yet arrived were empty and that the seats were right behind where Kennedy was to speak and so right in front of the television cameras. When I realized this, I went to the man in charge, keeper of the coliseum so to speak, who had a little office under one of the great cement block gates. I pounded on his door and he said, "Lady, I can't do a thing about it except on orders from Robert Kennedy."

So I got that straightened out and I got the dignitary seats filled; and just as they were filled, Paul Butler, the retiring chairman of the Democratic National Committee caught my arm in the crowd of arms and said, "Joannie, there's no seat for Mrs. Kennedy." I looked up and there was Senator Kennedy's mother, standing tall and straight and proud—and seatless. So we moved a dignitary from the dais and got a seat for the lady most appropriate for the title, and all came out well.

I said to Tom when it was over, "You'll have to go back to the hotel and change because we're invited to a party tonight." He was grumpy. He had counted on driving down to Oceanside and being home. I said, "No, Bobby has invited us and the party is to be at Romanoff's and the senator will be there and we're going." Sometimes I do this to my husband but only when I know I'm right. And I was right.

There is a moment in every man or woman's life that they hold in secret memory as though in their hearts. That memory is not to be revealed because the fact of holding it is a little embarrassing. To speak of it out loud would seem either boastful or pathetic. Would you say to anyone, "I triumphed"? And yet, the moment is of almost vital importance. Everybody has one and everybody looks back upon it and recharges batteries, or sometimes, reflects on the pillow. Until that night I don't know what moment I held in secret memory. Maybe it was as trivial a thing as being homecoming queen at Washington and Lee. But I know what I hold right now.

There was a small crowd outside Romanoff's restaurant, and to get to the restaurant you had to go up a flight of stairs. The stairs were jammed with people who thought they were invited by virtue of rank and long service but who weren't. Some of them I recognized as dignitaries who hadn't occupied their seats. So we got past these people, smiling and greeting as they looked at us in disgruntled envy. At the top of the stairs stood a burly gatesman in a dinner jacket; behind him was the small lean figure of Count Romanoff and the small stout figure of Prince Radziwill, and behind them was a quietly lit room full of white linened tables and place settings and seated people and sparkling glass. Suddenly John Kennedy came forward from one of them and took me by the arm, guiding me to an empty chair and instead of holding the back of the chair for me to sit down, he lifted my elbow and placed me, standing on the chair. At which exact moment, the orchestra immediately to his left, struck up "For He's a Jolly Good Fellow." There I was standing on the chair, blushing, and John Kennedy started clapping and the whole restaurant full of people were rising and clapping in imitation of John Kennedy and finally the orchestra stopped playing and John Kennedy guided me down off the chair. That was the moment. Triumph. I'm embarrassed to reveal it even now, but as I say, everybody bears in memory a secret moment. That is mine. Only now, it's not a secret anymore.

ELEVEN

The Boss

Those who worked on John Kennedy's campaign for president, who have outlived him to tell about it, say now in a kind of shorthand that they worked for John Kennedy. When they stop to think about it, they know better. They worked for Robert Kennedy. He gave them their orders; he moved them into their jobs. When they didn't perform as he wanted them to perform, he found ways to replace them or to ignore them, not always gratefully or gracefully. He was the boss, single-minded, never doubting his own decisions, never wavering in those decisions. With great reluctance, he would hear debate but not after he had made up his mind. He would ask questions about performance, "How is so and so doing?" or "How is it going?", but never, in all the days I spent with him on that campaign did I ever hear him say to anyone, "What do you think we ought to do?"

People would say, "Listen, Bobby," and he would listen if what the person had to say was directed to a better way of accomplishing what he wanted to accomplish, but they had to speak right to the point and very quickly. Usually, they never got to finish what he was supposed to listen to because, in an instant, he had discovered that what he was supposed to listen to was not worth his time.

Over and over I tried to get Bobby's attention to what Tom had told me on the telephone: that we were in danger of losing California. He wouldn't listen. Jesse Unruh, the campaign boss in that state, was assuring him daily that all was well. One day, I mentioned my doubts in front of the senator. Bobby cut me off, but his brother had detected "a problem." "Just a minute, Bobby, I want to hear what Joannie has to say." I told the candidate what Tom had reported, that Unruh was using the campaign chiefly to tighten his grip on the California legislature, that Governor Pat Brown was being cut out, that Paul Ziffren was being cut out, that campaign money was being diverted to Unruh lieutenants and Unruh base building, all to the detriment of an all-out effort for Kennedy.

John Kennedy was interested. He said to Bobby, "You'd better get out there." But Bobby was not. His brother had told him to get out there, so Bobby would go. But he wasn't really interested in hearing the other side, and maybe he was right, though in the end we did lose California.

"Ruthless" was the word his critics pinned on Bobby, and there was truth in it. But "ruthless" was the penalty he paid for being quick-minded, in a hurry, not suffering fools gladly, and not wasting time for fear of hurting someone's feelings or caring very much when he did.

I remember one incident, totally inconsequential, probably repeated many times in political campaigns and therefore not unique to Robert F. Kennedy; yet, when I think of him in the 1960 campaign, it seems to define Bobby as "the boss."

It happened in one of those vast, vacant buildings near the railroad tracks which get rented for a couple of months during a campaign or are donated by the building owner because they are about to be relegated to the wrecker's ball. We were passing through—the whole entourage, Bobby and assistants—and for some reason I happened to be in town. The man in charge of the campaign office—not the major politician who had the title of state chairman, but some young, aspiring politician who was actually running the show—came up to Bobby and asked for a private word.

It wasn't entirely private because I was there and maybe a couple of others, but it was about as private as campaigns usually are. Bobby listened while the man told him about his problem.

The volunteers were the problem. Volunteers were coming into the headquarters office by the hundreds, most of them old people but also some teenagers, and there wasn't anything for the volunteers to do.

So what do I do with these people? That was the man's question, and Bobby said, "Put them to work on lists." And the man said, "Lists of what?"

"Lists of anything. Have them copy out your mailing list, or copy out every other name beginning with *B* in the telephone directory. It doesn't matter what lists. Have the lists turned in every night; then tear them up and have a different group start again in the morning."

I told you it was a small thing, an unimportant thing. Some people would say it was ruthless. But it solved the problem of what to do with volunteers when there was nothing for volunteers to do.

I sometimes wish, looking back now, that I had been born with Bobby's lack of self-doubt. But I'm not sure I would have wanted what was in him, its corollary—a deep suspicion of anyone who doubted. Bobby could spot doubters at a glance. They were in the way. They were not to be trusted. They were to be gotten rid of or bypassed, ruthlessly.

Clad in a pair of gray trousers and a white shirt, the collar unbuttoned, the tie pulled down and askew, shirt sleeves rolled halfway up the forearm, tousled hair brushing his eyes, he stalked the floor on the balls of his feet like a cat ready to spring. Yet he had a wry, self-deprecating humor; he loved to use the word "ruthless" about himself, and where women were concerned, he had no sense of suspicion, no fear of being run around or outdone.

I had been enlisted during my "triumph." Shortly after John Kennedy had helped me down from my perch on the chair, Bobby had come up to me, kissed me on the cheek, and said simply, "I have two requests. One, will you dance with me? Two, will you come to work for me in the campaign?"

It wasn't until the next day that I had doubts about leaving our six children and leaving Tom, this time not just for a week or so, but for months. Maybe Bobby ought to know that I was pregnant again. Maybe I should tell him that I couldn't go to work until after the vacation Tom and I had planned with the children in Aspen, Colorado. Maybe he should know that I'd worked for many years for Nelson Rockefeller. Maybe for all those reasons he would decide that moving me to Washington was a mistake.

So when he called on the telephone a week later, I went through all these announcements, and he heard me out and said, "Come tomorrow." So I did.

"Write me out a list," he said on my first day in the office, "of what you think you should do in this campaign." There wasn't any banter and barely a word of greeting. "There's a typewriter"—he gestured—"over there."

So I made my list. One: Draw Jackie into the campaign as much as possible. People have criticized the senator for not mentioning her in his acceptance speech. Have her write a weekly "Campaign Wife" column for newspapers. Two: Start a "Calling for Kennedy" operation, asking people what they think are the important problems facing the country, and saying the responses are to be tabulated and given to the senator. And Three: Organize "Coffee for Kennedy" parties. Start by asking women to invite ten friends for coffee; ask each friend to contribute ten dollars; get "Coffee for Kennedy" cups and pour the coffee into these; have a campaign worker attend as many of the parties as possible; hand out pamphlets and Frank Sinatra's "High Hopes" campaign record at each party. And at the end of the campaign put John and Jackie Kennedy on television for a half-hour broadcast in which six or seven problems from the "Calling for Kennedy" operation get answered.

Bobby took my memorandum, wrote the word "yes" after each of the points I had enumerated and said, "I'll call Jackie. Start now."

Looking back, it was a breathless four months. It helped to be pregnant, knowing when I called Tom and the kids every night that I had something of theirs inside me, and since Jackie was just as pregnant as I, we had an instinctive and unspoken understanding of what we could do and what we shouldn't do or even try to do. Jackie had already lost one child through miscarriage. Campaign aides, particularly Ted Sorenson, wanted her on almost every campaign occasion. When she demurred, I fought on her side because I understood her fear better than they.

It was more difficult when Jackie's sense of good taste clashed with the tastes of others, including the tastes of the Kennedy family. Jackie did not like the Rat Pack trio of Frank Sinatra, Dean Martin, and Peter Lawford for whom the Kennedy family had an almost star-struck regard. After all, one of them, Peter Lawford, was an honorary member of the family and they were famous; so use them. Use them whenever possible.

But Jackie was certain that the Rat Pack was the wrong image; at least she did not want to be associated with the Rat Pack, didn't want to appear at campaign rallies with them, didn't want to appear on television with them, and though she was less demanding on this point, she didn't want her husband to appear with them either.

I was Jackie's liaison with campaign headquarters and I was to make her wishes known; and I dreaded what might be the confrontation. But it was done. The Rat Pack disappeared from the campaign. I have ever since credited Martin, Lawford, and Sinatra as possessing a quality not many people associate with their names. They showed understanding. They wanted very much to help. If they could help best by staying away, they would. There were no hurt feelings, or if there were they didn't reveal them.

I was discussing the Rat Pack problem with Bobby one evening in New York, where there had been a meeting, and afterward he asked me to have dinner. We were walking down Park Avenue. It was a late summer night, and suddenly, he took my hand, drew me close, and whispered, "Thank you." At that precise moment, a burly policeman pulled his squad car up to the curb and leaned out the window saying, "I sure hope your brother wins."

Startled for a moment, we walked on hand in hand to the side street where I was staying courtesy of Henry and Afdera

Fonda, who were away. I had the key and Bobby said, "Why don't I come in and have a glass of milk?" So we entered, and I went to the refrigerator and was pouring two glasses of milk when the police arrived. Suddenly, silently, and in numbers, there they were in the kitchen with us.

Bobby and I jumped like two bank robbers caught in the vault. I had failed to turn off Henry Fonda's alarm system and so the police put an end to the only moment during his brother's campaign when I sensed in Robert Kennedy a soft and caring mood.

Jackie and I went to call on old Mrs. Wilson, the president's widow. We wrote the newspaper column and were proud when it was picked up, mostly by weekly newspapers but also by some small dailies. Jackie started the "Coffee for Kennedy" campaign, and hundreds of thousands of "Coffee for Kennedy" paper cups were manufactured and shipped to campaign headquarters. Some of them got used, and more of them got stored in a vast New York warehouse. Steve Smith complained about the expense until one day I thought to ask him, "How many 'High Hopes' records are in that warehouse and how much did you spend on them?" When the campaign was over, thousands of my paper cups were still unused and thousands of "High Hopes" records, but at least the cups were used for Bobby's subsequent New York senatorial campaign and even for Teddy when he ran in Massachusetts. The "High Hopes" records are probably still in that warehouse.

I suppose it would have been fitting, and certainly it would have been crowd pleasing, if on the last night of the campaign, Jackie had appeared with her husband on the platform at Faneuil Hall in Boston where the final speech was made. The crowd overfilled the historic old building. People literally packed themselves in the elevator, stood on each other's feet, breathed in each other's nostrils, were wet with each other's perspiration. It was a quiet crowd, a polite crowd, because everyone sensed that to be unquiet or impolite was to be dangerous. It was that crowded. I was scared getting into the elevator because, as quiet and polite as they were, people couldn't help squeezing against each other so that there was no space even to sink to the floor. Here I was with a great bump protruding from my stomach and I knew that it was dangerous. Tom and Arthur Schlesinger had urged me not to come; but Bobby had backed me against their contrary urgings. When I got out of that place and could breathe again and the bump in my stomach was still there and I could feel it, still solid, in place, undisturbed, I thought how lucky Jackie was to have been in Hyannisport instead.

She had her baby that month, a month prematurely. I went home to California, and the next month had mine. It was Tommy. A boy. After five girls in a row, a boy.

Philip Graham, the publisher of the *Washington Post*, called me while I was in the hospital to remind me that I had other things to be excited about. There was the inauguration. We had tickets for that. There was the inaugural ball. Phil had purchased a box. Before the inaugural ball, Joseph Alsop was giving a dinner party, and the night before that was the grand gala, staged by Frank Sinatra and Sammy Kahn. I wouldn't have missed all of this for anything, and for once Tom was not being dragged along. He wanted to go. This was a party to which we felt entitled. We had been part of it. A grand victory. Everyone who works hard each four years for the man who turns out to be president feels entitled to the celebration. But this celebration was special.

Washington had had a record-breaking snowfall. Cars were abandoned in the streets. For a day nobody could move. The Army was called out to clear Pennsylvania Avenue, the Capitol grounds, and the streets surrounding hotels. Tom and I never saw Frank Sinatra's gala because we couldn't get out of Stewart Alsop's driveway. It wasn't a question of trying. It was an impossibility. I wonder seriously whether in all history a national celebration has ever been held against such odds.

There were other reasons for its being special. Robert Frost was special to Tom because he had been Tom's teacher at Dartmouth, and nobody who saw the inauguration of John Kennedy can ever forget the picture of Frost, standing at the rostrum in the bitter cold, trying to read the poem he had written for the occasion, blinded by the glaring sunlight, looking down at his white typescript with furrowed brow; Lyndon Johnson rising to try to help him shield the paper from the sun; then Frost, refusing to surrender, putting aside the poem he had written, and reciting from memory in a clear voice the lines he had written years before, "We were the land's before the land was ours. . . ."

There on the platform, buttoned against the cold, were figures from the past, gathered to honor the President. Dwight Eisenhower, ruddy-cheeked, polite, and looking almost benevolent; figures from the Truman days; and seated near the rear of the platform among the last surviving veterans of the New Deal was Vice President Henry Agard Wallace, pausing on his way into history. It was unforgettable.

It must have been about midnight when Joe Alsop came up to me at the inaugural ball, looking odd in a dinner jacket, black tie, and galoshes. "Darling," he said, "let's go to my house and have some terrapin and champagne. Afdera Fonda is coming and two or three others and it will be cozy." He looked around the ballroom, where people were dancing and chatting and drinking champagne. The president had come and probably gone to another ballroom but the evening seemed to me still young and Philip Graham, who had brought along a sack full of champagne, was holding forth from his box in high good humor. Nor did Joe seem tired or dispirited, which is the usual demeanor of those who want to go home early from a party. I should have paid more attention to Joe's demeanor.

But I did decide to accompany him and I sought out Tom, who disagreed. "In a way," he explained, "this is Phil Graham's, party, and we're by no means the big shots at Phil Graham's party. We shouldn't be the first to leave." So we stayed. On our way home I discovered how wrong we had been. We all got into Phil Graham's car, Chip and Avis Bohlen, Phil and Kay, Tom and I, and Graham maneuvered through darkened streets made narrow by banks of shoveled-up snow on each side. The Bohlens were to be let off first and as we approached their Georgetown street, Avis cried out in alarm, "Chip, there's a fire. Is it our house?" Suddenly we saw searchlights surrounding a house, their rays brightening up the neighborhood and lighting the sky. I, too, thought at first that houses were on fire, but as we came to an intersection on Dumbarton Avenue, I could see the house that was lit by the searchlights on all four corners, and I knew. "No," I said, "it's not your house, Avis, and nothing is on fire. The president of the United States has stopped at Joe Alsop's for a little terrapin and champagne."

And I didn't get to go.

On a winter vacation in Carlsbad, California, with my best friend, the gasoline station attendant.
BELOW: *A chat with Nelson in his office while he was vice president. (Note spelling of "grateful." Nelson was no better at spelling than I.)*

To Joanie Braden – A unique person with admiration and affection from an old & greatful friend – Very best wishes – Nelson A Rockefeller

ABOVE: *All ten of us on the beach at Oceanside where we swam and skipped and sang around evening cookouts. What a great way to grow up.*
LEFT: *I love him and he loves me. Taken on our deck, overlooking the beach in Oceanside, California.*
(Photo by Bob Morton)

RIGHT: *The whole family lines up for a bus ride through California during Tom's Democratic primary race for lieutenant governor. We marched with Cesar Chavez on behalf of immigrant workers, Tom made speeches, we sang songs, had picnics and fun. Except, as I didn't discover until we got home, we had endangered California. Tommy had the measles. Left to right: Tom, Tommy, Elizabeth, Nancy, Susan, Joannie, Mary, David, Nicholas, and me.* (Photo by Robert B. Shumway, Independent Press Telegram) BELOW: *On the beach in Rehoboth, Delaware, about 1980. Left to right: Susan, Mary, David, me, Elizabeth, Nancy, Tom, Joannie, Tommy, and Nicholas in front.*

RIGHT: *Tom with a copy of his newspaper, the* Blade-Tribune, *which vied with me and our children for his love and attention.*
BELOW: *Our closest friend, Stewart Alsop, and me on a picnic somewhere between Oceanside and Aspen, Colorado.*

ABOVE: *John Kennedy didn't carry California but he had the unanimous backing of my six—as it was then—children, David, Mary, Joannie, Susan, Nancy, and Elizabeth.*

LEFT: *Joseph Alsop, author, columnist, arbiter of taste, and me. (© 1980 Stuart Bratesman)*

RIGHT: *Our ambassador to India, John Kenneth Galbraith, with me on holiday while I was traveling with the first lady, Jacqueline Kennedy, in India. Being covered with brightly colored chalk by cheering crowds is hard on clothing but it lifts the spirits.*

Mrs. Nicholas Longworth on our trip to Japan, her second, my first. In her eighties, Mrs. Longworth still wore the broad-brimmed hat that had been her trademark since her White House days and still frequently adopted the lotus position while sitting.

David K. F. Bruce, handsome and elegant ambassador to more countries than any other man in U.S. history. One of the luckiest things that ever happened to me was that he chose me to be a friend.

BELOW: *Ethel Kennedy sent me this picture after Bobby died, with the inscription,* For Tom and Joan with Christmas love, from Ethel. *What woman wouldn't have fallen in love with Robert Kennedy? And who wouldn't be grateful to Ethel for sharing him with all of us who cared?*

ABOVE: *This is the picture John Kennedy didn't want to see in the newspapers: his wife, Jackie, with a Rockefeller. But John D. III was chairman of New York's Lincoln Center and so, on opening night, it was his job to escort the guest of honor. (That's me and Mrs. Rockefeller following along.) So far as I know, the picture did not make the newspapers and certainly the worst did not happen: Nelson Rockefeller and Jackie were not photographed together.*

BELOW: *Henry Kissinger was as exciting and fascinating to Elizabeth, Nancy, and Tommy as he was to world leaders.*

Kirk Douglas, Leslie Stahl, and me. With Kirk, you're always sure of having stiff competition. (Photo by Elizabeth Wackman)

Here I am with Robert McNamara, my adviser on river blindness in Upper Volta. We were on John Loudon's yacht, sailing the Greek islands after Bob had received an award for distinguished service in Athens.

TWELVE

Does It Matter What People Say?

More than any man I've ever known, John Kennedy cared about what people said. I suppose most successful politicians do. Their livelihood depends on what people are saying. And I suppose that presidents care more than most. But to me, John Kennedy's insatiable desire to hear what people were saying about him, about Jackie, about anybody in his administration, seemed curious in a man whose motives and goodwill were, again to me, unquestionable. I had grown up in the naïve assumption that if you cared about the big things, set goals, worked at them, and if your goals were good and you worked hard, it didn't matter what people said.

Nelson thought this way too. He never worried about what

people said because he had figured out that what he wanted to do was the right thing to do. When people disagreed with him or he heard that they disagreed, the fact was of no consequence to him. They didn't understand, and since they didn't understand, it didn't matter what they said.

Kennedy knew better. "What do you hear?" he would say to me, and once I said, "I hear you have Addison's disease."

An alarm went off somewhere inside him. "Where did you hear that? Who told you that?"

"A doctor told me. A doctor in New York."

"What's his name?"

I refused to say.

"What's his hospital? Where were you when he told you this?" I was blushing by this time and sorry that I had ever uttered the words. His startled reaction frightened me. Though I had not been told that the information was not to be repeated, I didn't want to get anybody in trouble and so again, I refused to say. But those who were within hearing at the dinner table looked at me askance as though I had made a dreadful assertion and then refused to back it.

In fact, I didn't know any more about Addison's disease than the name of it, but John Kennedy's alarm was such that anyone who didn't care as much about him as I did might have spread it abroad and at once. From that moment on, I never mentioned Addison's disease in John Kennedy's presence or out of it, though I know that he learned the name of the doctor by checking up on where I had dined in New York and who else had dined there. I know that the doctor was successfully admonished.

Once during the Cuban missile crisis, he asked me, "What are people saying?" and I responded, "They're asking why it took you so long to go public about the missiles." Which they were. I hadn't been in Washington more than an hour before I heard the question. Stewart Alsop said it was odd and Charlie Bartlett said it was odd and Philip Geyelin said, "What took so long?"

When I mentioned it to John Kennedy he went on instant alert. We were sitting—the president, Jackie, and I—in the small comfortable oval room in the White House which the Kennedys used as a private living room. I remember there was a fire and Kennedy was sipping a daiquiri. It was the first time he had dined with Jackie in several nights. He had been sleeping in his office and like everybody else, I suppose, he was scared.

Anyhow, there was a telephone on the little table between us and as he picked it up I heard him saying, "Get me Ray Cline."

I knew that Cline was the director of intelligence in the CIA and so I purposely turned to Jackie and started a low-voiced conversation. I didn't want John Kennedy to think I was listening in on intelligence matters. When he hung up and Jackie and I were still talking, Kennedy said, "Look, Joannie, when I go to the trouble to find out the facts and I repeat the facts for you in a clear voice, you might at least take the trouble to listen."

Whereupon in a clear voice, he went through the facts again: the date and the hour when it had first been reported that there were missiles in Cuba; the date and the hour when pictures had been shown to him; the date and the hour when he had conferred with McNamara and others; and the date and hour when he had announced the news.

It was all over that evening, and he had come home. But nobody was quite sure it was all over, and he was jumpy. My daughter Susan and his daughter, Caroline, were there to celebrate Halloween, and the president had helped them carve a pumpkin. The two little girls wanted to place the pumpkin in the window, where its lighted candle and grimacing frown would be visible to passersby. But the president, finishing the last touches on the frown, said, "Better not. People will think it's Castro."

Afterward, he carried Susan off to bed, making much of the fact that it was Lincoln's bed in which she was to sleep. It was soon apparent that Susan didn't like Lincoln's bed. She was frightened by Lincoln's bed. John Kennedy went back to her room, picked her up, and asked her where she wanted to sleep. "In your bed," said Susan, or at least so Kennedy reported to Jackie and me when he returned to the room. And I said, "So where is she?" And Kennedy said, "In my bed."

It has always seemed to me oddly comforting that while the Cuban missile crisis was winding down, while vast and powerful forces under his command were on alert, while his agents around the world were holding their ears to the ground, and while he and his countrymen and, for that matter, other heads of state and their countrymen, were holding their collective breaths, the president of the United States should be occupied—briefly to be sure, but with full attention paid—by the task of making a child comfortable.

There was at least one other time when Kennedy said to me, "What do you hear?" I told him what I thought was a funny story about Mrs. Chandler, the wife of the publisher of the *Los Angeles Times*. I said to Kennedy, "Mrs. Chandler called me and wanted to know when it would be convenient for a photographer from the *Times* to come to Oceanside [that's eighty miles] and take a picture of me and the children."

I told him that I didn't know Mrs. Chandler, had never met her, but that I had acquiesced and that the photographer had come and gone and there I was, photographed in the *Los Angeles Times* for no reason that I could see or that was apparent from the printed matter which accompanied the photograph. "I'm puzzled."

Kennedy was amused. "I know," he said, "what Mrs.

Chandler wants. She wants Jackie to come to the ground-breaking ceremonies for the Los Angeles Music Center if she is to help raise money for the National Cultural Center and she's putting the pressure on in any way she can."

Jackie didn't want to go to the ground-breaking ceremonies, I don't know why; it was just another thing she had to do, I guess, and she had much to do. But the president was very conscious of Mrs. Chandler and of the *Los Angeles Times*. So he promised me that he'd go, and he'd "bring John-John," and I was to tell Mrs. Chandler that.

He never did go because the missile crisis came along, but when Lincoln Center opened in New York, the president took careful interest, insisting that Jackie go and telephoning me to be sure that I'd go with her. Jackie and I stayed in the Kennedy suite at the Carlyle Hotel in New York. There was a White House telephone under my bed on which Pierre Salinger called to tell me that the president was worried by an afterthought. It had suddenly occurred to him that the newspapers might photograph Jackie in the company of Nelson Rockefeller, who was then in the middle of a campaign for reelection as governor and was running against a Democrat named Morgenthau. So a picture of Jackie with Nelson could be a political embarrassment, to be avoided at all cost. "Your life is on the line, Joannie, if she gets her picture taken with Nelson Rockefeller or for that matter with any Rockefeller."

Nelson's older brother John was chairman of the board of Lincoln Center, and it was his duty and privilege to escort the wife of the president of the United States into the hall; and Nelson was to be there at the reception for guests of honor.

So Pierre's frantic message made me frantic. How could I manage to keep the most celebrated guest at this celebration away from the two most celebrated hosts? I decided that the only thing to do was to talk to Nelson, and I never told Jackie that I had. Nelson understood at once. I didn't even have to explain. And Nelson talked to his brother John, who saw that all the formal greetings took place without a single picture. Jackie remarked to me later that John Rockefeller was the most self-effacing man she'd ever met.

In the course of keeping Jackie and the Rockefeller brothers away from each other while cameras were present, it never occurred to me to worry about Leonard Bernstein, who, as conductor of the New York Philharmonic at this opening concert in what was to be its permanent home, was rightfully the star of the evening.

I had met Lenny at the White House on the evening that John Kennedy had first broached the name of Roger Stevens to head the National Cultural Center, and I liked him at once. He hadn't thought much of the Stevens appointment, which had not yet been announced, and as Kennedy had put it to him in the form of a question—What would you think of Roger Stevens as head of the Cultural Center?—Bernstein had every right to give a straight answer. He had answered, "Mr. President, I think it would be a terrible mistake. I like Roger Stevens. But Roger Stevens is not an artist. He'd bring no stature to the job. He's a money raiser and oddly enough for a money raiser, he can't make a speech. He's a very shy man." I knew from Kennedy's face that he had already made up his mind.

But Leonard Bernstein's objections were important enough to Kennedy's ears to call for a formal response, even though there were only six of us in the room: the Bernsteins, the Kennedys, and the Bradens. The president rose from his chair and took a stance in front of the fireplace almost as though he were about to give us a speech. "I know, Lenny, that Roger Stevens can't give a speech. I know he's not an artist. But what the Cultural Center needs is money and success. You say Roger Stevens can raise money and I know that. Has it occurred to you that in the past few years almost every successful Broadway play has been produced by Roger Stevens, that he's produced more successful Broadway plays than anybody now living, and that if he can do that at the Cultural Center, the Cultural Center might get off to a successful start?"

That was that. Bernstein demurred politely. Everybody else thought of something nice to say about Roger Stevens, and we went in to dinner. It was the night Jackie started in first and the president teased, "Remember, Jackie, who goes first now."

But now Leonard Bernstein was to have his own moment in the sun, I suppose up to that time the very brightest of his career. He was to conduct Beethoven's *Missa Solemnis* at the opening of Lincoln Center. He had worked and polished and worked and polished for days beforehand. I went with him to the concert hall on the day before the opening, and he took me with him to various seats in the auditorium while he listened to the Philharmonic in rehearsal. He didn't like the sound from one seat and he didn't like the sound from another seat higher up in the balcony, and he would turn to me and shake his head in disapproval and then move to another seat. I went back to the Carlyle and he stayed to rehearse the orchestra again.

So I should have known that Leonard Bernstein would be excited when he finished the concert, but I didn't know just how excited a conductor gets. There he was bowing from the podium to thunderous applause; there he was leaving the stage, and the applause did not subside; and there he was coming out again, and again, and then a fourth time. Finally there he was at the reception, still sweating and flushed with the excitement and the passion, and he rushed past the cameramen and the crowd and up to Jackie, standing in the full lights before the cameras, embraced her and kissed her full upon the mouth.

God, I was naïve. Or unprepared. Or without knowledge. If Leonard Bernstein had done that to me, I would have embraced him back. It was a spontaneous act, full of emotion, and flushed with success and glorying in the Gloria of *Missa Solemnis*. But Jackie stiffened like Queen Victoria, and like Queen Victoria she was not amused.

Lenny sensed her disapproval at once and fell back. I suppose in retrospect that Jackie, who was after all only thirty-three years old, was trying hard to behave as she thought First Ladies ought to behave and Lenny spoiled the picture. But she was still wounded and angry several days later because she wrote me a note when I had returned to Tom and Oceanside. "Never let my husband seat me next to Leonard Bernstein again."

And Lenny, who sensed sudden cooling in his relations with the White House, explained to me, "I was up there doing the last measures of the Gloria and saying to myself, 'I will not kiss Jackie Kennedy; I will not kiss Jackie Kennedy; I will not, I shall not, must not kiss Jackie Kennedy.' I sang those words to the music as I waved the baton: 'I will not kiss Jackie Kennedy.'

"And then I did."

Jackie got over feeling put upon, Lenny got over his embarrassment, and the president got what he wanted, which was no pictures of Jackie with the Rockefellers.

As I say, John Kennedy cared more about what people said than any man I've ever known and took meticulous care in arranging public affairs so that people would say what he wanted them to say and appear as he wanted them to appear. As we now know, he also took meticulous care to keep private matters private. People didn't say anything about these private affairs because they didn't know about them. I never knew about them. I don't think Jackie ever knew about them. Or that if she did, it didn't bother her because she knew John Kennedy loved her. She once said, "All Kennedys, beginning with their father, have had their fingers in the cookie jar." I'm confident that members of the White House staff who had to do with public affairs didn't know about them. If I had to guess, I would guess that Kenny O'Donnell made the complicated arrangements which assured that private affairs would be kept private. It seems likely to me that he fixed such schedules as he was called upon to fix, asked no questions, and made no comments. He was a man who knew how to keep his mouth shut while appearing not to know anything worth shutting up about. Unlike Larry O'Brien, he never adopted the posture of the wise man. But that's only speculation. The fact is that John Kennedy managed his private affairs so carefully that there was no public awareness.

I tried to get Nelson to do the same. I remember telling him before he was vice president that he ought not to be seen so frequently walking into Nancy Hanks's apartment. He laughed and shrugged and was thereafter seen frequently walking into Nancy Hanks's apartment.

I remember that when he was campaigning for governor of New York, how Hugh Morrow, his press secretary, braved his wrath and mine by insisting that I not accompany Nelson on his private plane. I was furious and hurt. But Nelson simply paid no attention to Morrow's warnings. He didn't narrow his eyes or make any sign of denigration. He simply paid no attention, in itself a form of denigration, one to which Morrow was accustomed.

Through most of their adult lives, these two men, Kennedy and Rockefeller, were rivals in their own minds. They were interested in each other, had a wary respect and admiration for each other, looked forward to the possibility that someday they might have to vie with each other. Both were brought up as kings are brought up. Both were flattered and both liked to be flattered. Both surrounded themselves with courtiers, though because of their relative positions in public life or because Kennedy brooked more disagreement from his staff than Nelson did, Kennedy's courtiers had on the whole more brains, more ability, and more self-respect.

But Kennedy looked to men for advice. Women were for fun. Women were extracurricular. His relationships with them were in time-out periods which had to be carefully contrived. Nelson, on the other hand, treated women as part of every day. He looked to them for advice and counsel in the same way that he looked to men. A little more polite where women were concerned, not inclined to cut them down so readily as he cut men down, but totally open to what they had to say, totally open as to their abilities to handle affairs, and totally open to their attraction.

"Damn the attraction." Nelson must have thought that often as his mind wandered from what a woman was telling him to the way a woman looked. Kennedy never let his mind wander. There were time-out periods for the wandering mind.

I have sometimes thought that if Kennedy had had women in high staff positions, one of them might have kept him from his macho attempt to kill Castro, and thus, if my own speculation is correct, saved his life.

And I have sometimes thought that if Nelson had been less open, less boyishly brash, he might have contrived his final meeting with greater care and saved what he most wanted: his reputation as a serious leader free from any flaw. No matter. Both men died as they had lived.

●

THIRTEEN

Traveling
with Jackie

The first news of the grumbling came just before we were to meet the pope. We were waiting in a richly decorated anteroom—all gold and red brocade—and two cardinals in red robes were about to usher Jackie, her sister Lee Radziwill, and me through another long hallway, where Pope John was waiting for us. The time and place suggested a hush and Jackie's press secretary took advantage of the hush to bring me the news.

"There's been a lot of complaining," he said, "about your traveling with Mrs. Kennedy. They're saying you're a reporter like all of them and why aren't you in the rear of the plane with them? It's just jealousy, but I thought you ought to know."

I wished later that he had waited and told me after the

audience was over because the news worried me during a few moments which deserved full attention. Even the simplicity of John XXIII, the plainness of the tiny room in which he met us, his great calm, his weather-beaten face, his tininess—yes, he was a small, rugged peasant of a man—and the sincere interest he expressed when he talked to me of my seven (as it was then) children, all this couldn't down the irritation I felt about being the subject of complaint.

I asked Jackie about it on the drive back from the Vatican and she said not to worry; but I did worry, and I was right to worry. After all the purpose of this glamorous trip to India with a stopover in Rome was to spread goodwill, and how could goodwill be spread by angry female reporters whose principal concern, other than Jackie's reticence and reluctance to hold press conferences, was the question, Who does she think she is anyway?

It was one of the male reporters who told me how the question had been framed. He said, "Look, they haven't got anything else to do and they didn't get in to see the pope and you did; and so they're saying, 'Who does Joan Braden think she is anyway?' People," he explained, "who ask 'Who does she think she is?' always add the word 'anyway.' It makes the question sound as though it were of general interest."

Sometime later, after we had left Rome and were in India, I left the front of the airplane and went through the drawn curtain which separated Mrs. Kennedy and her party from the traveling press and joined the complainers, who at once ceased to be complainers. In fact, they were friendly and kind, and I made some good friends among them. But the change in the seating and therefore in the hotel accommodations and therefore in the proximity to Jackie and Lee made an enormous difference—putting me in what Tom would call a "hell of a hole."

You see, Jackie had called me in Oceanside and asked me to go with her. The president got on the line and was quite serious. He wanted me to go. I was excited and said, "Yes, of course I'll go," without even asking Tom. And when I told him, he was excited too.

But then there had been that crushing moment on the telephone when Tish Baldridge, who was Jackie's social secretary, called to say that the trip had been declared "semi-official" which meant that everyone would have to pay his or her own fare and expenses. "Six thousand dollars, more or less," Tish said.

Tom was crushed too. "Six thousand dollars, more or less, is more or less the weekly payroll at the *Blade-Tribune*." It was a figure not only beyond our means but also beyond speculating about or picking up a pencil and figuring about. It was out there, somewhere. It was beyond.

But I didn't call Tish back to change the plans, and I didn't call Jackie back. Maybe something would happen. One night, at dinner at the White House, something did. B. K. Nehru, India's ambassador to the United States, John Kenneth Galbraith, our ambassador to India, and some of the president's friends were at the dinner. The conversation was all about the trip and what B. K. had arranged and what Ken Galbraith had arranged, and it all sounded as glamorous as pink clouds and castles. Suddenly the president turned to me and said, "Joannie, does it sound exciting?"

"Yes, Mr. President. It certainly does sound exciting. But I can't go. I don't have the money."

John Kennedy looked straight at me and the slight frown that wrinkled his brow disappeared in the course of an idea. "Why don't you write a magazine article? Would it help if I asked Pierre Salinger [Kennedy's press secretary] to call some magazines in the morning? I'm sure something can be arranged. You make plans to go."

I went back after dinner to Stewart and Tish Alsop's house, where I was staying. They were still up. I remember Stewart was wearing his blue velvet jacket and a black tie, sitting by the fire and waiting to learn what had happened at the White House. As Washington correspondent for the *Saturday Evening Post*, Stewart always wanted to know what happened at the White House and who said what, particularly what the president said.

Excitedly, I told him. "Excellent," said Stewart. "But why have Pierre call magazines? What's the matter with the dear old *Saturday Evening Post*?"

And so it was arranged on the following morning. The *Post* would pay "six thousand dollars, more or less" and three thousand more for me and I would get to go.

So the complaining female reporters did have a point. According to the White House announcement, I was a "friend of Mrs. Kennedy who is accompanying her." In a burst of excitement, I told somebody or other, I've forgotten whom, that I was writing an article for the *Saturday Evening Post*. Sitting on the airplane across the Atlantic on the way to Rome, the female reporters had chewed on that, and the chewing made them angry.

I wondered from time to time why the male reporters remained unperturbed. Was it a feeling of natural superiority? Did they regard this trip as not particularly newsworthy and what difference did it make who sat where? Whatever the reason, the men in the press section were unperturbed and regarded the concern of the women with tolerant amusement. Barbara Walters was among the women reporters. She was the only woman who behaved like a man.

By that time Barbara had been a working journalist for

nearly ten years and a host on NBC's *Today* for two. She lived in a tiny apartment, arose at 3:15 every weekday morning, dressed, put curlers in her hair, a scarf around her head, and was on her way to work in a taxi at four. Maybe the daily grind inured her to such minor pains as jealousy. She didn't care where she sat. She observed, and when she got home she had a lot of interesting stories to tell her listeners and a lot of people to put on the air, least important me.

Nevertheless, the female complainants had a point. I was on assignment for the *Saturday Evening Post*, and if I hadn't been on assignment for the *Saturday Evening Post*, I wouldn't be there, "friend of Mrs. Kennedy" or not. So they were right and I was wrong, and Tom would have told me to shut up about it and try to have fun.

I did have fun. B. K. Nehru and Ken Galbraith were both nice to me. I reported on what Jackie did and what she saw. I tried to get the red dust of India into the stories I wrote for the *Blade-Tribune* and sent back to Tom by airmail, but for two whole weeks I never saw Jackie again except at a distance. As the trip was ending, we came to the line on the schedule which read, "depart for London." I realized quite suddenly that I had nothing—absolutely nothing—for Stewart Alsop and the *Saturday Evening Post*. Nothing that hadn't been printed in three-week-old newspapers; Jackie at the Taj Mahal; Jackie and Lee riding elephants; Jackie behind wrought iron fences gazing at statuary, the tall white-clad figure of Prime Minister Nehru standing beside her. The cameramen had been very kind to me. They had big cameras with telescopic lenses; Tom had given me a camera from the *Blade-Tribune* such as you might use to take a picture of the new baby. The cameramen always arranged for me to get up close to the wrought iron fence so that I had a chance of a discernible picture.

But it was no use. Tom told me later that he and the reporters in Oceanside went through the negatives carefully, enlarged them, examined them, and examined them again. Even under the magnifying glass, the best they could do was to make out some tiny figures off in the distance, and up front, so he said there were excellent views of magnificent wrought iron.

So what could I write for the *Post*? The *Saturday Evening Post* was not to be taken lightly. Even in that year of 1961, it was as much a national institution as the Post Office, and though some people must have known that it was being slowly strangled by television and had only a few years to live, it still had a sound ring, like "pay to the bearer in silver on demand." To say today, "I wrote an article for the *Saturday Evening Post*," is to draw from those with long memories a polite, "Oh, did you?" To say the same in 1961 was to gain instant approbation and envy.

I couldn't let the *Post* down. I couldn't let Stewart Alsop down. But the fact was I had nothing to write. Would the *Post* be interested in the wedding party to which the handsome and dashing B. K. Nehru had escorted me? Would its editors exclaim over my description of the groom dismounting from a white horse while the bride waited against a vast, colorful background of flowers? I doubted it.

Would the *Post* be interested in the story of Ken Galbraith and me being covered in colored chalk during the ceremony of Holy Day?

That had been a return to childhood, getting all dressed up, even to white gloves, and then hurling mud pies at each other.

But would the *Post* be interested? No. Probably not.

Then what would interest the editors of the *Post*? What would repay them for their investment?

Well, the answer was obvious. Jackie would interest the editors of the *Post*. What Jackie thought of the pope, what Jackie thought of Nehru. What Jackie thought of Madame Nehru. What Jackie thought of India. What Jackie thought about anything.

And the trouble was that I didn't know what Jackie thought, or even if she thought. I hadn't seen her since I had gone to the back of the bus.

There had been that one time when Keyes Beech, of the *Chicago Daily News*, had succeeded in averting the Secret Service and the Indian Security and had managed to get close to the wrought iron gate when Mr. Nehru and Jackie chanced to be standing near. Keyes Beech had actually heard the conversation, or so he told us. We all crowded around him and wanted to know exactly what Jackie had said to Nehru and what Nehru had said to Jackie. So Beech made a great show of not wanting to share his information. He said, "I wasn't a pool reporter. I got this story on my own and I intend to use it. Why should I tell you what Nehru said to Jackie and what Jackie said to him?"

To which everybody responded with groans and entreaties, and finally Beech said, "All right, I'll tell you but you have to promise to give me a twelve-hour lead before you write anything."

So everybody agreed. There was silence while Beech told his story. "Nehru and Jackie were viewing the monuments side by side, and Jackie said to Nehru, 'What century are these?' And Nehru said, 'I'm not sure but I believe that they are of the fourteenth century.' And Jackie said, 'Oh.'"

Would the *Saturday Evening Post* be interested in that? Maybe Art Buchwald could have done it, but not me.

So now we were nearing the end of this two-week journey and I had nothing. Stewart Alsop's reputation was on the line. My reputation was on the line. And the *Post*'s six thousand dollars was on the line. When we arrived in London, I was scared.

But as I looked out the window of the airplane, I could see a small group of figures standing on the pavement, waiting for our plane to pull up to the painted markers. I thought for probably the hundredth time on that trip how very fragile human beings look when they are standing on cement pavement waiting for giant planes to pull into place. Then I noticed that one of the figures was recognizable. Tall, militarily erect, wearing a chesterfield with a black homburg. Those around him seemed to defer. Yes it was, it was David Bruce.

Well, naturally. He would be meeting Jackie and Lee as was his ambassadorial duty. Maybe I'd get to see him, but probably not, not with the long line of reporters standing in the aisle, waiting to get off that plane. By the time I got off, Jackie and Lee would have departed for Lee's London house and I'd be left alone with my problem and my typewriter.

So I stood in the long line and went down the steps and over to the long wait for baggage, and just as I was picking up my typewriter to take some more steps forward, the typewriter disappeared and it was under the arm of David Bruce.

"Come on, Joannie. I'll take you back to the residence and I'll send around for the baggage later. Tell me, was it fun?" There were those brilliant blue laughing eyes; there was the elegant and impeccable dress, the shirt an off-white, the tie a bright blue that matched his eyes and with a pattern not bold but quiet, singular, as though he'd had that tie made especially for him. There was the friendly, kindly smile, the smile of the man who knew exactly where he was and where he was going and how he would get there with the least possible difficulty and with every turn in the road plotted and mapped in advance and the way made smooth.

There was about David Bruce an air of gentle command. He

was never flustered. He never raised his voice. He was imperturbable. He always got his way.

Except once. I remember once when he didn't get his way and when it seemed to me for the first time that he was out of his element in a strange new world. That was at an airport too, and Tom was there. David and I were going off on a short trip to his ancestral estate in Virginia, to the place he loved, a place called Staunton Hill, and I was going because he wanted me to see it. After the short-hop airplane had been canceled, the three of us stood before the Hertz counter so that David could rent a car.

The lady behind the counter asked David for a credit card and David replied, "I'm sorry, I don't carry a credit card. Would a check do?"

"No," said the lady, "only a credit card."

David reached into his wallet and withdrew four hundred-dollar bills, laying them on the counter before her, each bill separately. "Would this suffice as evidence of good faith?"

"No," said the lady, "only a credit card."

By now, a line was forming behind us and several people recognized David, including a young man whom I took to be a foreign service officer. He spoke up from his place in line, a couple of steps behind my shoulder. "Ma'am, Mr. Bruce is well known to me and perhaps you will permit him to use my credit card."

I could see that David was not about to let himself be extricated from an embarrassing situation by someone he didn't know. I looked at Tom, who shrugged his shoulders and held out his hands, palms up. He had gotten out of bed early to drive me to the airport and didn't even have a wallet with him.

David put his wallet back in his breast pocket, bent down and picked up his briefcase, a highly polished, dark leather briefcase with clasps. He put it on the counter and opened it deliberately; out came a roll of parchmentlike, heavy paper tied with a red ribbon. David untied the ribbon and smoothed out the roll for the lady to read. It was engraved, with long flowing script. "To all to whom these presents may come: Greeting." Then down below in smaller script it read: "Reposing special trust and confidence in my ambassador"; and typed into the blank, "David K. E. Bruce"; and then script again, asking that the reader of the parchment repose special trust and confidence too. It was signed by the president of the United States, and over on the left at the bottom was the presidential seal.

David was a little embarrassed, I could see. We were holding up the line. But he was composed and gentle in voice. "Perhaps this will identify me and provide you with sufficient reason to accept a personal check."

The lady behind the counter looked curiously at the parchment. "No," she said, "only a credit card."

Dejectedly, David rolled up the parchment with the seal and the red ribbon, tied the other red ribbon around it, and put it back in the briefcase. Politely he thanked the young stranger behind us, and we walked off to Tom's car and Tom drove us back to our house, dropped himself off, and David and I took Tom's car to Staunton Hill.

That was the only time I ever saw David Bruce unable to command. But now, here in London, he was a presence. He took me to the residence and showed me to my room. I called Tom and asked him what to do. Suddenly in the middle of the phone conversation, I already knew what to do.

Tom had just said, "Joannie, if you can't get to Jackie and have a long talk with her, I don't see how you can write a piece. That other stuff is last month's news stories. You have to know what she thought about the trip and what she felt and what she thought was funny and what she thought was sad, and to do that you've got to get to Jackie."

And I had just said, "Nobody can get to Jackie. She's spending the night with Lee and there's no time because we leave in the morning."

Right there, it came to me. How stupid of me. What did I mean, "Nobody can get to Jackie"? David Bruce would see Jackie. I could write a note, explaining all this to Jackie, and David would deliver it and she would read it. I got off the telephone, wrote the note, and went downstairs to find David.

"Mrs. Kennedy said she would be more than pleased. Delighted if you flew home with her." That's the message David brought back and that's how I found myself on the airplane the next morning, side by side with Jackie Kennedy, drinking gin and tonics and talking and asking questions and talking some more. After a while, Jackie went off to sleep and I stayed up and wrote the *Saturday Evening Post* piece.

I looked it up the other day. It's almost one long quotation from Jackie, "I just pray I was all right and that the trip did some good. I'm glad I went but I'd never make a trip like that again without Jack. There were moments like that time in Lahore at the governor's house when I sat in the window and looked at the fantastic lighted trees reflected in moonlight pools when I wondered what I was doing so far away without Jack. . . . Jack's always so proud of me when I do something like this. . . . He spent the whole last day of his vacation screaming over the telephone on a poor connection with Ken Galbraith, telling him he had to shorten the schedule. . . . He spent the whole last day of precious rest helping me."

There are some White House glimpses in the piece. "When I start to ask him whether I should wear a short or long dress, he just snaps his fingers and says, 'That's your province.' And I say, 'Yes, but you're the great decision maker. Why should everybody but me get the benefit of your decision?' "

"Sometimes," I wrote in that piece, "she seemed to me very much a queen. As she walked through the Vatican for her audience with the pope or listened to 'The Star-Spangled Banner' in India or Pakistan, her shoulders were back, her eyes were straight forward, and her face was composed with only a slight smile.

"And sometimes she seemed to be Alice in Wonderland. When she saw the Taj Mahal for the first time or when she watched two thousand men march with flaming torches in Pakistan, her eyes were bright with excitement.

"Now on the plane back, as we talked about her husband and her children, I saw that she was still Jackie. . . ."

As I say, the piece is mostly a long quotation, but I think the long quotation showed how much she cared about representing her country well and how hard she tried.

I was there and I can attest that she succeeded, succeeded brilliantly and beautifully. I hope the piece showed that.

Back in Washington, the president went over it and changed a few words, writing in the margin in his fine hand. He didn't like the word "ratted" to describe what Jackie had done to her hair. He preferred "teased." He made a note at the end of one paragraph, "Say something nice about Provie," who was Jackie's maid. Provie, as I reported in the piece, had sent the president a postcard from India, "Dear Mr. President. Having wonderful time. That's me on the back of the camel. Love Provie." Stewart smiled when he read that. "The dear old *Post*. Straightening out relations with the White House staff. Well, I suppose there are worse missions for men and magazines."

Come to think of it, there was one more quotation from Jackie in that *Post* piece which strikes me, now that I look at it again, as casting a shadow before. She is talking about the presence of the Secret Service, not just in India but back home, at the White House. "I sometimes fret at the Secret Service restrictions . . . but I don't know what we'd do without them. They are usually right and every single one of them is so kind and dedicated and bright. Every president and his family must drive them mad, as it's such an adjustment to go from private life to constant surveillance. When the Secret Service tries to stop Jack from doing things, he just says no and shakes hands with whomever he wants and does what he wants, but usually I can't get away with it."

But none of us—not Jackie nor Stewart nor I—was thinking then about shadows. The world seemed very bright when the piece was published in the *Saturday Evening Post*, "An Exclusive Chat with Jackie Kennedy," by Joan Braden. Tom was proud and Stewart was proud and only I knew the secret, which was that after I had been cut adrift by jealous women, a man named David Bruce had saved me from disaster.

FOURTEEN

Making Ends Meet

Mrs. Longworth never spoke of Cincinnati. The years in which she had been forced to live there, because she was the wife of a congressman from Ohio and speaker of the House, were unhappy years. She spoke to me of Oceanside as though it were my Cincinnati, a distant place to which I had to go because my husband had gone there but a place which, once entered, became oblivion.

Not that she had particular antipathy toward the town in which I lived. She mentioned its name in the same way she would say, upon being introduced to the wife of a visiting congressman, "Oh, yes, Pennsylvania," as though she had heard the name of that place, perhaps in school, and had always meant to inquire further. "Oh, yes, Oceanside," maddened Tom; and as she saw that it did, she would twist the knife a little, and her head too, in order to look up at him, birdlike, "California?"

I'm ashamed to admit it but a little of her attitude toward places not within afternoon driving distance of the nation's capital had rubbed off on me. When I was not about to have a baby, I was in Washington. When I was on the telephone, the call was to Washington. When I was looking forward to the arrival of guests, the guests were usually from Washington. And when I began to know interesting people from California, it was because I had met them in Washington.

I blamed my fixation for Washington on Tom. I remember the first time he came home from the *Blade-Tribune* at 6:30, happily picked up a copy of his own newspaper, and settled into a chair. "How was your day?" he asked. "Did you take the kids to the beach?"

"Tom Braden, don't you ever again come home and ask me that question. Is that what I'm supposed to be? A nursery? Do you know that I can still think? I can still read? I still have a mind? I can still call people and know what's going on in Washington?"

But, in fact, I don't think my fixation was entirely Tom's fault. He tried to get me interested in the newspaper. I was to become the society editor or the woman's editor, title to be selected. An entire page and sometimes more of the paper was devoted to society or women: club news, a little bit about fashion which came off the wires, weddings and engagements, women's fishing contests, women's golf tournaments, PTA meetings at several elementary schools and the high school, and bridge clubs. That was the page and I was to run it.

I did for about ten days, and I found it a stultifying bore. Tom would say, "Well, there's something interesting in every person, Joannie, and you have to get to know them to find out what it is."

"You find out, Tom. You spend an hour and a half at the bridge club. Come back. Tell me what is interesting. Is it interesting that the wife of the city councilman has three scotch and sodas in an hour and a half? If you find that interesting, will you print it?"

Tom's job was more interesting and more like Oveta's description of what she did when she ran the *Houston Post*. He got up in the morning and from 6:00 A.M. until noon, he put out the paper, handling the wire copy, assigning stories, editing them when they came in. Sometime after 2:00 P.M., when the presses rolled, he took care of the business side or walked around town, collecting bills, saying hello to merchants, sometimes playing golf with one of them. I could have done that. Then what would Tom have done?

The fact was, as I had seen from the beginning, we had two reasonably intelligent and ambitious people consigned to the job of publishing a ten- or twelve-page newspaper (fourteen on Wednesdays), and it was not a big enough job for two reasonably intelligent and ambitious people to do.

Tom was also having troubles with adjustment, and his troubles were a lot more important to both of us. I learned about them one morning at 2:00 when Susan cried and it was time to nurse her. Tom went to get her, as he usually did, but he'd been sitting up in bed, waiting. He said he hadn't slept at all. When the nursing was finished, he paced around the house, picked up books from the shelves, and put them back and counted to himself, out loud, "Thirteen, fourteen, fifteen."

"What are you doing? What thirteen, fourteen, fifteen?"

"I don't know, Joannie. I guess that's how much we owe, or maybe it's how much we have that we can pay on what we owe."

"Is it enough?"

"No."

There began a long time with Tom unable to sleep, sitting on the edge of the bed, counting to himself, and then getting up and going out and pacing in the living room. It was not so bad during the day because the paper had to get out and he had to get it out; but every night was painful, desperate, as though some horrible event in the shape of a monster were driving us both to despair. I worried and wore a pretty white nightgown, and said, "Don't you like my nightgown?" but it didn't do any good.

In retrospect, it is clear what the larger problem was, clear to me and clear to Tom. When you don't have enough money to pay your bills, there's a reason. If you can get at the reason in time, maybe you can turn it around so that you will have enough to pay your bills in time. But when it happens that you can't pay your bills, that becomes the problem. Such reasons as you can think of for why you can't pay your bills don't take hold of the mind, or don't matter anyhow because it's too late to think about why.

The larger problem, as I see it now and as I think Tom does too, was that Tom's ambition far overreached his judgment. He wanted to publish the best small newspaper in the country. So he bought the best features and the best services and the best machinery in order to make the *Blade-Tribune* the best small newspaper in the country. He was excited about it. And I was too. I went down to the plant to see the new Linotype machine, and listened as Tom pointed out how much time and labor it saved by running on tape, and I took an interest in the installation of a secondhand press which would print more pages faster, and I was pleased when Tom printed the full texts of the president's news conferences.

"If you read the full text," Tom told me, "you get a very different impression of what the president is doing than if you read only what the *Los Angeles Times* says the president is doing."

I knew what he meant and I knew he would give me that quotation again. Which he did.

"The Eisenhower administration took a sharp turn toward socialism yesterday as the president signed a bill increasing social security benefits." And then Tom added his punch line: "Lead story, lead paragraph, front page, leading newspaper in California."

The story had appeared in the *Los Angeles Times* on the day that Tom bought the *Blade-Tribune*, and he never tired of quoting it. "That," he would say, "is what newspaper readers in southern California get every morning."

Tom didn't think he was going to beat the *Los Angeles Times* with a ten-page newspaper, but he was going to beat the *Los Angeles Times* in Oceanside, which he soon did. He was so proud that it always seemed to me a shame that the *Los Angeles Times* didn't publish the fact, probably because no one at the *Los Angeles Times* noticed it.

It's sad when I think back upon Tom and that newspaper. Sometimes I wanted to get up on the roof and shout at the town of Oceanside, "Do you care? Do you care that you're getting a good newspaper? Doesn't anybody care?"

Tom did. And that was Tom's problem. And now it was my problem too. Tom didn't have enough money. The *Blade-Tribune* was going broke.

I remember the time of the crisis very clearly because the Republican convention of 1956 was to be held in San Francisco in July, and Tom was to make a thirty-four-thousand-dollar payment on the newspaper in August. I knew that Nelson would attend the convention. I remembered Oveta's story about how the *Houston Post* was about to go broke and about how Will Hobby had become desperate and about how she had gone, unbeknownst to Will, to call upon Jesse Jones, who owned the opposition paper, the *Houston Chronicle*. Oveta had told me that Jesse Jones had lent her the money and she had saved the *Houston Post*.

I never knew why Jesse Jones did this. It seems to me magnanimous, almost beyond belief. But that's what she told me and I don't doubt it for a moment. I said to myself, "I will save the *Blade-Tribune*, and since Nelson does not publish a rival newspaper in Oceanside, I have an easier job than Oveta had." So I went to San Francisco with Tom, who was covering the convention.

Nelson and I had a picnic lunch on a green hill, a spot that he found, way up overlooking the city. I've been to a lot of beautiful hills on beautiful days in beautiful countries, but I think this particular spot on this particular hill that Nelson chose was the most beautiful I've ever seen. We had blankets to sit on and we had the lunch and we had the city down below to gaze at and we had fun. And when I brought up the newspaper and the problem, it was as though something very minor had been mentioned, something that was hardly worth interrupting the flow of conversation about Tom Dewey, "the saddest man in the world," according to Nelson, and about how Nelson might, just might run for governor of New York and about not saying anything about that, and about Harold Stassen putting up Chris Herter's name as a replacement for Richard Nixon on the ticket and about how silly Stassen was becoming, and then about the *Blade-Tribune*.

"Tom wasn't adequately financed," Nelson said. "I lent him fifty thousand dollars and he used it all to make a down payment.

He should have told me or I should have known it. Would it help if he stopped paying interest to me?"

"I think it's worse than that."

"Not worse, Joannie. If you weren't adequately financed, you made a mistake. When you find it out, it's not worse, it's better. I'll send Tom another fifty thousand dollars tomorrow."

"That's too much. We don't need that much."

"You'd better have the cushion. It's not too much for me. You know, it's funny about Stassen. I used to think he had ideas but once I got to know him, I got to know one of the most boring men I've ever met."

So the lunch ended. I had saved the *Blade-Tribune*.

I went back to the hotel and told Tom. I know he thanked Nelson. By letter and later in person. But he never thanked me. I wonder if Will Hobby ever thanked Oveta.

And isn't it funny how things that matter to one person, almost as life and death matter, mean nothing much or very little to another?

Many years later when Tom decided to sell the *Blade-Tribune*—and he made the decision, not I—he insisted on taking an airplane to Albany: Los Angeles to New York, New York to Albany. He took a cab ride which he described to me—"through a dingy, drab, little New England town and suddenly to this great, new center called the capital of New York which Nelson had built—it was like stopping by woods on a snowy evening and coming upon the pyramids." As he mounted the steps, Nelson came down the steps, and the two of them stood there. Tom produced a check from his pocket and handed it over—one hundred and twelve thousand dollars—something like that. Then he turned around and got into a taxi and back on the airplane and to New York and to Los Angeles and home.

He refused to use the mail. He made a great journey of it. A significant journey.

And I saw Nelson a couple of months later. "Joannie, I've been meaning to ask you. Why did Tom pay me back that money? Nobody else ever has."

FIFTEEN

Bobby

W henever I think of Robert Kennedy, which is pretty often because I loved him a lot, I think of him the way he was before his brother died.

I think of Frank Sinatra knocking at the front door of Bobby and Ethel's house on the night before John Kennedy's inauguration gala. I don't know how we heard the knock because the whole house was echoing to the voice of Frank Sinatra, played with the volume turned all the way up, on the record players of the Kennedy children. If a stranger had selected a particular spot in that vast house, it would have been possible to hear Frank Sinatra loudly singing one song on one of the children's record players, another song on another, and a third on yet another.

I don't know how Bobby and Ethel put up with the racket, but they had been doing so for a number of weeks because Frank Sinatra was the rage among the Kennedy children, who wore his recordings out almost as fast as he could produce them.

This was a small, private dinner of family and friends and many, many Kennedy children. Since Frank Sinatra was coming to dinner, I guess Bobby and Ethel thought it not inappropriate to let the children do what they normally did in the evening, which was to put Frank Sinatra records on again.

Through the din of Frank Sinatra, somebody heard Frank Sinatra's knock; and he came in the door, greeted effusively by Peter and Pat Lawford who knew him best, enthusiastically by the rest of us, and Bobby and Ethel's children just stood around him and stared. And stared. A miracle had occurred. Frank Sinatra was in their living room. Himself. They turned off the record players, gathered around him, and stared some more.

Bobby performed introductions for each child, and each child came forward shyly while Frank Sinatra, who had settled in a comfortable chair, shook hands with each one until one of the older children came forward and said to this god who had dropped out of the sky, "My Way." And Sinatra said, "What did you say?" And the child said, "My Way," and then there came a chorus of shouting voices from the other children. "The French Foreign Legion," "All the Way," "High Hopes," "Chicago." It went on and on until the names of the songs were indiscernible in the frenzy of anticipatory demands.

I paused in conversation with one of the adults at the party to see what Frank Sinatra would do because obviously he didn't want to do what the Kennedy children were demanding. He had not expected it. He didn't have accompaniment. He didn't have any of those cute little girls with cute little voices who in that particular year were doing trills in the right places and at the right times to Frank Sinatra's most popular songs. Moreover, he had just gotten off an airplane from a long trip across country.

But I didn't pause long. First Frank Sinatra took off his toupee, then he leaned back in his chair, and then he sang first one song and then another and still another. He then stood up and said, "That's enough of Frank Sinatra. Bobby, get me a drink."

It was, I suppose, embarrassing for Sinatra. It was awesome for the children and admirable for the adults. I look back upon that evening as one of the times I saw good taste under pressure, and whenever I hear or read about how Frank Sinatra misbehaved in public or about somebody's view that he was crass or a bully or a male chauvinist pig, I think back upon the night that he sang for the children and I have my own view.

But it was Bobby's house, Bobby's party, and Bobby being gay and getting drinks for people and laughing that slightly mocking laugh. "It's not Sinatra's voice, it's his stamina. I wish I had Sinatra's stamina."

I remember Bobby at the Hickory Hill seminars, a series of evening lectures for members of the Cabinet, their wives, and other guests, which he held usually at his home and at which world-renowned intellectuals reminded the assembled that there were more important things than government. Stewart Udall almost invariably fell noticeably asleep during these occasions, and Bobby ended one of them by telling the guest speaker that while "we had all appreciated his efforts, he could not help noting that the level of intellectuality must have been lower than that to which we are accustomed because the secretary of interior has remained awake throughout."

There was about Bobby, even when he was working very hard on his brother's campaign, a sense of fun and play and gaiety. With John Kennedy's death, all that disappeared.

In its place was a laconic bitterness. I had the feeling that I was talking to a desperate man and that the desperation went very deep. It was, I thought, the desperation of knowing that life always ends in defeat, that it must therefore be lived at breakneck pace before defeat becomes a nearby apparition and then a reality. Friends noticed the change and were sorry—for themselves because they missed the sarcastic wit and the sense of fun that had marked him in the past, but also for him because he bore a grief that was so deep as to be untouchable and so explosive that nobody wanted to grope for it for fear that he might find it.

Once I said to him, "Bobby, why keep making fun of Lyndon Johnson? Why keep bringing up Johnson's pompous announcement?" (Johnson had declared, as though after long deliberation on the Constitution and the separation of powers, that he would not choose a vice-presidential candidate from among his Cabinet, thus ruling out Bobby and, for that matter, Wilbur Cohen of HEW.) "All that's past," I said, "and forgotten by everybody except you."

He dismissed my admonishment with a grunt. I realized that I had stumbled upon a suspicion and a distrust that was consuming.

I saw him often enough to know that he privately regarded the war in Vietnam as a disaster, and I knew that as the war went on and got bigger, the restraint of keeping his opinion private (he was still a member of Johnson's Cabinet) was beginning to hurt. But how much of Robert Kennedy's aversion for the war sprang from his aversion for Lyndon Johnson? I doubt that he himself knew. As Bobby came to detest the war, the war became more and more "Lyndon's war." The two aversions grew hotter until they fused.

In those days when I traveled to Washington people talked

about Vietnam at every gathering and almost to the exclusion of any other public subject. Senators and congressmen who had doubts usually kept their mouths discreetly shut, but those who saw the war as a necessary burden to be borne patriotically and as a public duty were welcome at Joseph Alsop's house. When rumors began to spread that Bobby, having left the Cabinet and won a senate seat in New York, might run against the war and against Lyndon Johnson in the primaries of 1968, no one could have been more dismayed that Joseph Alsop. At bottom, Joe thought that the United States of America simply did not "bug out" of wars. He argued the Chinese menace and when that appeared to be without substance, he argued the Russian menace. People who opposed the war were "soft minded" or did not understand the complexities of the balance of power.

Then came the public defection of Robert Kennedy. It was a blow from which Joseph Alsop might never have recovered had he not chosen to disbelieve it. "I always thought," he told me long afterward, "that the minute Robert Kennedy got to the White House, he would tear into Vietnam like a tiger. Robert Kennedy would not have permitted his country to lose a war."

I cannot honestly say that Robert Kennedy's views on the war mattered more to me than Robert Kennedy mattered. Besides, out in Oceanside the war did not seem to throb in everyone's conscience as it did in Washington. And in our family, other things were throbbing. Tom had decided to sell the *Blade-Tribune*, a wrenching decision from which it took him months to recover. It was not the money he would get for the *Blade-Tribune*, he explained to me. It was the fact that he didn't have enough money to keep the newspaper as it should and eventually would have to be kept. Newspapers were switching from letterpress to offset, and the switch cost more money than the newspaper had originally cost. He had a choice. Either he could go out and raise the money to make the change in the typesetting process or he could sell. He chose to sell, and for a long while he pouted about it. "Sad, but so," he would say, repeating himself, "sad, but so."

"Look," I said, "it's not the end of the world. A lot of people sell newspapers. You've built the newspaper to nearly twenty thousand circulation. You've made a lot of money. The fact that you don't want to go out and raise more money to switch over all the machinery seems to me the 'so' part of it. There is no 'sad' part of it. Why don't we take the kids to France for a year and everybody learn French and then come back here and see what we want to do?"

We talked about it and talked about it, and one time when we were talking I turned on the television set and learned that Robert Kennedy had decided to run for president. I turned to Tom, "Well, that settles it. That's what we're going to do."

At that moment the telephone rang. I was excited and said so. I was thrilled and said so. I wanted to help and said so. Bobby, on the other end of the line, was terse, tough, almost bitter. "We're going to chase Lyndon's ass all over this country."

Looking back now, there was something about Robert Kennedy and about his campaign for the presidency which was raw and desperate and lonely right from the beginning. He was driven by a sense of obligations unfulfilled. Obligations to black people, obligations to people who had been left out of a share of the American dream, obligations to soldiers who were fighting and dying in a war for which there was no definable purpose, obligations to the families of those men, obligations to his brother and his brother's aims, wasted by the war. Robert Kennedy was running for president out of a sense of duty, and duty, when tested, is always lonely.

But I said it was desperate and raw. It was desperate

because Bobby had to play catch-up against Eugene McCarthy right through to California. It was raw because Bobby had no political base other than opposition to the war and to the head of his political party; and by the time he had run whirlwind visits to campuses in seven states and had said that Lyndon Johnson "was calling upon the darker impulses of the American spirit," his hands were bleeding, his shirts had been torn off his back, his cuff links were gone, and the surging crowds against the war had become his political base.

I gave Tom a souvenir of the raw emotion which marked Bobby's campaign. I lent Tom's brand-new convertible to Bobby to make a drive through the black Watts district of Los Angeles. It was a last-minute need. There was no other car. I didn't have time to tell Tom. Tom watched from a second-floor vantage point as Bobby pushed into a packed, frenzied humanity, reaching out from the open convertible to touch hands, standing in the open car. Fred Dutton and Bill Barry were holding Bobby's belt against the peril of his being dragged into the street. The crowd was pressing against the car, beating upon it, and clambering upon its rear end to get at the candidate. One of Tom's friends who was standing with him by the window remarked, "Say, that looks like your car." Tom looked again. "Now that you mention it," he replied, "it *was* my car."

Part of my job as cochairman of Robert Kennedy's California campaign of 1968 turned into a contest with the McCarthy forces to get out the black vote. This was surprising to all of us. Bobby considered that the black vote ought to be his. But when we began to count black churches, which in those days was a pretty good way of assessing which way blacks would vote, we were stunned. McCarthy and his team had gone after them hard, lining up the ministers and being introduced at the largest Sunday services, McCarthy standing before the congregation and receiving good wishes from the pulpit.

I said to Bobby, "We've got to do something about this."

And he said, "John Lewis [now a congressman from Georgia] is working on it but pitch in." So I called Charles Evers in Mississippi and Roosevelt Grier, a former member of the Los Angeles Rams' fearsome foursome. Both were friends, and both said they would help undo the damage. Evers went to work on the ministers, and Rosy organized an endless series of block meetings in Watts, where he got his first experience at being the preacher he was later to become.

I organized—it's silly to use the word "I" because in a campaign there's seldom any truth in the first person singular. Though I was in charge, I should say "we" organized a Kennedy day in California. To each town of any size we brought senators, congressmen, movie stars, football players, and anybody who was a "name" and who was for Kennedy; and held local rallies, parades, and walk-the-street fiestas: "Shake hands with Joe Tydings of Maryland. He's a United States senator. He's for Robert Kennedy."

Bobby asked me to take care of California because it needed it.

And then just as I was getting up to my neck in California, he called me on the telephone. He wanted me to drop everything for a week and go to Indianapolis to organize a rally in a black district. His instructions were to try to make it more than just a black rally. Bobby wanted some white local government officials there to show that Roger Branigan, Indiana's governor, who was Lyndon Johnson's stand-in, was less than powerful.

I remember a small neighborhood park. The small neighborhood park was surrounded by houses, and all the windows of the houses were open. Some of the occupants of the houses were leaning out the windows, not cheering, not enthusiastic, just watching silently. All the faces at the windows were black, and the people in the park were black too, and they were all silent.

In front of the sidewalk at one end of the park, across the street from the houses, a stand, based upon a big flatbed truck, had been erected, a kind of dais for the speaker. There were chairs on the dais, all filled, and some of the bodies in the seats had white faces. I had said that the mayor would be there and some of the city council members; and some of them, I noted, were there. But overall, it was a sea of black faces, all silent. Then I noticed that in that sea of black faces, there were transistor radios covering some of the faces and that people who had them were listening and talking in low tones to the people around them.

So they knew. The crowd knew and had known for half an hour what I had learned on the telephone about an hour ago. I was at the Indiana headquarters of the Robert Kennedy campaign for the Democratic nomination for president and Pierre Salinger had called me. "Now listen to me carefully, Joannie, and don't say anything or let your expression change. Martin Luther King has been shot. We don't know for certain but we think he's dead. The senator is coming to your rally. I don't think you ought to go and the senator doesn't think you ought to go. But if you think you must, Adam Walinsky will pick you up at the headquarters. So pray for the country. Good-bye."

I was balancing myself on the hood of a car when the entourage entered the park, Bobby riding in the backseat of a convertible as it wound through the silent crowd. Not a cheer. Not a hand clap. Just silence. He got out and made a gesture to me to go to the platform with him. "No," I said, "there's no room up there. Just go." And so a path cleared for him through the crowd and he made his way up the steps to the dais and stood there, looking out at a sea of white shirts and black faces. Just then a man sprang onto the hood of the car where I was balancing and took my hand. I felt the hand before I saw it. I remember looking down at my hand, and it was enfolded in a black hand.

Fear was palpable. You could see it in people's faces, feel it, though it was unspoken. It hung in the air, a warning of an event about to happen. The man who had his hand over mine knew it and I knew it and Bobby knew it as he spoke for the first time about losing his brother, and about grief and pain—soft words in a soft voice, deeply felt and coming slowly, with great effort from one who had suffered as people in the crowd were suffering now; and somehow the words were above anger and retribution and revenge. I looked down again at my hand and suddenly I knew that we were all flesh and all blood and all the same. And I also knew that I was safe.

The crowd didn't cheer and didn't clap when Bobby finished but dispersed quietly and sorrowfully into the twilight, people nodding to each other in quiet affirmation of commonality and community and sorrow. I got back to the motel through the crowd and very shortly after there was a knock on the door.

It was Bobby. He looked at me, saying nothing, and pulled his tie off. Then he spoke. "It could have been me." He put his arms around me and pulled me down on the bed alongside him, and we lay there for a long while and cried.

Yes, I love Tom. Yes, I've always loved him. I am married to him. I'll love him as long as I live. But to say that because you love your husband, it's impossible to love another man is as silly as to say that because you love your son, it's impossible to love your daughter.

"Meet me," Bobby said to Tom and me and to John Glenn as we stood in his room while the California returns were being announced on the television, "at the Factory," which was then a popular and swinging Los Angeles nightclub. He didn't say it as a gesture or to the room as a whole. He came to each of us, stood before each of us, and said, looking each of us in the eye, "Meet me at the Factory." There was something quite serious, personal, and wistful about that invitation. Then he left the room to go downstairs, where the celebration in the ballroom was in full swing. And that was the last time I saw him.

Provie, the maid whose name John Kennedy had inserted into my *Saturday Evening Post* piece, came rushing out of a side room as we started down the hall toward the elevators, and she was sobbing. Her face contorted in anguish, "Mrs. Braden, Joan, they've killed him. They've killed him. They've killed him."

We went to the funeral, and I thought at the time that it offended grief. Maybe I thought that because for me it began with those reporters outside the cottage where Tom and I had taken two of Bobby and Ethel's children. The reporters took no notice of grief or the curtain of privacy which grief draws around itself and which most people honor as grief's due.

Tom was hurt most by those reporters; perhaps because he was a reporter, he considered that a reporter's role was honorable. To get the facts, that was the reporter's role, and what more important and honorable a role could there be? Yet here were reporters getting the facts, and the job of getting the facts seemed to him disgusting and revolting, cruel and insensitive.

We were in a cottage on the grounds of the Beverly Hills Hotel in Los Angeles. Tom and I had driven there with Teddy White, who was showing Tom the way, reading the directions he had scribbled at the desk at the Ambassador Hotel before bedlam broke.

I never saw any man so calm and clear and precise in a

moment of mounting chaos as Teddy White was on that evening. He was perhaps the best-known reporter in the world. What was the job of a reporter? His answer was, in effect, The hell with the job of a reporter. Being a human comes first.

So he saw at once that the one thing we could do was to see that the children, who were in bed in the room adjoining Bobby and Ethel's at the Ambassador Hotel, were shielded from the mob. He looked around him, and there we were and there was John Glenn; and he gave us our orders, firmly, without raising his voice, without the slightest sign of panic.

Here I must ask the reader's indulgence, for it is possible that in what I am about to recite, I am mistaken in some details. When bedlam breaks, the logic of immediacy takes hold. All else is forgotten, and afterward the memory is vague about details. But I think John Glenn was to call President Johnson and arrange for a plane to come out and pick up the children, and get them back to Hickory Hill in Virginia. In the meantime, those children who were asleep next to Bobby and Ethel's room had to be taken from the Ambassador Hotel and driven to the Beverly Hills Hotel, where Bobby and Ethel had rented a cottage for the family.

Teddy turned first to Glenn, and I remember Glenn's face in expressionless assent. He would go to his room, and get on the telephone to the White House at once. To the hotel clerk, Teddy said simply, "My name is Theodore White and I'm a friend. I want the directions to the Kennedy cottage at the Beverly Hills Hotel." The clerk understood from his manner of speaking, picked up the telephone, called the Beverly Hills Hotel, and got the information. To Tom, Teddy said, "Go get your car and bring it up to this door, the one I'm pointing at, and Joan and I will go up and get the kids and we'll meet you right here."

All this was immediate. It was while the ballroom downstairs was chaotic and just a moment before the lobby of the hotel was to erupt. We went upstairs and Teddy and I picked up two sleeping children and we got to the door just as the lobby was beginning to explode. We drove up Wilshire Boulevard and made a right turn and a left turn into the Beverly Hills Hotel entrance, and then a left, and then to the second cottage on the right. Teddy was reading the directions out loud while Tom drove. By this time, the children were awake and we got to the cottage, where we found little David Kennedy and a baby-sitter watching television. Teddy snapped the set off at once and said, "Whatever you do, don't let them turn this thing on again."

He then sat down and made telephone calls to the schools where other Kennedy children were still in blessed oblivion and talked to headmasters and wives of headmasters, and then left.

I sang songs and Tom read a book of fairy stories. I've forgotten who had the presence of mind to bring the book of fairy stories, but we read them and then we read them again; and I made hot chocolate, and finally the children went to sleep.

The telephone call came just as dawn was breaking. A car was to pick up the children and take them to an airplane. So we bundled them up and Tom opened the cottage door.

To a hail of popping flashbulbs, to faces pressed against the children's faces as we hurried down the sidewalk toward the car, and to a string of questions, loudly put: "Have you prayed for your daddy? Do you know your daddy's been shot? Do you think the man who shot your daddy is a mean man?"

That was the way the youngest of the Kennedy children learned what had happened to their father. It was callous, cruel, and inhumane. Tom found a word for the reporters. They were, he said, churls.

Death was too long in coming to Bobby. There was time for grief to give way to pettiness, to quarrelsomeness, for people who wished to be seen entering the hospital, wished to be noted as having been admitted to the room, who vied with one another to get on the list for the funeral train. And then there was the long plane ride to New York, the funeral at Saint Patrick's and, after that, the endless train ride to Washington, with the long pauses because the tracks were lined with people and three people died on the tracks.

Why did anybody do this? Why did anybody plan this? Why did anybody go to Ethel and make the suggestion and get her approval if she was sane enough at the moment of approval to know what she was approving? That's what I asked myself at the time.

And yet I'm not sure that my own feeling of distaste and revulsion was only a selfish feeling. Do processions such as this one bind Americans? Does a child who was taken down to the tracks by his parents, who stood there with them and waved a flag as the train passed slowly—does that moment, etched in his memory, serve, in later years, his country?

Was that train and the long, long ride a necessary ritual, marking the end of the process by which Robert Kennedy's campaign for the presidency stirred the country to its better self and to the recollection of its own ideals, and so set in motion a protest against a war of which the country was ashamed?

In later years I have mused about grief, an experience so common to all of us yet so demanding of individual expression. Everybody on that train grieved. Some were somber-faced, staring grimly out the windows at the open country and at the crowds of people at the stations. Some cried silently but quite openly. Some reflected conversationally, and I was glad for older people who had experienced grief and who knew how to help. I remember, for example, white-haired John McCone, the director of the CIA, going up the aisles, stopping before silent younger acquaintances, saying to them, "I know how important Robert Kennedy was to you. Will you tell me about it?"

And some grieved with a laugh, standing in the aisles and remembering, "Were you there that time Bobby was telling us all what a horrible mess O'Brien made of that appearance in Trenton and all of a sudden the door opened and in walked Larry O'Brien? Did you see the expression on Bobby's face? I laughed until I thought I'd die."

Young Joe Kennedy came through the aisles and shook hands with each person on the train, and to each person on the train he said, "My father would thank you for coming," and nobody who was there will ever forget that he did that.

So, on second thought, I guess I was selfish. I thought it was *my* grief. It was everybody's grief, and everybody needed an end to grieving and the train ride was the end.

Jackie sat with Bobby's casket during the train ride. She had come out to California, I met her at the airport, and we drove to the hospital. She had not been told that Bobby would certainly die. When I told her that death was coming very soon, she was frantic.

She insisted on going through red lights, though we had no police escort and no markings on the car and nothing but the horn to signal that we were racing death. It was a long drive through so many red lights that I thought if something happened, if we hit somebody or somebody hit us, the string would break, in me and in her.

But she got to see Bobby while he was still alive. I know that meant something to her, and I pray that it meant something to him.

SIXTEEN

—•—

Oh, Well

Someday along the beach at Oceanside, some stranger may find an emerald ring I once laid down in the sand for just a moment while I ran to get a child out of crashing waves. There is a gold watch there too, and a whole lot of silverware, dropped by children and forgotten when we picked up everything after the camp fire had died down and the bright orange ball in the sky had descended below the vast expanse of dark blue water and we all went up the long flight of stairs and into the house and to bed.

I like to think that these almost forgotten and long lost objects will someday testify that a family once lived along these shores and that the family was careless in the true sense of the word.

We ran and we skipped, the children and I, and we liked to hold hands while we skipped; and for some reason which is inexplicable except to mothers, the words, "How would you like to skip with me all the way up to the pier and back?" were words joyous beyond measure, eagerly awaited and greeted, with arm-flailing excitement.

And we sang at night, raising our voices against the crash of the waves, and the deep bass songs were the best because they were the best match against the rumbling of the waves.

We picked up shells, the children and I, and carried them carefully up the stairs to be glued together for picture frames, and the pictures were colorful drawings of pink ducks and red lions. "A red lion, my, have you ever seen a red lion?"

Sometimes I wish we could go back and live it all over again, but, of course, it wouldn't be the same because we aren't.

And there came a time, or Tom said there came a time, when we had to go.

Looking back on it now, I can see that Tom thought we were beaten, beaten by events and beaten by our own reaction to events. Death takes its toll on the living, and death was certainly one thing that seemed to defeat us.

First Jack. Then Bobby. I doubt that anyone who knew them, or millions of those who didn't know them, escaped the feeling of hopelessness and defeat. It seemed to me that it hung upon the country like a great and heavy shroud during those five years. And Martin Luther King. What was the point of dreams? What was the point of enthusiasm? Of what purpose was goodwill or brave effort?

Well, maybe Mrs. Longworth escaped it. She was old and so she must have known many defeats and many deaths; and she observed them with the practiced equanimity of one who knows they occur and will occur and who knows that hopes, goodwill, and brave effort will rise again.

She waved almost merrily when she spotted Richard Nixon from her car on the way to John Kennedy's funeral, lowering the window to lean out at the lone dark-visaged figure standing on the corner of the bridge. "Dick, oh, Dick." And then she turned back to me. "I wanted him to see me because I wanted him to know that I saw him." There was a little dig to that gesture. Did she think that Richard Nixon, standing there alone, was putting down some self-suspected moment of triumph? Did she want him to know that she suspected it?

And the next day when Tom and I, breakfasting at her house, announced that we were going to visit the grave, she decided at once that she would go with us, although it was a gray and chilly, spitting rain kind of day. So we drove out to Lee's mansion, high over Arlington Cemetery, and we walked down toward the grave—where a man in a trench coat approached us. "Mrs. Longworth, I'm from the Associated Press. Are you visiting the grave?"

"No, no, young man. I just came out to see Lee's mansion. Very interesting. Have you visited it?"

And then, in an aside, as we turned and walked back up the hill, "I can hear it now. All those New York Roosevelts, 'Silly old fool. Grave sitting in the rain.'"

But that night as we sat by the fire in her living room, watching over and over again the killer of dreams himself being killed—the police station, the man in the wide-brimmed hat, the sudden blow to the stomach, the death grimace—she rose, went to her bedroom, and produced one of the slim volumes of Shakespeare she kept piled up at bedside. She found the page and read aloud:

"A lioness hath whelped in the streets;
And graves have yawned, and yielded up their dead;
Fierce fiery warriors fought upon the clouds,
In ranks and squadrons and right form of war,
Which drizzled blood upon the Capitol. . . ."

"Yes," she said, sitting back in her chair, "that's about it."

Tom ran in the Democratic primary for lieutenant governor of California in 1966 and was beaten the moment Lyndon Johnson put a third man, Lloyd Hand, in the race; and Bobby, although he knew that a third man in the race made Tom's campaign impossible, had given me ten thousand dollars and said, as he handed over all those bills, "What does he want to do? Make a statewide name for himself so he can sell soap?"

I never quite forgave him that cut but he was right; neither the children nor Tom was particularly sad about being beaten because they knew Bobby was right. I was the only one in the family who expected to win and always played to win, and I was shocked when we didn't and angry at Bobby, who thought losing was for other people. Including Tom. Including me.

To be fair, Bobby, who was already watching carefully every political move that Lyndon Johnson made and regarded Tom's candidacy as something of a harbinger, was more kindly after he'd looked at the final totals. He wrote to me that he believed that Tom would have won if Hand had not been in the race.

And then, as I said, Tom decided to sell the *Blade-Tribune.* Why didn't he plan ahead so that he could know what he was going to do after he had sold it and would not be reduced as he was to playing golf in the daytime, writing articles for magazines, and sitting up all night reading? Once I remember getting out of bed and finding him in the magnificent long book-lined room we had built under the old beach house so that we could look out at the waves and saying to him, "What do you intend to do for the next year, read every book in the house?"

So it was time to go and the going was wrenching for Tom but I think honestly less so for me, probably because I had spent so much time in Washington. When Tom was president of the state board of education and when we traveled the state during his campaign, I had come to know California pretty well. But as I look back on it, my life there was having babies (by now it was eight), and shuttling back and forth to Washington, helping Roger Stevens and Jackie raise money for the Cultural Center and listening in while John Kennedy talked with his artist friend Bill Walton about where it was to be. Bill envisaged the center as a group of separate buildings along a run-down portion of Pennsylvania Avenue, a building for the opera house, a building for the concert hall, a building for the big theater, and one for the small theater, and he thought of it as transforming the main thoroughfare of Washington—the street between the Capitol and the White House—from a long dreary line of four-story brick buildings containing second-hand shops and dark-in-the-nighttime small businesses into a brightly lit bustle of crowds on their way to theaters.

I was taken by his vision, and so was John Kennedy. I remember Jackie and the president and Bill and I talking about it over dinner one night just a week before they were to go to Dallas, and to his death.

It doesn't matter how the Walton concept lost out to the big structure under one roof along the Potomac, but I think it was easier to raise money for a big single structure, and Mrs. Chandler's Los Angeles Cultural Center was to be big and under one roof and it was, well, the fashion.

Anyhow, I was part-time Oceanside, part-time Washington,

and Tom's decision about the newspaper seemed to me to be his, though when I think of how much he put into it, how much he cared about it, the little flourishes—the quotation from George Washington over the masthead: "Let us raise a standard to which the wise and the honest may repair"; the big flourishes—the sports editor to cover the World Series, even when the games were played in New York—the addition of a Sunday paper, the book review section, the colored comics on Sundays, his insistence on perfection, even when perfection meant extending deadlines and making over the front page. After all that, to sell to "a chain." You would have thought to hear Tom talk that a newspaper chain was something to be despised. But now the *Blade-Tribune* was to be part of a chain. I'm sure it's not at all the worse for it, but at the time it seemed like paper towels.

Paper towels was a private joke between Jackie and me. When she went off to Paris for a state visit with her husband, she was excited by what she called the exquisite taste of Charles de Gaulle. For example, she said that in de Gaulle's box at the opera there had been Porthault towels in the washroom. It was a small thing, but it startled her because it was, she thought, just right. "Remind me, Joannie, to be sure that the Cultural Center has Porthault towels in the washrooms of the presidential boxes. Some day de Gaulle will return the visit and everything should be in perfect taste."

That was, of course, before the Cultural Center became the Kennedy Center and before de Gaulle returned the visit by attending a state funeral. Years later, Tom and I went to the ballet at the Kennedy Center one evening with Henry Kissinger, and we sat in the president's box. A question suddenly occurred to me and I had to know the answer. So I went through the doors to the rear of the box and into the private washroom. The president's box at the Kennedy Center has rough brown paper towels.

The next time I talked to Jackie, I told her. She didn't seem as disappointed as I was. Her attitude was "Oh, well," which was, I think, the way she felt about much that happened in Washington. The plans she had made for recovering the White House furniture that had been removed over the years by various occupants, the plans for beautifying Lafayette Square, the plans for the Cultural Center—they had all to one extent or another gone agley, and there wasn't anything she could do about it. "Oh, well" was not only the best response, it was the only one.

"Oh, well" was the way I felt about leaving Oceanside.

SEVENTEEN

How I Became a Socialite

tewart Alsop was Tom's best friend. Best man at our wedding, he soon became one of my best friends too. Stewart and Tom had served together during the war and had worked together after the war. While Tom went into the CIA and then to Oceanside, Stewart became one of the best, if not the very best, political columnist in the country. Along the way, Stewart thought of the three rules essential to being a political columnist.

I remember very well the night he formulated the rules for Tom, who, having sold the newspaper in Oceanside and having decided to become a political columnist, regarded those rules as having been handed down from the high mountain and engraved in stone.

We were sitting in Stewart's living room, just the four of us, Stewart's wife, Tish, Tom, Stewart, and me. I had just walked across the living room rug, an old Aubusson which had been handed down to Stewart and Tish from some long deceased relation and which Stewart was in the habit of repairing almost nightly. In crossing the room I had caught my high heels in one of the threads and had ruptured it. Stewart, clad, as was his custom when he dined at home, in a blue velvet jacket, a bow tie, dark trousers, and ancient ornamented slippers, was down on his knees, repairing the damage. Shortly we would play bridge, and Tom and I would be severely defeated, as usual. But for now the fire was warm, the day was done, and there was time to have a scotch and soda, repair old Aubussons, and listen to wise saws and modern instances.

Having stitched up the rug and reproved me for wearing heels that were too high and too pointed, Stewart sat down in his chair (nobody else ever dared to occupy that chair) and discoursed upon his rules.

Rule one was: See, not just talk on the telephone with but actually see, at least two and preferably three important government officials every working day.

Rule two: Don't write thumbsuckers. Stewart adopted a mock serious pose, extending his hands so that the finger tips of each touched lightly at the tips of their opposites while he expounded his example of a thumbsucker. "The situation in Afghanistan appears at first blush to be fraught with peril."

Thumbsuckers, he explained, were what political columnists are reduced to writing when they are too lazy to get out and see people; and thumbsuckers, though they may be quite logical and contain much wisdom, make columns that are dull and that, therefore, nobody reads.

The third rule also had to do with seeing people: If you don't invite people to dinner, nobody will invite you.

Those were Stewart's rules and Tom listened intently. Perhaps they are wise rules. I will leave that question to political columnists, but the reason I remember this winter evening so well is that it has seemed to me ever since that the rules fall with some severity upon the columnist's wife, particularly if the columnist's wife is possessed of eight children.

To go out to dinner three or four nights a week, to have people in to dinner, say, one night each week, even when Washington's unwritten regulation of an 11 P.M. witching hour is strictly followed, constitutes a pretty stiff regimen. It was clear to me that I had to have help, and since help had to be paid for, I would have to go to work—which, I suppose, I would have done anyhow. Except for brief spells in Oceanside, I always had. Up to now, I'd always gone to work for the work itself or for somebody I cared a lot about or because I cared about what he cared about. This was different. I had to go to work because we needed the money.

I don't like to do that. I like to work for the work and not the money. Every time in my life that I've gone to work where the money was more important than the work, I've been sorry.

This time I was lucky. I got a job on the air for a half-hour show on a local television station. The local television station was just waking up to the fact that Washington was a predominantly black city still operating under such a thick crust of white supremacy that even the blacks didn't really understand that it was a predominantly black city. But the television station did, and so the reporters for that station took on the job of pointing out the fact to Washington's population, black and white.

Black schools, white teachers and administrators. Black population, white government. Fires in black homes, white fire fighters. Black crime, white policemen. Pointing it out was a job. It had to be done delicately. I played a very small part in doing it, but I enjoyed it so much that one Saturday afternoon, Tom, rummaging through a drawer in search of spare change, found three weekly pay checks I had forgotten to send to the bank.

So I got a job and I hired the help. Tom or I chauffeured the little kids back and forth to school, and the bigger kids took busses. As the youngest, Tommy and Nicholas were in one school; Elizabeth, a little older, was in another; Susan and Nancy in a third; and going up the ladder, Joannie in a fourth; and Mary and David in a fifth. The younger children were frightened. They didn't have any friends. They didn't know anybody in these new schools. Moreover, the new schools were gargantuan compared to the school they'd known back in Oceanside, and they felt lost. Maybe the bigger kids felt lost too, but I'll always remember the morning that Mary, my oldest daughter, waiting to be driven to her new school, watched with me as Susan and Nancy got out of the backseat of the car and walked up the wide concrete pathway to their new school. They were very little girls in their new blue dresses, white ankle socks, and black shoes. We watched them go up the pathway to the school door and when they reached it, they both looked back, as if for help. And Mary said, "Wait a minute, Mom," and opened the door of the car and ran after them. I saw her bend down to Nancy's ear and then to Susan's, and I saw the school door open and Nancy and Susan go in, and the door close. I said to Mary when she returned, "What did you say to them?"

"I told them, Mom, that they were the best-looking girls that had ever entered that school and also that they were two of the brightest, and that they had the best-looking dresses of anybody I'd ever seen in any school."

I'll never forget that Mary did that.

But even I was a little scared about all the new schools. A principal would call me at the studio to tell me that Tommy had come to school without his shoes (children from small southern California towns sometimes do forget their shoes) and I, apologizing and promising rectification by lunch time, would have to ask for the name and address of the school.

An embarrassing question from Ethel Kennedy settled the matter. Ethel didn't mean to ask an embarrassing question. She simply asked, "What school does Susan attend?" And I couldn't remember whether it was Woodrow Wilson or Theodore Roosevelt or William McKinley or James Garfield. I said to Tom that night, "Either we have to get them into one school or I have to quit this job."

"That will cost an awful lot of money, Joannie, because it means a private school."

So we made a compromise of sorts. David and Mary, the eldest, were to go on in public high school and the younger six were sent to a private school.

It still cost an awful lot of money.

It was now time to get to work on Stewart's third rule: If you don't invite people to dinner, they won't invite you.

It wasn't long after I began to pay attention to this rule that I got into a terrible fight with Tom. Tom would pick up the *Washington Post* in the morning and then take his wrath out on me.

"Joannie, the newspapers are calling you a goddamn socialite." If there is a word Tom regards as the ultimate in opprobrium, it's the word "socialite." It stands for everything he dislikes: snobbery, misuse of money, misuse of time, people who don't do an honest day's work, drawing room people, empty-headed people, people with yachts, people who have never mowed their own lawns or put a spade into the ground.

"Socialite" conjured up for Tom everything he didn't want to be or know or have anything to do with.

And I said, "Look, I'm not a socialite, whatever 'socialite' means, and you know I'm not a socialite, and just because the newspapers say I'm a socialite doesn't make me one. I'm doing this for you. You said you wanted to have people in to dinner. Stewart told you to have people in for dinner. He and Tish have people in for dinner and the newspapers don't call Tish a socialite, so get mad at the newspapers and not at me."

So Tom did get mad at the newspapers. He got mad at the *Washington Post,* where his column appeared and which never used my name without appending a comma and the word "socialite"; and he got mad at *Newsweek,* which picked up the habit from the *Post*; and he got mad at *New York* magazine and the *Los Angeles Times*; and then he got mad at the *Washington Star,* which said I was "the chic superwoman who has established one of the most exclusive salons in town and is regarded as perhaps the most powerful hostess."

I don't know who coined the word "socialite." The dictionary dates its first usage as 1929, which puts it in the F. Scott Fitzgerald era. I wish it would stay where it belongs. Almost invariably it is used with a sneer, calling to mind a person of empty head and no occupation other than to make herself conspicuous by giving dinner parties. Almost invariably also it is used to describe a woman. The National Organization for Women, which has succeeded in eliminating the word "girl" as used to describe any woman over twelve from the vocabularies of television anchormen, ought to go to work next on the word "socialite."

For, as Tom kept pointing out, whenever he picked up the newspaper to find me so described, "You're a reporter, damn it, doing the same job in a different way as the person who wrote that story. Besides that, you're raising eight kids. When we can scrape together the money to have some friends in to dinner, does that entitle anybody to refer to you in public print as an air-head?"

In fairness, I must say that "having a few friends in for dinner" was something of an understatement. I remember one time during the oil crisis when people were lining up for miles to get to gasoline pumps, Art Buchwald walked over to my corner of the room and said, "Why have all these meetings and presidential proclamations? We could settle the whole problem right here in this room."

He was referring to the guests of the evening, who included the secretary of state, the Iranian ambassador, the British ambassador, the chairman of the Federal Reserve, the assistant to the president for national security affairs, the secretary of treasury, and a couple of White House advisors.

I won't pretend I didn't enjoy having some friends in for dinner. And it may be that Stewart's rules gave me an excuse to do what I wanted to do anyhow.

We have a big barn of a house, painted bright yellow to satisfy the children, and the house has nine fireplaces. Fireplaces make a difference between a dinner party and having friends in for dinner. The children make a difference between a dinner party and having friends in for dinner. The children had animals. At various times we had three sheep, two goats, a parrot, a crow, a monkey, three dogs, and a boa constrictor. They certainly make a difference.

And in the fourth place, the fact is that I didn't really know how to give a dinner party. I had the tablecloths and the flowers and the candles, and Tom lit the downstairs fireplaces, and we rented the extra chairs and the extra place settings, but I didn't know—in the Washington sense—where to seat people and who took precedence over whom. I made mistakes which at other people's dinner parties would have been regarded as insults to flags. I have seen ambassadors turn away at the front door of other people's houses, when after examination of the seating arrangement posted on the front hall table, they discovered that if they actually sat down to dinner they would be subjected to the degradation of occupying a chair two places further to the right of the hostess than the place which by seniority and rank was their rightful due. It took me a long while before I even knew that there ought to be such a posting on the front hall table and even longer to hunt one up and purchase it at one of the Washington stores which purveys such items. I seated the ambassador of Israel above our own secretary of state. I didn't know that ambassadors and their wives are seated not according to their country's power or size or friendliness or even whether you particularly like them, but are seated according to the length of time they have been ambassadors to the United States. I didn't know, for example, during the Nixon years when Hungary became suddenly important because it had been kind to Richard Nixon after his defeat in his race for governor of California, that Hungary's ambassador could not be seated near the head of the table because he had been a very short time in his post.

I once seated Nelson, who was then governor of New York, ahead of Henry Kissinger, who was the secretary of state; and was amused to discover later that governors rank next to last in Washington protocol and that secretaries of state take precedence over anybody except the president, vice president, and Chief Justice of the Supreme Court.

That was an error among friends. When I seated the new ambassador of India ahead of Henry, he noticed it and admonished me gently and in good humor. I had thought that the Indian ambassador, whose name was Tiki Kaul, being new in town and among strangers, deserved the place of honor, but I later suffered through the discovery that Mr. Kaul, at his own dinner parties, was in the habit of rising at the table and toasting each of his guests, calling each by name and reciting his or her past accomplishments. The whole thing took well over half an hour, and I made up my mind that the best way to avoid the after dinner toast at Mr. Kaul's table was to give him no place at mine.

The worst mistake I ever made was when the Soviet ambassador, Anatoly Dobrynin, paid his respects to détente by arriving for dinner at our house preparatory to a Frank Sinatra concert. The foreign minister of Mexico was in town, and Henry had called to ask that he be invited. I was so impressed by the fact that the Dobrynins were coming for dinner—as far as I know they had not been seen at a small private Washington dinner in many years—that I had in mind that the occasion was important because Dobrynin was important. I seated him on my right with Henry on my left and the foreign minister of Mexico down the line. The foreign minister of Mexico made no sign of umbrage, nor did Henry, but after dinner Mr. Dobrynin made a conspicuous acknowledgment of diplomatic rank by bowing at the door to permit the foreign minister to go out of the room first and later at the theater, he did it again, standing aside and gesturing for the foreign minister to precede him into the hall.

These little signs of rank and stature, which were of no importance to me whatever, are of enormous importance in Washington. Yet I don't recall over all the years that I was a "socialite" that anybody ever complained. If anybody felt insulted, they didn't reveal it. I should have known better than to make the mistakes I did make, and I do know better now. When I'm in doubt I call the office of protocol at the State Department and find out who outranks whom. Tom says, "Who cares where he sits so long as he sits next to an attractive woman?"

But diplomats care a lot. As one of them pointed out in rejoinder to Tom, "It's my duty to demand my rightful place on behalf of my country; and for my country's sake, I must, if protocol demands, sit next to a most unattractive woman."

It seems to me that the reason I was never confronted with my mistakes was that Tom and I never really gave dinner parties. We had some friends in to dinner. The distinction was obvious.

When a sheep walks into the living room, folds his legs in the deliberate fashion sheep do and lies down at the feet of a Supreme Court justice, when Mrs. Longworth insists that the children bring the boa constrictor down to the living room so that she can wrap it around her neck and "warm it," when the two Nubian goats balance themselves on the windowsill to stare in at the guests, the distinction is obvious. Officials who came to our house were not attending a dinner party. They were friends gathered for dinner.

But it was not I or Tom, spaciousness, fireplaces, the children, or the animals that drew the attention of the press to our house during the latter years of the Nixon administration and the beginning of the Gerald Ford administration. It was Henry Kissinger. Henry became, during those years, America's most sought-after man. The press followed him like children after the Pied Piper. Ambassadors and senators and congressmen who sat near him at the dinner table took notes. I watched them surreptitiously do it under the table but not surreptitiously enough nor far enough under the table to escape my eye. Henry Brandon, a Washington reporter for a London paper, published a book consisting largely of Henry's ruminations by the side of a swimming pool. Once I gave a party for Tom to celebrate publication of a book he had written, and the house was mobbed with TV cameramen, and the headline in the Style Section of the next day's *Washington Post* was, THE CALL. Larry Eagleburger,

Henry's closest advisor, had placed a call from Paris, and Henry had taken it in an out-of-the-way room but not far enough out of the way to prevent at least twelve reporters who had followed him into the house from trying to listen in.

Tom writes a book and CBS, NBC, and ABC cover its publication with cameras? Barbara Howar moves from Washington to New York and holds a much publicized garage sale, listing one of the items as "toilet seat used by Henry Kissinger"?

It wasn't Henry's fault. He did not seek public attention, and he shunned people of bad taste as soon as he learned they had bad taste. The reason he was the most sought-after man in America during those years was not only his intelligence, his knowledge of history, his self-deprecating humor, his ability to discern the aspirations and probable courses of action of great powers (characteristics which Henry possessed in high degree), nor the fact that he was single. (Washington loves singleness in powerful officials.)

It was rather that during those years we were engaged in a seemingly endless war—sad, horrible, and purposeless—and that nobody in the administration could or would admit that it was purposeless and Henry's job was to try to get us out of it without endangering or dividing the country. He was, along with the two presidents he served, the country's most important man.

And maybe before he married Nancy, also the country's loneliest. I remember the first time he called and asked himself for dinner. It was not a startling request. Henry and I had been friends during many of the years I spent with Nelson Rockefeller. It was as natural for him to say, "May I come over?", as it would be for anyone else to call any good friend and ask the same.

But I hesitated momentarily. It was one of those breathless days Washington suffers during July. Tom, in the course of his rounds, had run into the senator from Wisconsin, Gaylord

Nelson, and the senator from South Dakota, George McGovern. Learning that both their wives had sensibly left town, Tom had invited the men to dinner. They were both Democrats, both opponents of the war, which Henry, as head of the National Security Council, was even then trying to wind down without "bugging out." Would it be awkward for them and for Henry?

So I told him that Tom had invited these friends and Henry replied, "Do you think that they would like me?"

I found his question wonderfully Washingtonian. Obviously he did not know either Nelson nor McGovern. They were his foes, politically and ideologically. But Washington is unique— perhaps apart from London, the only place in the world where foes smile at each other, where even bitter enemies, men who have just finished denouncing each other to the press or to the galleries or in some other public forum, must meet on common ground, at somebody's dinner party or at somebody's cocktail party. They must behave with civility. They must listen to each other's jokes; they must jibe each other in jocular fashion—and often they find themselves in some corner of the room where they learn to their mutual surprise that neither of them have horns.

It was such a plaintive question—"Do you think they would like me?"—such a little-boy question. I told him that I knew Gaylord Nelson and George McGovern very well and that I was certain they would like him.

So he came to dinner and we sat outdoors in whatever coolness we could find in the evening, and neither senator suggested, as some of their constituents were doing at the time, that Henry Kissinger was murdering babies. We talked about the war, which was the only subject anybody in Washington talked about in those years, and I think the senators did like Henry and that Henry liked them.

That was the first of many similar and larger gatherings at

our house, which to me meant having friends in for dinner, and meant to Henry, I guess, a way to get away, and meant to the press, "Joan Braden, socialite."

I liked a man named Bill Fulbright, who came to dinner often. Sharply intelligent with a questioning, appraising cast of mind only partly disguised by a courtly manner; I found him charming. I laugh even now when I recall his constantly reiterated answer to all questions having to do with his post as chairman of the Senate Foreign Relations Committee. His brow would knit and he would turn to the questioner in mock astonishment. "I wouldn't know the answer. I'd be the last person to ask. You see, they never tell me anything."

Bill Fulbright had given Lyndon Johnson's war his initial support. Indeed, he had introduced the famous Gulf of Tonkin Resolution, which gave Johnson legal underpinning for the vast expansion of the war, but his doubts had grown proportionately to the untruths emanating from the White House. After conducting committee hearings which exposed some of those untruths, he had bolted into fixed opposition. But Bill Fulbright was responsible in opposition. He wanted out of the war, but he wanted out as gracefully as possible. He needed to know what the administration was considering, what courses for departure might be open, what courses closed, what attempts at finding courses were being made.

His opposition to the war had made him a foe of Lyndon Johnson, and when Nixon and Kissinger took over Johnson's war Fulbright became their foe as well. The chairman of the Senate Foreign Relations Committee and the assistant to the president for national security affairs were on cursory speaking terms only. "They never tell me anything."

Bill Fulbright repeated the complaint perhaps a little ostentatiously at our house one evening when Henry Kissinger was at the table, and Henry responded by turning to me. "Joannie, why don't you ask the senator to have lunch with us some day?"

Fulbright followed suit. He didn't respond to Henry. He turned to me. "I'd be glad to accept an invitation from Joannie anytime she wishes to extend it."

How odd it now seems, this preparation for the waltz between two grown men using me as the pillar around which they carefully circled. But it's true. I don't know to what extent I helped to repair a breakdown in communications between two branches of government, but I took my cue from Henry, who called me one morning at my office and said, "Now is a good time to have lunch with Fulbright."

Pillars, as is well known, do not take part in waltzes. They simply stand there and are danced around. And so it was probably rude of me to speak up in protest. "My God, Henry, I can read the newspapers. We're bombing Cambodia. Do you want to have the lunch now?"

The voice on the other end of the line was dry. "Sometimes," it said, "when something big breaks, a pause ensues, and it is time to reflect. See if you can get Fulbright for tomorrow."

Which I did. "The chairman would be pleased to join you for lunch tomorrow," said his secretary. I made a reservation at Sans Souci, then a popular Washington restaurant, for 12:30 P.M. the next day. When I arrived, Fulbright was already there, looking around the room, appraising, nodding to acquaintances, obviously enjoying himself. "This is the first time I have lunched outside the Congress in nearly thirty years." Then Henry arrived. After greeting him, I don't think I opened my mouth, other than to ask for bread, for three and a half hours.

They sat at the table and talked about the war for precisely that length of time. The restaurant filled and emptied. At 3:30 P.M., we were still at the table; they were still talking; I was not bored and neither were they.

I was pleased a couple of weeks later when David Bruce and I, lunching together at the same restaurant, were politely approached by the waiter. "The two gentlemen in the far corner of the room ask if you will stop by their table before you leave."

I looked up and across the room. The table for two in the far corner was occupied by Henry Kissinger and Bill Fulbright.

Having friends in for dinner was not always so satisfactory. One occasion broke a Washington rule. At least I thought it was a Washington rule and Tom thought it was a Washington rule, but maybe I should say it used to be a Washington rule. The rule is or was that nobody ever reported to a newspaper what was said at a private dinner party. The rule applied to everybody: host, hostess, guests, and reporters—if reporters were among the guests.

A reporter, according to the rule, could use a private conversation at a private dinner party as an excuse for a follow-up. He or she could call a man's office and say, "You were telling me the other night that you thought the president made a mistake. Would you tell me some more about that?" But he or she could not report what the official had said in private at dinner.

It is a good rule. It protects people. It permits an official to relax, to converse freely, to speak as he thinks, and to have his thoughts countered with the thoughts of other people. All this, according to the Washington rule, he could do without fear that his unrehearsed thoughts would be reported in the next edition of the newspapers.

The rule was broken at a dinner one evening at our house, to my dismay and to the dismay of a lot of good friends. I remember that Henry Kissinger was there, Robert McNamara was there and Barbara Walters (she had come down from New York to do something for the *Today* show), Averell Harriman was there and Stuart Symington, the senator from Missouri. I had picked up the newspaper one morning to learn that Richard Helms was in town. Tom had known Dick Helms since his CIA days, and Helms, who had gone on from those days to become director of the CIA, was now ambassador to Iran. So the dinner party was for him and his wife, Cynthia.

I don't know whether he thanks me for it or whether he'd like to forget it ever occurred. But I'm sure he hasn't forgotten that the private party became one of the most public ever given in Washington. Obviously the presence of Dick Helms stirred the emotions of many of those at the table. Helms was under indictment for perjury. Testifying under oath in 1973 before the Senate Foreign Relations Committee, he had been asked a question by Senator Symington of Missouri.

"Did you try in the Central Intelligence Agency to overthrow the government of Chile?"

Helms answered, "No, sir."

Symington pressed him. "Did you have any money passed to the opponents of Allende?"

"No, sir," Helms had replied.

"So the stories you were involved in that war were wrong?"

"Yes, sir."

Tom used to argue that the moment Symington asked his first question, Helms should have demanded an off-the-record session. But no matter. Here was this tall, taciturn, intelligent, and friendly man surrounded by friends or enemies, he didn't know which, just off a flight from Iran and pausing at the edge of an abyss. It must have looked very black down there.

Everybody was conscious of that. Tom rose after dinner, recalling an episode in which Dick Helms had stepped beyond the line of duty to protect an able and much respected CIA officer from unwarranted attack by Senator Joseph McCarthy during Tom's days in the CIA. He toasted Dick Helms for courage.

That started an outpouring. Symington, Helms's interrogator rose in praise. McNamara and Harriman, Henry Kissinger, who was secretary of state, and Bill Simon, who was secretary of treasury, did the same. It must have been a moment of warmth for Dick Helms, and the warm feeling may have lasted for a day or until the *Washington Post* ran the whole story, toasts and all, on its front page.

Now there's no law which makes private dinner parties off bounds to newspapers, and I guess it must be said that no custom dictates against newspaper intrusion upon privacy, except of course the privacy of the newspaper's editors and publishers. But I was shocked when I found this party on the front page, and I didn't like the tone of the piece, which clearly suggested the entire Washington establishment had rallied around the right of a CIA director to lie to Congress. Tom didn't like the suggestion that he and I were not only a part of the establishment but also had the money to go with the role. "White candles gleamed and rich red wine flowed freely," as I remember the *Post*'s story began, and Tom's comment was that the rich wine was three dollars and fifty cents a bottle.

I felt wronged and angry, and I spent too much time feeling wronged and angry and probably too much time speculating on who had talked to the *Post* and too much time calling guests to apologize.

The story was accurate in innuendo but not in fact, and no laws were broken. But it seems to me that when you go to someone's house for dinner, you don't expect to have your dinner table conversation reported in print. When it is, you have a right to feel violated and the person who asked you to dinner has the right to feel wronged.

Confronted by exasperating events over which he had no control, Stewart Alsop used to ease his exasperation by reciting an old saw he had learned as a boy: "The cow kicked Nellie in the belly in the barn; didn't do her any good, didn't do her any harm."

Maybe that's the way I ought to have felt about that dinner party. But speaking for Nellie, it was a pretty hard, swift, unexpected kick.

———•———

New Facts; Old Innuendos

*D*uring the seventies, the press tended to beat up on any woman who was appointed to a post of public prominence by a man. It raised its eyebrows and suggested the questions it would have been crass to put in print—Is there anything between them? did she get the job because she's sexy? are they sleeping together? The press didn't ask these questions; it suggested these questions. Worst of all, the people who did the suggesting were most often women.

Every time I read a speech by a female leader denouncing our sexist society, the sexism is blamed on men. But the next time you see a nasty and suggestive piece about some poor Matilda Brown who has just been appointed assistant to a

Cabinet secretary or press secretary to a congressman or head of the advisory board for some department of government, take a look at the byline in the newspaper or the face of the reporter on television. Chances are it's that of a woman.

I speak from experience. There I was on a Friday evening, sipping a predinner cocktail and sitting on a bed surrounded by three children and three dogs, Walter Cronkite had just finished his broadcast and I had said to the children, "Let's go down and have dinner." That morning I had been to the State Department to see the under secretary for economics, a man named Charles Robinson, and he had offered me the job of consumer advisor to the Department of State. As far as I know, the jobs were President Ford's idea, and whether he saw them as fulfilling a real need or whether he saw them as a means of placating the strong consumer movement and shunting off Ralph Nader's demands for a Department of Consumer Affairs, I don't know. I had been to see Robinson several times, submitted résumés, written letters, called friends—the kind of things anybody does when a job is the object, and now the job was mine. I told Tom, and I asked, "Will this make the newspapers?"

"Yes," he had said, "page twenty-six."

The telephone rang. It was Maxine Cheshire, gossip columnist for the *Washington Post*, the woman who had made national news as a symbol of downtrodden femininity when Frank Sinatra responded to her questions by handing her two one-dollar bills.

I was wary of Maxine. She often called me to ask such questions as Is Happy Rockefeller pregnant? or Was Jackie Kennedy wearing an engagement ring? That's the reason I was wary.

"I understand," she began, "that you accepted a job this morning as consumer advisor at the State Department. When did you last see Henry?"

I suppose right there I could have said—maybe I should have said—Maxine, it's none of your business when I last saw Secretary Kissinger. But I didn't. "Let's see," I answered, "I think it was on Thanksgiving Day."

"And when did you last see Nelson?" She used the word "Nelson," and I almost corrected her. I almost said—maybe I should have said—I can't remember when I last saw the vice president. Perhaps two months ago. I didn't. I said, "I can't remember, perhaps two months ago."

I was catching the drift. I was to be portrayed by Maxine Cheshire as the "close friend of Henry" and the "close friend of Nelson," and that's how I got a job for which I was totally unqualified. Which was the gist of Maxine's next question.

"You say in your résumé that you have a degree in economics from Northwestern University. But the registrar at Northwestern doesn't confirm that. Do you have any degree at all?"

There was a final question. "You're a Democrat. Do you have any idea why you should be chosen for a plush job by a Republican administration?"

"Plush job" seemed to me the final straw. "I don't know that it's a 'plush job,'" I said. "I intend to work very hard at it before I decide whether it's plush."

It didn't matter what I said. Maxine had revealed by her questions what line she would take, and she took it high on page one of the *Washington Post* the following day. I was quoted as referring to "Henry" and "Nelson" as though they were two boys who had accompanied me on a hayride and as though the hayride had been great fun. The word "socialite" appeared again, along with the word "chic," along with the not very faint suggestion that I had lied about my education. In short, I don't see how any casual reader of the *Washington Post* on that day could have escaped the conclusion that a woman had been appointed to a high post in government for no other reason than that she had pull and that the pull was in being a woman, and that in fact she was totally unfit not only for this job but also for any other line of work which high-minded people who care about ethics in government might consider to be "respectable."

I don't think I can blame Maxine Cheshire for the backache which sent me into the hospital and into traction. I've had a backache ever since having eight children, and I wouldn't trade any one of them for relief from an aching back. Nevertheless, as I look back now, the pain in my back seemed to mount along with the press storm and to reach an apex about the time somebody named Joy Billington began her piece in the now defunct *Washington Star* with the lines, "Before having her picture taken, Joan Braden unbuttoned the top button on her blouse and raised her skirt above her knee."

Bill Simon, secretary of the treasury, called before I had even read the papers—Simon went to work very early—and told me not to worry. Worse things, he said, had been written about him. But my son Tommy, as I leaned down to kiss him that night, said, "Mom, I'm worried about two things. I haven't been wearing my retainer and you'll have to pay more for braces. Even worse than that, Mom, what am I going to say at school? My mom is a sex symbol?"

Before the storm reached its full fury, my friend Larry Eagleburger, who was under secretary of state for management and Henry's most trusted advisor, told me not to take any more calls from the press. "The hubbub will die down."

That intelligence assessment must rank in Larry's mind as his most erroneous in the nearly thirty years he has spent in the State Department. The *New York Times* joined the furor and then the magazines—*Time, Newsweek, People*. Clayton Fritchie and Art Buchwald tried to calm things down with funny columns, making light of my predicament and of the press storm which created it. But the storm continued.

Eagleburger called again. "You can't hide so you might as well talk, and I'll check in with Henry."

Sally Quinn of the *Washington Post* came to the hospital to interview me. She made it clear in a hand-delivered note that if she couldn't interview me, she was going to write a piece anyhow. A piece by Sally Quinn can be feline. I have seen people clawed deeply enough so that it hurt. She came—on two successive days—and besides the interview, we took time out to discuss marriage and children, and she avowed that she would never have either (she since has). I, apropos of something that came up in the conversation and undoubtedly wanting not to seem as square as she thought me, said I didn't think monogamy was the most important thing in a marriage, that love and truth and trust were more important.

Sally put this aside into her piece for the *Post*, and I've never been allowed to forget it. It comes up every time I come up, and I wish I hadn't made the remark. But as I've said before, I think it's true.

I heard about Eagleburger's checking with Henry after I left the hospital and the traction, and the newspapers had become, once again, something I looked forward to reading in the morning. Kissinger was in the Caribbean, taking a rest, and Larry chose his words carefully, not wishing to disturb. According to Larry, the conversation went like this: "Henry, Chuck Robinson hired Joan Braden for that consumer advisor job. There have been a number of press inquiries and I've told them you knew nothing of the appointment."

Dead silence.

"Henry?"

The heavily accented words of the secretary of state then wrote an epilogue to the whole affair: "Larry, even *I* wouldn't believe that."

There was a great big room with chandeliers hanging from the ceiling, and it was packed with people seated on chairs. Up in front of them were newspaper reporters and cameramen kneeling, standing, and sitting. Up still further were six chairs, one for me and one for each of five other consumer appointees from five other departments of government. We sat, our necks craned to the ultimate "up," seven congressmen around a table above us. Congressman Ben Rosenthal of New York started on the left of the single row of chairs before him and called out the name of the appointee from the Department of the Treasury, went on rapidly to the next appointee, and the next. Now it was my turn. But he skipped me and went on to the next appointee and the next. Then he paused, a measurable pause. "And now, Mrs. Braden, you. Will you step up to the microphone please?"

I was terrified. I rose and went to the microphone. Cameras clicked from all sides of the floor. They seemed to be clicking from overhead. I found a voice. "Mr. Chairman, my name is Joan R. Braden. . . ."

It was all over in less than ten minutes. The great green glob was long gone and so was the pain in the back. But now the terror was gone too and the embarrassment. In their place were friendly faces. Who in the world is that distinguished-looking man rising from his chair and coming forward? Good heavens, it is—it's David Bruce. How kind of him to come and be with me in my moment of fright. The face of David Bruce was wearing a half-amused smile.

NINETEEN

Sex and the Working Mother

Maybe I have been unfair to women journalists. I blamed them for putting me through trauma and, in fact, they did put me through trauma. But women journalists, like other working women, have good reason for knowing that the great American workplace is full of attractions to sex, propositions for sex, and adventures in sex. Women journalists have joined what used to be the man's world, and they too have to make decisions about how to handle that fact.

I think they tend to overemphasize sex, to look for it as the reason behind the reason, and sometimes to allude to it, point to it, when it isn't there.

Sex is not sinful. It is not sensational. It is everyday. It is matter-of-fact. I think, for example, of the airport at Wausau, Wisconsin, in 1960.

At 2:00 in the morning in Wausau, during the month of March, it is commonly cold; and on this particular March morning the airport was frigid. It was also dark and lonely. Hubert Humphrey's plane had landed fifteen minutes earlier. A more tired, more dispirited group of travelers has not, I think, before or since, ever shivered through the baggage unloading, wandered across the cement, and sought refuge from a biting wind inside the dimly lit shed, which, at that hour, was all that was doing business in Wausau's airport. There were not very many of us because Humphrey's Wisconsin primary campaign was not catching on. This was a state in which he had to beat Kennedy. It adjoined his own state of Minnesota. It was part of the Midwest, and Humphrey had to show he was strong in the Midwest.

I had decided to cover a week of Humphrey's campaign because Tom was covering a week of John Kennedy's campaign and our stories appeared side by side in the *Blade-Tribune*. Fairness. Fairness even on small newspapers which shouldn't have afforded the money for that kind of fairness. We each spent a week covering Richard Nixon's campaign too.

By that time, Hubert Humphrey was running out of money and almost out of spirit, a resource which had hitherto seemed inexhaustible. I stood alongside him one morning and listened to him plead over the telephone with Mary Lasker in New York for fifteen thousand dollars so he could pay for the airplane to make a final sally around the state. It was to begin at Wausau, go to one town and then another and then to another where crowds would greet him at each airport stop. It was to end in Milwaukee, where we were to spend the night.

First, he had secured Mary Lasker's promise, and then he

had boarded the airplane. Right there, before the reporters from the Wausau paper, the Minneapolis paper, the St. Paul paper, and the representatives of the wire services, he had staged a little dance in the center of the aisle.

The dance was a sort of knee-bending exercise much like the ones football players engage in when they are told by the coach to get off the bench and get ready to go into the game. It was also running in place; and the running in place ended with a pounding of his chest and a shout, "I am a Tiger. That's what I am, a Tiger. I'm Hubert Humphrey, the Tiger, and I will not—cannot be beaten." Then he went to his seat and sat down.

That had been about 10 in the morning, and now it was 2:00 A.M. on the following day. All day and all night we had bucked and plunged in sick-making suddenness through the snows and winds of northern Wisconsin, and only once had we managed to land, only one crowd had been greeted, and here we were back where we had started, fifteen thousand dollars of Mary Lasker's money and a whole day of campaigning blown away by the winds.

So it was not the Tiger who stood next to me as I dropped coins into a slot and called another number for another motel. It was just a senator from Minnesota, kindly, sweet, dejected, and wearing a brown hat. I remember the hat because he removed it before he spoke. "I have a suite, Joannie, with a living room. Why don't you take my bed and I'll use the living room?"

You know, I almost wish I had. No, I don't really. But the man was so beaten and so tired and so kind and so obviously lonely. It was so dark over by the phone booths and so cold; and tomorrow he had to get up and try to be a Tiger all over again, and I felt so sorry for him.

Maybe I wear my sympathies on my face. Tom was shocked when he learned that on the Humphrey campaign stops, I was handing out pieces of paper entitled, "Muriel Humphrey's Recipe for Beef Stew." He said no reporter should do that. But there was nobody else to do it. Hubert had brought stacks of the recipes along on the plane, and I was the only woman on the plane. The sole staff member, a man, was otherwise occupied, and Hubert wanted the recipes handed out. So I did it. And Hubert thought it was a friendly thing to do. Does being a reporter mean you can't do a friendly thing? No male reporter, nobody from the *Minneapolis Star Tribune*, the *St. Paul Pioneer Dispatch*, the *New York Times*, or the Associated Press would have done it. You know why? Because they're too damned self-important and they think their newspapers are too important. If the candidate's car had a flat tire, I'll bet that not one of them would have helped to change it. Helping to change the candidate's tire so that he could get to the next stop would have been an act of partisanship. Not for the *New York Times*. Not for the *Minneapolis Star Tribune*. They were non-partisan: wish we could help, but it's not our job. Our job is to observe the candidate undergoing the stressful experience of a flat tire and to report thereon.

I'm not made that way. I'm not a first-class spectator as Mrs. L. was. I want to help. So I handed out recipes for Muriel Humphrey's beef stew. Though I didn't accept the candidate's invitation to share his suite on that bitter cold night in Wausau, I have since reflected that I should have been more appreciative of a warm bed and less worried about what others might think.

I like warmth on a cold night as well as the next person. But I don't know a thing about sex. Despite having eight children, I don't know as much as the next person. Because the next person always seems to know and to confide in me that they know all manner of mysteries and techniques. Particularly men. And men assume, I don't know why, that I must know all these mysteries and techniques that are said to touch the passions; the correct arrangement of lights, the eroticism of perfume, the sensualness of clothing, the gentle touch of fingers.

Why do they assume it? I don't know. David Bruce used to suggest during quiet dinners that I was a walking encyclopedia on these matters. And when I told him I wasn't, that I didn't know any more about it than a Briargate girl on spring vacation, he dropped the pretense of polish which had distinguished him for fifty years in at least five diplomatic posts. "All right," he said, "you're an ignoramus. Then let's have a toss in the hay."

I loved David Bruce. I revered him. I think of him still as he thought of George Washington: "Striking in appearance, fastidious in dress, courtly in manner, dignified in bearing, skillful in field sports, hospitable as Timon of Athens, he was the ideal Southern cavalier." That's what David wrote about his hero in his book *Sixteen American Presidents*. The description fit its author as well as its subject, and I caught his point at once. He was far too distinguished, experienced, and sophisticated ever to be caught tossing in the hay.

Tom was not experienced, not sophisticated, and had grown up, as I had, in the Midwest. Tom was a hay tosser, as he had demonstrated during a weekend at the Judge's house on the lake in New Hampshire. That was very early in our long relationship. In fact, it was not more than a month or two after I had met Tom. I consented with some reluctance to go off for the weekend and a college kind of reunion at the Judge's lakeside house, the Judge being the father of one of Tom's closest college friends.

The reason I was reluctant was that the Judge's son had made it clear when he extended the invitation that only people who were married or engaged to be married were to be invited. I'm not sure why this stricture was laid down. I suppose the Judge and his wife, having been persuaded by their son to consent to a house party, wanted to be sure that the mingling of the sexes during the house party would not result in gross embarrassment during months to come. The man was, after all, a Judge.

Since the rule was laid down, Tom insisted that we become engaged in order to comply. I thought the notion silly, unnecessary, and suggestive. I refused to become engaged in order to go to a house party. I was nevertheless invited, welcomed, and assigned a room with a bunk bed in the long dormitorylike arrangement of small rooms which abutted the lake and served as underpinning for the main house, the Judge's house, which constituted "upstairs."

In my room and everybody else's there were bunk beds. I chose the top bunk and closed the door. I don't know what bunk Tom chose in his quarters far down the long hall, but I hadn't been asleep very long before I learned that he didn't intend to stay in his quarters and that my top bunk had not been built for two.

"Tom Braden, get out of here; somebody will hear you." I remember I whispered hoarsely as he clambered into my bunk, one long step up, one bare foot resting on the lower bunk and then the leap upward, into the hay.

It was the leap which finished off the bunk bed, splintered the wood, broke the bed posters, split the underpinning for the hay, and caused the bunk to come crashing down upon the lower bunk with a sound that was like a clap of thunder in an electrical storm.

The mattress saved me. It was still under me after its four-foot plunge, and Tom somehow leaped to safety. I could see him standing over me observing the ruins. Outside the room, in the brightly lit hall, was the Judge in his pajamas, his flannel-nightgowned wife with her head covered in the kerchief of her

New England generation, and our friends—a circle of mutual embarrassment.

Concern hid embarrassment. "Joan, are you all right? Is anyone hurt?" Concern also covered the need for apology, accusation, and guilt. Everybody went back to bed and said whatever they had to say in the privacy of their own rooms. I said nothing, and Tom said nothing and went on down the hall, and the next day an incident which had aroused an entire household in the middle of the night went politely unmentioned.

I don't know why I married this hay tosser. I might have become skilled in the art of seduction. I might have played the role of the courtesan. Instead I married a hay tosser and had eight children and learned to love a toss in the hay.

For months I was ashamed of what happened that night by the lake in New Hampshire. Even today, I can see the kindly, startled, red face of the Judge's wife under the kerchief; and when I do, I cringe. That bed crash saved me from disobedience of the strictures. I was a virgin when I married Tom. I have four married daughters and I think—I'm not positive about this—but I think that one of them may have been a virgin on her wedding night.

Through the years I have found on the subject of sex that I am much more modern and also more open and frank with my children than is Tom. Where Tom says, You must absolutely not, I say, Don't you think it would be wiser? Tom thunders in Victorian fashion, and I discuss and suggest and point out. Never once did I tell my teen- or college-age daughters that the stern strictures they were hearing from their father were the same strictures he tried to persuade me—and no doubt other young ladies—to ignore. Most fathers are hypocrites on the subject of sex, particularly in conversations with their daughters. Somehow their daughters know it or suspect it. Tom admits this, but he thinks that nevertheless there is a certain value in pronouncing the strictures.

I think, for example, of my son David and the girl Jennifer, for whom we lovingly and carefully prepared a separate room. The room had been a luggage storeroom until David announced that he was bringing Jennifer home for a weekend; but David's sisters went to work on it and by the time they had finished, there were lace curtains on the windows, flowers from the garden on the night table, a bookcase with books, and a single bed with a flowered spread. Clean too. Not a speck of dust from those old suitcases.

Kirk and Anne Douglas were staying with us, and on Sunday night, as Jennifer was to depart, the whole family and Kirk and Anne were at the front door to say good-bye. So it was a large assembly which heard Tom address a polite question to the pretty young lady who was going out that door. "Was your room comfortable?"

And a large assembly which heard her reply. "Oh, yes, Mr. Braden, but the bed was awfully small for two."

Nobody laughed out loud, though there were titters from the children. But nobody ever laughs out loud at the true faith, even when they doubt that the preacher believes it. I, on the other hand, aware that the faith is long lost, preaching common sense, reason, caution, get laughed at.

I say to those of my children who are still not married that they shouldn't unless they know the girl or boy very well and have known the girl or boy very well for a long time, have come to like them and admire them a lot, or think that maybe they love them.

To which Nicholas, my youngest son, responded only the other day. "Mom, how do I get to know her very well unless I've slept with her?"

To be laughed at is somehow better than to be completely ignored, as Tom and other exponents of the true faith are now ignored. You can react angrily to laughter and explain once again your point of view which, as is well known, constitutes the facts of life. But then, every once in a while, you have a conversation with children (I shouldn't use that word anymore because they're all grown up, but that they are my children is also one of the facts of life) that reveals that angry responses to laughter haven't done any good at all, that everything you said in that response or in a lot of angry responses, reasoned responses, quiet responses, has been wasted, lost—words spoken as from another world and in an unintelligible language.

One of my unmarried daughters came home for a while, and during a long respite between jobs in faraway cities, occupied her old room and once again joined the family.

"Mom," she said, as she was sitting on the end of my bed one morning and we were reading the papers, "it's fun being home again. I just love it. But one thing bothers me. Suppose I want to spend the night out. Yesterday morning Dad came down the hall with a cup of coffee for me. What happens if I'm not there?"

"All right," I said, adopting the role of one who has long ago lost the battle, "what you should do when you go out is let me know the night before where you're going to be. I'll cover for you."

"But how do I know when I go out whether I'll want to stay out and where I'm going to be?"

The question, innocently put and intended to settle a practical matter for purposes of mutual convenience, struck me as a final blow. I had no answer. It was no use talking. I hadn't merely lost battles, I had lost an undeclared war.

The cause of the war? The cause, I suppose, is virginity on

a wedding night. Is it worth all those battles? Is it worth a war? Well, I fought the battles. I lost them. And now that I've lost them, I'm not sorry I fought them, but neither am I despondent that I lost. The cause strikes me as having been worth a skirmish line, worth putting out pickets and sounding alarms. But not worth losing the confidences of my children, not really worth a declaration of war.

Those of us who were born under one set of rules and saw the rules disappear have to rewrite them for ourselves. The facts of life have changed. The pill is a new fact of life, reminding everybody that sex doesn't have to produce pregnancy. People live longer. That's a new fact of life, meaning that successful marriages, those that are worked on, can last fifty years or more. Women have gone to work. That's a new fact of life. In another generation, it will no longer be a man's world. People will have two or three children; no more. That's another new fact of life.

Is it possible to believe that, under the conditions brought about by these new facts of life, a husband and wife, both working, married for forty or fifty years and attracted, as both will be, to someone of the opposite sex, will never carry that attraction beyond a pale sigh or a kiss on the cheek?

I don't condone extramarital sex and I don't recommend it. But I don't believe it should wreck a marriage. Love and truth and trust are more important than strictures.

But getting back to that night in Wausau, it is certainly true that a woman is flattered when a man who is famous pays attention to her. I admit to excitement when Nelson called for me in a bright red Lincoln convertible and we drove out to his father's estate at Pocantico and walked along the brow of the hills over the Hudson River. I admit to excitement when Henry Kissinger called to say he'd be working late and could I go out to dinner. But unless a woman is a fawner or has a secret desire to see her name in a gossip column, a walk by the river is fun or not fun and dinner is either interesting or not interesting. Neither is innately sexual.

I guess I think a man who is sexually attractive is one with whom I've shared a lot of experiences, one with whom I've worked and worried, laughed, seen a point, shared a triumph, tossed off a defeat, stood side by side, on common ground. "You do this and I'll do that and see if we can't solve this problem, make this go." That kind of experience. And when you have that kind of experience, you feel very close and as one. So Nelson had a point. Sex is part of working together. Which means that sexual attractiveness has to be deserved. But that takes a long time. One long hard day of shared hard time, and standing in a wooden shed and being very cold besides, almost qualifies. But not quite.

—•—

TWENTY

A Goddamn Woman

There is a muffled atmosphere about the seventh floor of the State Department that is deceiving. Rooms full of fine antique furniture and ancient paintings; enormous heavy doors opening noiselessly on well-oiled hinges as though out of respect for those whose titles surmount them in large block letters: THE SECRETARY OF STATE, THE UNDER SECRETARY OF STATE, THE UNDER SECRETARY FOR MANAGEMENT.

There are also rooms for the walking wounded. One runs into half-forgotten names, recalls later who they are, and then reflects that they deserve the massive doors through which they unobtrusively slide. Here, for example, is somebody named Ambassador Graham Martin. Who was he? Oh yes, of course, the last man off the roof of the embassy in Saigon. He must still be writing his final report. Appropriate that he should write it on the seventh floor.

One dresses up on the seventh floor—no long pants for women and no sport jackets for men—and one treads quietly. If you see an old friend down the long corridor, you do not shout in greeting. "Quiet please, statesmen reflecting" is not stated anywhere in the corridors of the seventh floor. It doesn't have to be.

It was to the seventh floor that I repaired after the newspapers had turned to less juicy subjects and after the congressional hearing and after the effect of the great green glob's visit had worn off and my back had stopped hurting. I went in to see the secretary of state and remembered to address him as "Mr. Secretary." Henry was kindly, informal, and interested. But the kindliness, informality, and interest hid a warning. "Joannie, you are now the consumer advisor for the Department of State. You can tell the Congress and the press that you have complete access to me; but when you testify before Congress or speak up at trade and commodity meetings, you're on your own."

Henry Kissinger was telling me to be careful; that if I said or did something foolish, he would have to correct me in public. He was also telling me that I wasn't really on my own, that I could count on him for help and advice and goodwill.

But don't get into a real jam, where I won't be able to help you. That was what Henry meant, and I was as careful as he intended me to be. In speeches before trade associations, in conversations with individual congressmen and senators, in congressional hearings, I remembered that the views of the consumer affairs advisor are not supposed to make headlines. Only once did I say something that I feared might cross that line.

The price of coffee was soaring, principally because Brazil, our chief supplier, had suffered a drought. American consumers, shocked at the weekly price increases over the counter, suspected that Brazil was gouging them. "It isn't true," I told one consumer group, and if it were true, I would walk into the office of the secretary of state and say, "Mr. Secretary, you have to drop everything else and lead a boycott of Brazilian coffee." That remark did hit the newspapers. Henry only smiled.

But I said the muffled atmosphere of the seventh floor was deceiving. It is. The seventh floor is where the final battles are fought. It is where the arguments, the ideas, the wordings, and the orders are hung out for inspection and reconsideration. It is where turf-consciousness, personal rivalries, and personal ambitions are either exposed for what they are or, passing unnoticed for what they are, become the business of the day.

So behind the massive doors of the seventh floor tense passions run, and sometimes run amok. I had not been behind one of those massive doors for more than a week before I was tense with passion too.

As was Jules Katz, down on the sixth floor, a scholarly-looking, wiry man with glasses and fringes of red hair at the temples and at the back of his neck. Jules was the assistant secretary for economics and business, and had risen to his sixth-floor post after many years of handling trade negotiations. Quite naturally, he resented the addition of a seventh-floor advisor for consumer affairs to the long list of people to whom he had to explain, justify, or criticize the myriad of complicated, complex trade agreements, adjustments, and problems which govern the ways in which the United States does business with countries abroad.

Jules Katz probably knew more about these agreements, tariffs, and adjustments, and problems arising therefrom, than any man living. They had been his business for many years. What was a woman doing in his business? For that matter, what was anybody doing in his business? If a man had butted into his business, Jules would have known how to take care of him. Give him an office, let him read the files, occasionally send him copies of the correspondence of the assistant secretary for economics and business.

But I was not a man. I was a woman. You have to be polite to a woman. You have to be sure you don't treat her unkindly. Worse than that, I was a woman who had just been appointed to a highly publicized job and was on friendly terms with the secretary of state.

So Jules had a problem for which his many years in the bureaucracy had not quite prepared him. He chafed and grew red in the face whenever I spoke at meetings. His staff paid scrupulous attention to what I did, what I said, what I wrote, and who wrote to me. His staff kept him informed, or so I ascertained, and I could understand his pain.

On the other hand, I had my own pain to take into account. All those agreements, tariffs, adjustments, and problems arising therefore made the price of breakfast, lunch, and dinner for the American consumer either rise or fall; and I was the consumer advisor. So these matters were my business too. Moreover, I was, as Jules once indelicately put it to his staff—or so I was told—"a goddamn woman!" And being a "goddamn woman," I was goddamned if I was going to be shoved around, put down, or ignored even by somebody who had reached the rank of assistant secretary of state for economics and business.

Mrs. Longworth used to take great interest in the habits of simians. When she traveled abroad, she invariably visited the apes in the zoos and read about them with fascination. It was, she told me, the habit of these most manlike beasts to smile quickly at each other when roused by anger, jealousy, or fear. That's the way Jules gestured to me—a quick smile—when we passed each other in the hushed corridors of the seventh floor.

I didn't mind the smile as much as I minded the assistance of Jules's assistants. One or another of his young men kept dropping in from time to time during the day, asking to read the embarrassing first drafts of my speeches, paying particular attention to my correspondence with congressmen and senators.

My consciousness of their presence reached a blow-up point one evening (all blow-up points on the seventh floor are reached at about 7:00 in the evening) after I had received a call from the chairman of the House Foreign Affairs Committee, asking me to testify as to the effect of certain commodity agreements on the prices of coffee and sugar.

The assistant secretary of state for economics and business was to testify at the same hearing, so the chairman informed me, and I went down to discuss the hearing with Mr. Katz.

Jules blew up first. He pointed out that it was his job to give testimony to the House Foreign Affairs Committee, that it had always been his job, and that I should call the chairman back and tell him so. I replied that I had already told the chairman that I would be delighted to testify. He made some mention of my "being in the way." I countered with the observation that his assistants were daily in my way. He then said that he would be willing to let me testify if he wrote my testimony and I agreed not to deviate from the text. I said that under those circumstances I would call the chairman back and decline to testify on the grounds that the consumer advisor for the Department of State was not permitted to say what she thought.

Clearly we had reached an impasse. Higher authority must be consulted.

Which meant that Bill Rogers, under secretary for economic

affairs, a tall handsome man with a patient sense of humor and an unruffled exterior, had to be called upon. Rogers was in his shirt sleeves, in acknowlegment of the lateness of the hour, and he sat back in his chair, listening first to Jules and then to me, smiling quizzically at us both. Then he put in a call to the secretary of state and explained the problem. He hung up and we all waited. Rogers tried to turn the conversation to uncontroversial matters; he tried football and he tried the weather. He failed. There was no conversation. At last Larry Eagleburger, Henry Kissinger's under secretary for administration, entered the room. "The secretary says let Joannie testify, but tell her she's on her own."

Thus are matters of high importance and great consequence settled upon the seventh floor. In retrospect, the entire affair seems silly and juvenile; yet, I would venture that more than half of the tense and passionate meetings which take place on the seventh floor seem, in retrospect, equally silly and juvenile to those who take part in them.

Retrospect, that great leveler, plays tricks with the mind. It denies the importance of the moment. It denies me the victory I felt I had fairly won. I had stuck to my guns, preserved my integrity and the integrity of the post of consumer advisor. I had preserved the independence of consumer groups. Moreover, I had delivered a blow for the rights of a "goddamn woman." I will not permit retrospect to deprive me of the exultation I felt at that moment and at a later moment which was to come.

"Will there be consumer representation at the upcoming negotiations on sugar and coffee at Geneva?"

The voice was that of Congressman Rosenthal of New York, and the question was not addressed to me. I had already testified. I had said there would be consumer representation at the upcoming negotiations on coffee and sugar.

But now the question was readdressed to the assistant

secretary of state for economics and business. Right in front of me, occupying the witness chair which I had just vacated, sat the slight figure of Assistant Secretary Katz. I could see the back of his neck growing red. And then I heard his answer, delivered in a soft voice, "Yes," said the assistant secretary.

The hell with retrospect.

I didn't rub it in, and Jules Katz behaved like a thoroughbred. I became one of his close advisors on everything that affected consumer prices, which meant that my opinion was sought on most matters. I was often invited to attend his staff meetings, and his staff who had frequented my office faded into the woodwork so rapidly that it seemed like old times when I ran into them in the corridors of the sixth floor. Today I respect Jules as my friend and as the very best in his field.

Moreover, the goddamn woman got to go to Nairobi along with the secretary of state, the deputy secretary of state, Charles Robinson, the under secretary of state for economics, Bill Rogers, and various economic advisors for bilateral meetings, including one with the Russians on the subject of agricultural exports and imports. The delegation didn't expect to settle anything, but the idea was to find out what the Russians wanted so that President Ford and the National Security Council might engage in informed speculation about what the Russians might be willing to give.

The meetings with the Russians began with the exchange of toasts with vodka. M. Polichev, chief of the Russian delegation, brought out a bottle of the best at the opening session, placed it on the green baize table, poured a glass for the three Americans in attendance, then one for himself, and in a voice of command, ordered the Russian equivalent of bottoms up.

The four of us around the table complied, and he did it again and again. The third time, I did not comply, nor did the two other Americans. That didn't faze M. Polichev. He poured a third glass for himself, said bottoms up to himself, and drank it down.

No notes, M. Polichev said, were to be taken because this was to be a free and easy discussion, and he went on to discuss freely and easily. Doubtless, the vodka helped his volubility, but I was sorry that he had swallowed three and I two because when the meeting ended I went back to the hotel to find a note from the secretary of state asking me to transmit to Washington at once what M. Polichev had said.

So if you wish to possess, for a certain length of time, a ready flow of words, I recommend three glasses of vodka; and if you wish to remember a ready flow of words, I recommend two. I was surprised at myself. I remembered and cabled back to Washington everything that Polichev had said, as translated by the official interpreter; and a month or two later when the Russian desk wanted to know what he had emphasized in what he said, I was able to recall. I'm just joking about the vodka. Three glasses undoubtedly added to M. Polichev's readiness for conversation, but this was my first international meeting. I was so alert that even if I had joined M. Polichev in his three "bottoms up," I think I would have recalled every detail of what everybody said.

We worked in those days on sugar, coffee, textiles, and shoes—consumer items on which price counts more than quality. We tried to keep the prices down by cutting tariffs, cutting subsidies, keeping the United States open to foreign goods and foreign commodities, even though the foreign goods were not made by union labor, even though the foreign commodities competed with our own products.

Ideally this is what the consumer wants or should want. But it is a never-ending struggle. Ralph Nader is right: Big companies, powerful interests with great sums of money to spend and expert lobbyists on which to spend it are often lined up on one side and consumers, which is to say the entire population of the United States, lack the strength and the organization to defeat them.

The best the State Department can do, and only when it is constantly prodded by consumer groups, is to keep the principle of free trade alive—whittling, hedging, and pecking away where it can.

I had the idea of getting the department's attention to free trade by holding a consumer conference to be attended by the country's leading economists and by the middle-to-top echelon of the department. It was to be off the record, no press participation, and it was intended to bolster the principle of free trade within the department, which nominally at least is partially in charge of trade. For weeks my proposal for a conference was batted around in the bureaucracy but I got no definitive answer, and at last, as the Carter-Ford election neared, I realized I was unlikely to get one. Still, it seemed to me, the principle was important no matter who won the election. People then in the Department of State would be holding important jobs in the Department of State under Ford or under Carter. They would be holding important jobs after Ford and Carter were both gone. To hear the country's top economists on the subject of trade might fix their minds and affect policy for years to come.

So unbeknownst to the secretary of state, I pulled a string. I went to see the vice president of the United States. Nelson was enthusiastic, as I knew he would be. Nelson loved gatherings of experts. He loved them so much he couldn't stay away from them. So I wasn't really surprised when after we'd talked about my plan and after he had made a few suggestions and just as I was about to leave, he said, "Joannie, I think it's a great idea; not only that but I'll come."

Bill Rogers entered my office a few evenings later. It was

7:00 or 8:00 again and he was in his shirt sleeves again and he had just been in to see the secretary again. He sat down and relaxed, leaning back on the couch, and said, "I asked Henry again about the economic conference. He thinks it would be better to wait until after the election."

"Okay, Bill, but you tell Henry he'll have to uninvite the vice president."

We had the conference.

I think it did some good. As I say, you have to keep pecking away.

When the election was over, my friends were gone. The secretary was gone, Bill Rogers, though nominally a Democrat, was gone. Larry Eagleburger would soon be gone. I stayed on because I thought the job was important. But advisory jobs are only important if there's somebody to advise, and in the Carter administration there wasn't. I knew Cy Vance, the new secretary of state, but I also knew that he had a lot of things besides consumers on his mind; and the man who replaced Bill Rogers, Richard Cooper, as under secretary for economic affairs, had been a professor of economics at Yale. Though he wrote brilliant comments on my memoranda, he saw his own role as advisory, and I was redundant.

I don't mean to suggest that the new Carter team thought prices for consumers were unimportant. (If they did, they were soon to learn better as inflation soared.) But the post of consumer advisor had been a Ford administration initiative. I had been appointed by Henry Kissinger. Anything that had to do with Henry Kissinger was suspect. So I was suspect.

George Shultz once told me that in the course of a long career in government, teaching, and business, he had once been forced by circumstances to sit in an office with no telephone and with absolutely nothing to do for three whole months. George used the time to read and write without interruption, but even so he fidgeted.

George Shultz is possessed of enormous self-control. I had a secretary and I had a telephone; but I had nothing to do. I was being paid and my secretary was being paid, and I can't fidget and read and write at the same time. So I resigned and reintroduced myself to the world of the bottom line.

—•—

TWENTY-ONE

Twice Damned

For me the bottom line as well as the words "public relations" will always be personified by a slim, brisk, perfectly
groomed man of medium height with flashing blue eyes named
Robert Keith Gray.

Bob Gray greets you as though you were the one person in
the world with whom, at that particular moment, he most wishes
to converse. Just as you are beginning to converse, he greets
somebody else in precisely the same manner. For nearly seven
years I watched him bowl over hundreds of people—clients,
government officials, employees, even friends. They all get the
same treatment and it is charming, intelligent, seemingly guileless,
and effective.

Tom says that Bob Gray is a booster. That is true, but he is also up to the minute on the news and up to the minute on the person to whom he is talking, quick to discern whether the person to whom he is talking has a problem with the way the news has broken for him, wishes to confide his problem to Bob Gray and have Bob take care of that problem.

Bob Gray can make the world view that person in a better light. Who doesn't wish to be viewed in a better light?

Moreover, no booster that I know about has provided himself with a more perfect background for keeping up his self-esteem or making others wish they had as much of it. As you walk into Bob Gray's Power House (that's the name of his building) in Washington's Georgetown, you have a sense of the awesome and you realize that there is no ceiling. You look up, and there it is high in a loft like a church belfry. But it is way up, skyward, and here on earth there is nothing but red brick, three clocks mounted on brick showing the time of day around the world, a television set turned on with the sound low, and a pretty receptionist.

"Mr. Gray will see you in a moment." You sit down in a comfortable antique chair and look up at the winding staircase. The ascent to power is marked by pictures of Bob Gray with every president of the United States since Eisenhower, pictures of Bob Gray with every famous person you can recall, and suddenly, there at the top of the stairs, looking down at you from the threshold of power and welcoming you into the inner sanctum of power, is Bob Gray himself: friendly, keen-eyed, perfectly groomed, brisk. He is power.

Bob Gray wanted me to be a vice president of Gray and Company and I accepted without ever finding out about the bottom line.

I don't mean that I was not on speaking terms with the

bottom line. Nelson Rockefeller's IBEC had a bottom line and so did Tom's newspaper. But I was under the illusion that to some extent at least, if you worked hard and did a good job, the bottom line would take care of itself. To the contrary, I learned from Bob Gray, if the bottom line looks good, the work will take care of itself.

And I didn't denigrate the work. Bob Gray had some clients which seemed to me worthy to stand in the sunlit uplands in which he tried to place them. NBC was a client of Bob Gray. So was American Airlines. Others I thought were worth working for because, in trying to improve their image, you might possibly persuade them that the way Americans looked upon them had a lot to do with the way they behaved; Turkey, for example.

But there were those among Bob Gray's accounts about which it seemed to me there was nothing to say except abandon hope. I would agree that Jackie Presser, president of the Teamsters Union and under indictment for embezzlement, racketeering, and fraud, was in need of public relations. People tend not to think highly of a man who is under indictment for embezzlement, racketeering, and fraud. Bob Gray's job was to make them think highly.

The same with Adnan Khashoggi, the Saudi arms merchant and "world's richest man," later charged with helping Imelda Marcos take the millions she allegedly stole from her country and hid by investing in New York real estate. Those charges gave Khashoggi a bad name. Bob Gray's job was to turn a bad name into a good one. Bob Gray deserves a lot of credit. He tried and, to a certain extent, succeeded.

Bob Gray had a lot to do with persuading Khashoggi to give American University in Washington, D.C., a new gymnasium. That is, to give the university the Adnan Khashoggi Sports and

Convocation Center. For a while, just a little while, the gift made the name Khashoggi stand for benefactor. But not even Bob Gray could have persuaded Khashoggi to give away enough money to compete with continuing revelations about Khashoggi.

Then there was Haiti under Duvalier and Puerto Rico under Romero.

I thought about all this for a while after I became vice president of Gray and Company and had settled into the Power House. I decided that as much as these clients and others of similar ilk needed public relations, they didn't need my public relations. I was embarrassed every time I read one of the names in the newspapers listed as a client of Gray and Company. But they didn't embarrass Bob, and they didn't embarrass the other people who worked for Bob. Bob said, and so did the other vice presidents and executive vice presidents, that every man was entitled to public relations in the same way that every man was entitled to a lawyer.

The argument has weight. It has merit. I can feel the weight and see merit. But after you've felt it and seen it, you get down to the nitty-gritty. You have to say to yourself, "I don't care what Jackie Presser did to get to be head of the Teamsters. I don't care what he did after he became head of the Teamsters. I don't care anything about his alleged relationships with murderers and goon squads. I believe he is an elder statesman of the labor movement and a fighter for the rights of the working man and woman."

I couldn't say that. So I went to Bob Gray and told him I didn't want to have anything to do with the Teamster account, didn't want to have anything to do with the Khashoggi account, didn't want to have anything to do with the Haitian account, or the Puerto Rico account under Romero. Now working for Puerto Rico when it was governed by Rafael Hernandez Colon would have given me pleasure. But how could Rafael, a good friend, hire us after we had represented Romero?

Bob was gracious. Bob was understanding. But when I left him, I said to myself, "Now what?" I had cut myself off from the bottom line. There was only one thing to do. Go out and get some accounts for Gray and Company that I wanted to work on, somebody or something in need of good public relations, in need of recognition, in need of favorable mentions in the press, and worthy of them.

I went to Roger Stevens. The Kennedy Center, sad to say, sometimes stages performances before half-empty halls. Theaters have to advertise; and this one, dependent on private funds, needs public relations. I signed up the Kennedy Center and I think the bottom line went through the roof. We didn't ever make any money on that account, partly because Bob Gray, pleased and proud to have it, lavished upon it the attention of his staff, set up a small advertising agency with myself in charge, and then underbilled the center, refusing to charge overtime costs for last minute changes in the ads. We even produced a television spot that could be used either for ticket sales or as a pitch for contributions to the center. It was, I thought (and still do), a triumph. But it cost more money than it brought in. Bob Gray never once complained.

I had another idea. If ever a country needed the kindly attention of the American public and the American congress, that country is Canada. Canada gets treated in Washington like a younger brother who is away at school—a fine boy and doing well but nobody in the family gets around to writing.

In my view, that's the way not only the Congress but also the whole country thinks of Canada. When I began to turn my thoughts to Canada, I was startled by the facts. Canada, I discovered, is our largest trading partner. Largest by far. So large a trading partner that when you look at the list of trading partners according to dollar volume, Canada ranks first and Ontario, a province of Canada, ranks second.

Why not Canada as a client? The Canadians were building a new embassy right across from the Capitol, and Canada had an ambassador, Allan Gotlieb, whom I knew and admired.

I admired him partly because of all the ambassadors I have known in all the years I've spent in Washington, Allan Gotlieb cared the most about the town. I remembered the first time I ever met him, we were in conversation about Washington's buildings. "By the way," he said, "have you ever seen the sun rise over the old Treasury Building? I went down to see it last week. Magnificent. You ought to go."

Any ambassador, I thought, who cared enough about the capital city of the country to which he was accredited to rise at 5:00 in the morning and watch the sun come up over one of the city's ancient buildings deserved to have his country thought of as something more than a younger brother away at school.

So I went to call on Allan Gotlieb. I pointed out the importance of public relations and lobbying and how much better it could be done by a United States firm and how much less expensive it would be to hire a United States firm than to try to do it with an embassy staff. Allan was polite and I got a personal tour of the etchings and lithographs he has collected since his youth and with which he had adorned the walls of the Canadian residence.

Much instructed in art but none the wiser as to his business intention, I departed. Several weeks went by and I decided that I was not good at the hard sell. But I had been reading Canadian newspapers and one morning I picked up the *Toronto Globe* to read a lengthy piece by Allan Gotlieb on the duties and opportunities of a Canadian ambassador to the United States.

Glancing down the columns, paragraph by paragraph, I found my own words as spoken to Gotlieb, repeated in the *Globe*; my opinions had become his opinions.

I saw him next at the Swedish embassy. "I have," I said, "been reading the *Toronto Globe*."

Allan laughed. "I know what you want. You want me to put my money where my mouth is."

I worked hard on that Canadian account. I led a study proving that the use of steel leg traps by Canadian hunters was costing Canada more bad publicity than the number of animals caught were worth. I did a similar study on the killing of baby seals. "Slaughter," United States newspapers called it. We got results. I learned a lot about Canada. I loved working on that account and I'm sorry that it ended with me in the role once more of "a goddamn woman."

But it did. I told Bob Gray that I thought the person who brings in an account, and who is the account executive, should be in absolute charge of the account, at least that nobody should do anything or send out anything without his or her approval. I fought this out on the Kennedy Center account and won only because Roger Stevens, unbeknownst to me, said he wouldn't continue the contract unless I was in complete charge.

But the Canadian account was a bottom line account. Everybody who could fancy the slightest reason for piling on, piled on.

The bottom line kept receding. Why were six people from the press department attending a conference in Ottawa? Why not two people or one person? And why not consult me? I could have told them that it was not necessary for the Canadian account to pay for more than two people to go to Ottawa. Or I could have asked Allan Gotlieb how many people he thought were necessary.

Anyhow, I said all this, and before long I became a "goddamn woman who happens to know the ambassador socially and thinks she knows public relations."

And then it all blew up in one of those intraoffice feuds which probably lie behind half the headlines in the Business Section of your local newspaper reporting that company X has switched its advertising account from company Y to company Z.

Somebody in the press department sent out a notice to a reporter from the *New York Times* about a lunch which Ambassador Gotlieb was to have with Art Buchwald and Mordecai Richler, famous as a humorist in Canada. The name of the reporter from the *Times* was misspelled. The name of Allan Gotlieb was misspelled. The name Mordecai Richler was misspelled. The reporter from the *Times* thought the press release with the misspelled names was funny and ran a story about how Gray and Company, public relations consultants for Canada, couldn't spell the name of the Canadian ambassador or the name of Canada's most famous humorist or even the name of the reporter to whom the press release was addressed.

Canadian newspapers took note. Canada's prime minister and MPs took note. Allan Gotlieb took note. None of the above thought it was funny.

And neither did I. Ambassador Gotlieb canceled the contract and I behaved as, in my view, a goddamn woman should behave when she is ignored because she is a goddamn woman. I quit.

There is a certain satisfaction in quitting. But this must be said: When a goddamn woman quits, she can no longer fight to prove she is not just a goddamn woman. I'm sorry for that.

—•—

Tribal Instinct

Through all the generations of man, it has come to pass that the children of man have grown up. The odd thing about this is that throughout the generations of man, the children's parents have been surprised by the discovery that those to whom they have referred in endearing terms—"adorable," "beguiling," and "lovely"—are in fact heirs to the sins as well as to the misfortunes of man.

This discovery is a shock. It will always be a shock. It is the reason why people who do not have children invariably look younger and less worn than those who do.

The shocks began right after we moved back to Washington. The children were growing up. Some of them were barely children. The oldest was sixteen; the youngest four. In between were six others and it doesn't matter how old they were. They were growing up. So the end of innocence didn't come all at once, though it seemed that way. As every parent knows, the end of innocence can be frightening, horrifying, dark, and desperate.

Oh, we had had our share of what parents in the safety of retrospect call "close ones." Nicholas at age three had fallen out of a car going seventy miles an hour and skidded along a busy highway and into the brush at the side of the road. Bruised, burned, sore, and sound.

Tom and I had both been away from home when an eighteen-year-old girl whom we had hired as help put Nicholas in a bathtub and left the hot water running while she talked to a boyfriend on the telephone. Mary, my oldest daughter, made the telephone call to Dr. Harvey. "His skin is coming off," was her accurate description of Nicholas's condition.

Nancy, at two, had crawled one hundred and fifty yards across the beach and was bobbing up and down in the sea when Tom, who had gone for a walk along the beach, spotted "that funny white thing bobbing up and down in the waves. My God, it's Nancy." He ran the fastest half mile he'll ever run.

There were broken arms and broken ribs and broken windows, and the accidents can be counted as our fault. You can't blame a child for "close ones."

But what do you do when you don't know for sure whether to blame him or her? When is it possible to do so? When is the child grown up?

Tom was the first to face this question which is the aftershock to the shock of realizing that your children are growing up. He was coming up the stairs one noon, having lunched downtown with what newspapermen call "a source." Not having learned much from the source, he was musing, he said, on what he could write for a column. As an observer of Tom, I would venture the guess that columnists spend twenty minutes of each day in writing their columns, and six hours in trying to decide what to write about.

At any rate, Tom was musing when he saw a folded piece of paper on the staircase leading up to his office on the third floor of our house. He bent down to pick it up and because he had nothing more urgent to do than to muse, he unfolded it to see whether he should throw it in the waste basket. Finding that it contained writing in an unfamiliar hand, he read it. "Thank you for sending me the lovely gold bracelet. I have never in my life had anything so beautiful nor so valuable and I shall treasure it always, always wear it, and always be reminded of you."

The letter went on and Tom explained later that he read on with increasing guilt born of the knowledge that the letter was not intended to be read by him. Finally, the guilt overwhelmed him so that he ceased reading, folded the piece of paper into the state in which he had found it, returned to the staircase, and placed it carefully in the exact spot where it had been.

He went back up the stairs, the word "valuable" intruding upon his musings. Where had the boy gotten the money for a valuable bracelet? And then, what did "valuable" mean to an eighth-grade girl? And then, he must have earned the money cutting lawns. And then, but hadn't his mother said that he ought to be cutting lawns?

That was it. The thought of his mother was what did the boy in. His mother's voice, raised over and over again these past two weeks, raised in a querulous tone, raised in the nighttime as we were getting into bed and raised again in the morning as I was dressing. "I simply cannot understand what happened to that bracelet. You know the one I mean? The plain gold one that Nelson gave me; the one I wore on that Saturday night when it rained. I wore it with the black dress. And I'm sure I put it right here. It's absolutely disappeared and I can't understand it. It's just gone."

Over the years, Tom has learned not to pay much attention to these exclamations. He is patient and polite, but not really attentive. He has learned over the years that the thing will turn up and attentiveness will have been wasted.

But the constancy of this particular complaint had penetrated. And, of course, it was obvious. Back down the stairs he went, retrieved the folded paper, and spread it out that evening for me to read when we were alone in the bedroom.

I didn't know how to handle this revelation and neither did Tom. Of course we would tell the boy we knew what happened to the bracelet. But what would follow the confrontation? At fourteen, a boy is too old to spank. Do we ask him to get the bracelet back? What does he say to her with whom he is smitten and whom he believes to be the love of his life: "I'm not what you think I am. I'm just a little boy who steals gold bracelets from my mother's dressing room table"?

Do we put him through degradation? A psychological wound? Perhaps lasting harm?

So we did nothing. Aside, of course, from telling the boy that we knew, that we regarded it as a serious matter, that the loss was a serious loss, that he'd have to pay it back over years. What was the right thing to do? What would you have done?

It's odd that growing up, as painful and shocking as it is, strikes me, now that I think about it, as a cohesive force. I don't recall that Tom and I ever talked to each other or to the children about sticking together. But shocks that came from growing up made it clear that sticking together was something that needn't be mentioned. It was just there. Each member of the family knew that the family would come to the aid of each of its members against all enemies, foreign and domestic, against all critics, in all defeats, in all misfortunes, in all adventures, including the adventures of growing up.

Not that we made a show about it. I don't think we were ever chauvinistic. I remember once in Aspen, Colorado, when we were all on a ski vacation, watching Bobby and Ethel's children coming down the hill and racing up to the head of the long line of skiers waiting for a lift. Somebody said to one of them, "Hey, wait your turn. This is the top of the line." And one of the Kennedys said, in self-assured explanation, "We're the Kennedys."

Bobby and Ethel would have winced if they had heard that remark. And I winced when I heard it, and I'm not sure that the man who complained was correct to let them go ahead to the top of the line because "they were the Kennedys."

I remember my daughter Elizabeth, who has red hair and freckles, used to make an announcement when she was four to the man at the desk or the headwaiter in a motel dining room on the road or in Oceanside or in Washington. "We," she would say as she hurried ahead of seven brothers and sisters, "are the Bradens." The tone was breathless, expectant of immediate attention. She did that when she was four and when she was five and when she was six. We thought it was amusing at first and so did the headwaiters, but Tom eventually put a stop to it before Elizabeth got to the age where headwaiters would be annoyed rather than amused.

There is something about large families which reaches into dim prehistory, a time before there were nations, before there were loyalties to anything but the tribe—or the family.

I presume there were struggles within the tribe. There were certainly struggles within ours. Eight children are jealous enemies of each other. And critics. My daughter Susan said when she was fourteen, "What makes you think you're such a big shot?" She said it to her brothers and to her sisters and she said it to her father and she said it to me and she said it so often and over so many years that the line still taunts me. "What makes you think you're such a big shot?" It's a useful question and everybody ought to ask himself that question once in a while, some more frequently than others.

My point is that criticism, jealousy, and fighting, while endemic to the tribe, are put aside instantly when the tribe or any member thereof is confronted with animosity or criticism or opposition by any member of another tribe. Or by threat from outside forces, natural, contrived, or imagined.

Then the tribe is all for one and one for all, so much so that in my imagination I have seen the various members of my family as clad in animal skins, bare legged and barefooted, each armed with a club or a sling over the shoulder marching over hill and dale on some long trek in the prehistory of man.

Maybe tribalism exists in small families too and is less evident to the stranger's eye. But I don't think it exists to the same degree. The tribal family requires a certain quantity of numbers, and so it is dying out in America along with its unattractive aspects—its chauvinism, its jeering oppositional instinct—and along with its attractive aspects too—its closeness in adversity, its variegated unity.

Tom wrote a book about all of this and, remembering the question Dr. Harvey had addressed to me just before Nicholas was born, called it *Eight Is Enough*. When the book was made into a television series in which the characters took the names of all the family, I sensed a certain discomfort among the children. Were those transgressions, misadventures, errors, and omissions of olden days to be reenacted, names named? Were the actual authors of letters purportedly signed by me and asking for excused absences from school to be revealed? Elizabeth, for example. Her teacher had once called and said, "Mrs. Braden, by my count, your mother has died twice this year." She sent me the most recent note over my forged signature. Tom had it framed and hung it on the wall of Elizabeth's bedroom. Was all that to come out—and on television?

So I sensed a certain tension in the family, a certain "us" (my children) against "them" (Tom and me). I remembered that David Hartman, for many years the host of ABC's *Good Morning America*, had told me he thought it a mistake to permit my children to be portrayed on television. I worried.

And I remember with great pleasure the day the tension broke. There was a knock on the front door one afternoon about four. Nicholas, just home from high school, answered. Standing before him were three tiny girls from the nearby parochial school. They were dressed in their best: white socks, lovely little dresses, bows bobbing at their waists, asking if they could see Nicholas. Nicholas was the hit of *Eight Is Enough*. But in *Eight Is Enough*, Nicholas was about four. Now the real Nicholas, nearly six feet tall, looked down at the little girls standing in anticipation outside the door and answered, as honesty required, "I'm Nicholas." The look of astonished disappointment on the faces of the three little girls broke the tension in the family. It had all happened a long time ago and was not to be worried about. It could be looked back upon with a certain detachment. In fact, it was funny.

I remember only one other time when I felt that we were not all together in a time of trouble. That was on the ride to the hospital at three o'clock in the morning. There were the three of us, traveling the empty, darkened streets because one of the girls had a sharp pain in the stomach. We were discussing the pain and I said, "Well, is it like what I've told you about labor pains? Does it come at more or less regular intervals?" Tom, who was driving, commented that of course that was not a possibility. He said it with the impatience of the man who wants to speculate upon realities and thus not waste words on silly suppositions.

"Well," said our daughter, "I suppose it could be."

We had been there, sitting in the dark, bent upon an errand of mutual concern, and the dark night and empty streets had added to the feeling of oneness. And then came the storm, not a threat from the world outside but something boiling, surging, raging within the "us" part of the world. "What? Who? When? What have you done?"

Tom raged as he drove and the little girl in the backseat started to cry, and crying, she said the name, Peter, and the steam kettle who was driving the car blew its top.

"You mean the kid down the block with the hair in front of his eyes? You mean him?" And the little girl sobbed out, "I don't think so, Dad, I don't know what happened." Right then we reached the hospital.

Where we discovered that nothing had happened. I don't even remember the cause of the illness. But the night sticks in my mind because for a moment it split our world; we had been one and then there was the little girl and me against the steam kettle. I think it was the only time our world was split. Once the steam kettle had become a man again, he apologized to his daughter and to me. It was the shock he said, and we said we understood. It was the shock.

There was more to come. I don't like to remember the growing-up shocks, but they happen. They're part of every parent's life, and sometimes they're so horrible that you know they cannot be forgotten. How many times I've said to myself, "Face reality. It happened."

We who are not very rich but not very poor tend to think the horrible stories we read of rape and drugs happen only to the very poor and the very sick or the famous—professional football players, entertainers. They don't.

A few years ago another of my daughters attended an enormous Fourth of July celebration at the Washington Monument. It was a free show with fireworks, flags, and entertainment; and, according to the newspaper account, the large crowd behaved well.

But as my daughter strolled alone off the Monument grounds and entered a side street, a car rolled up next to the sidewalk. Two men emerged from it, seized her roughly, and before she could do more than utter a half-stifled cry, put her in the backseat, where two more men held her to the floor.

She was tied, gagged, and taken to a house, the location of which she could not identify. She was kept in the house for the rest of the night during which she was struck and raped. The next morning she was blindfolded, driven back to the Monument, and shoved out of the car. Sobbing, she called me to please come and get her.

During the time she was gone there was, of course, no sleep at home and a great deal of worry and anxiety. Had something happened to her that we should call the police, or should we assume she had gone to a friend's and forgotten to call?

Having her home and safe was enough for me, but Tom rightly insisted she should call the police. The policemen tried to be helpful to a hysterical girl, but couldn't be because the hysterical girl could only estimate the time she had been in the car, describe the inside of the house, and sob out some meaningless first names. All four assailants were black men and a hysterical white girl's repeated description of them as being black was not definitive.

That's really the end of the story. Except, of course, we immediately took her to our doctor for a pregnancy test. When it came back positive, there was no question in my mind, nor in Tom's, nor in our daughter's. She would have an abortion. Except for the most firm or most strident believers in the Right to Life, I think most parents would have done the same.

Shocks mount. They mount in number, and they mount in intensity, and the greatest of them is the discovery that one of your children is a drug addict.

Now I will argue that it is perfectly possible for the mother in the family to be the last to find out. Because I was. But what if the boy is doing well in his job? What if he did well in his last job? What if he graduated from college with good grades? What if he's healthy and strong and only recently has begun to have a gray pallor and sunken eyes?

In short, what if the boy has everything going for him, including a love affair—a nice girl and pretty—and the only thing you've wondered about recently is the gray pallor and the sunken eyes?

People tell me, my friends tell me, "Well, Joannie, it's wrong for a boy who's out of college to live at home."

But this boy had not been living at home until very recently. He'd held two jobs away from home, and now we know that he'd been using drugs all through those jobs and all through college too. So why was living at home a sign of danger? Because it was cheaper? Because he would have more money to support a growing habit and an increasing appetite? It may be that friends are right.

Anyhow, I was the last to know. Tom suspected and one of his brothers knew. He had seen syringes and needles in his brother's room. Once, early in the morning, he had seen tiny blood splatters in the kitchen sink. He hadn't told. Can you imagine blood spatters in the kitchen sink? Can you imagine jabbing a needle into your forearm and shooting cocaine into your veins? The thought is disgusting. Repulsive. Impossible.

The dark streets were lined by two-story brick houses, side by side, hardly space between them for a person to walk through. The streets were empty at three o'clock in the morning, except for the long lines of parked cars. Once in a while a lone young man would walk slowly past the parked cars and pause on the street corners to look about him.

Tom and I had been up and down the dark streets for nearly an hour, cruising slowly, studying the lines of parked cars at the curbs to see whether one of them might be "the" car, glancing at the young men on the street corners to make sure they were alone.

And then we turned one corner and suddenly one of the young men was not alone. He was leaning into the window of a car which had pulled up alongside him and it was "the" car. We came to a dead stop half a block away and I watched my son get out of his car, follow the young man into a darkened house, and emerge a few minutes later.

Tom met him on the sidewalk before he could get back into his car, and Tom told me the boy looked up at him, eyes wide. "I didn't expect to see you here."

"I don't want to be here."

"I'm sorry, Dad. Neither do I."

The craving must be extremely powerful.

And so, next morning we had to face reality. Our handsome, loving son, with dreams and high expectations, was addicted to drugs. All of us were hurt. How could it have happened? He certainly didn't want to be addicted, but the addiction was stronger than he was. It is a disease but, unlike other diseases, only the afflicted can find the cure. That very day he went to a drug rehabilitation center for a month and then continued with counselors and meetings every single day.

That was a long time ago; it's all right now. I mean the boy is all right. But it still hurts to think of what he had to go through, and it still hurts to think of how much money it cost to help him through it, money that could have helped further his career.

When something like that happens in a family, I suppose everyone reacts individually. You don't think ahead as to how you should react. You just react. My reaction was to weep and write letters to my son, telling him how proud I was that he was sticking to his program, urging him to call often, and, though keeping it a secret from Tom, sending him tiny bits of money. Tom reacted in utter silence, constantly wondering what he could have done to keep this from happening—had he not been strict enough? The other children reacted with disbelief and sorrow. How could their brother have done this to himself? How could he have done it to them and to his mother and father? Should they have told us sooner—as soon as they knew? Should they have protected him even though they were angry at him for hurting us all? After all, they had lived with it as Tom and I had not. Addicts are not likable people; they lie, they steal, they tear at the bonds of love and of family until those bonds are frayed.

But although the love and respect are intact, the memories of those days will be with us forever. And the questions. What did we do wrong? I had faint, guarded suspicions, which as soon as I had them, I put down. Over and over I said to myself as I used to say about my father back in Anderson, Indiana, "He will be all right." I would then pray that he would be all right, and go ahead and put a face to the world that said, All of my children are perfect.

Tom tortured himself with the guilt that maybe he could have found some way to save him. But how? He probably wasn't even in the vicinity when it started. And how did it get started? Some dare? Some older boy? Some desire to "get with it"? Tom and I never faced these things when we were young and if we had, who knows whether one of us might not have succumbed.

"One day at a time," is what drug addicts say to each other when they are trying to overcome the habit. Six years have now gone by and our son still says to himself, "I'm an addict. One day at a time." He made it through the day, and the next day, and the next two thousand one hundred and ninety days. And once again, he's all right.

So are all the rest. They grew up. They tell their father, when they come over for dinner, that the opinion he has just expressed is "what people used to think." Or they say to him that the view he holds about this or that problem is a view that was commonly held in "olden days."

I enjoy that.

Each night when I go to bed, I pray for each of them. First I put a picture of each of them in my mind. Then I think of something that each of them did at some time in the past that was in its way remarkable, strong, admirable, and individually his or her own. Then I pray that God will give each of them the strength and the confidence to do that kind of thing again.

Tom turns the lights out and says, "You haven't said anything for fifteen minutes. Are you praying?"

And when I don't answer, he says no more. He knows it takes me a long time to say prayers for eight children.

TWENTY-THREE

•

A Special Friend

*A*m I keeping Robert McNamara from getting married? The question bothers me enough that I have discussed it with his daughter. She said she didn't know. Neither do I.

But I think I'm objective enough to understand that in some ways I have, since Marg McNamara died, taken the place of a wife to Robert McNamara. You'll notice I don't say I've taken Marg's place.

I travel as a friend with Bob. I share his joys, his puzzlements, his disappointments. I notice that when I have lunch with Kirk Douglas, Bob's a little jealous, and when he tells me that he's taking Katharine Graham to the theater, I'm a little jealous. I read his speeches and his articles, and I make suggestions before they're public. I argue with him about everything from serving smoked salmon every time he has people to dinner to whether the United States risked the security of West Germany by removing the Pershing missiles. I share his friendships, and I've never known a man whose friends love him more dearly or of whom it could be said more accurately that the friends of his youth are the friends of his maturity. I've never known a man of higher intelligence nor any man who cared more deeply about other people or felt a greater obligation to put his best efforts to helping mankind.

I know that sounds high flown. My rejoinder is that Robert McNamara flies high above most men. I prize him highly and love him very much.

It was Bob's wife, Marg, vivacious, blue-eyed, sparkling Marg who invited Tom and me to Bob McNamara's sixtieth birthday party, where I got up the nerve to ask him about river blindness in Upper Volta, a country from which I'd just returned. He knew a lot about river blindness in Upper Volta. He was a walking encyclopedia about river blindness in Upper Volta. Standing in the center of the room at that birthday party, he answered my questions for a full ten minutes. When ten minutes had passed, he said, "Come over here and sit down for a minute and I'll tell you all about river blindness in Upper Volta."

I remember saying to Tom, when we left that party, "Robert McNamara is the squarest man I've ever met." Was it that he had his hair cut short like a Marine? Was it that he combed it straight back? Was it that he had moved through the crowd at his party as though running to catch a train? Was it those rimless glasses shielding his eyes? Or was it that in the course of his lecture on river blindness in Upper Volta he was totally absorbed in the subject? I think that if someone had dropped a drink onto his lap in the middle of his lecture, he might have paid no more attention to the shock than you or I might give to the momentary annoyance of a passing fly. First, he cited the latest medical information on the source of the disease, its course, and its treatment. Then the statistics—how many people had it and how many people were likely to get it.

There followed the consequences, to the economy, to the food supply, to the stability of the government of Upper Volta. When he finished, I decided that when a man knows a lot, it's possible to overlook the fact that he's square.

At the State Department, I was desperately trying to become an instant expert on trade and commodities, and how the interdependency of world economies affected the consumer. Coffee was the big problem; the price of coffee had gone rocketing. Then I thought of Bob McNamara. And when I discovered that in order to fight for free trade on behalf of the American consumer, I needed to be able to argue from facts of history—the Hawley-Smoot Tariff, the fight for free trade as waged by Cordell Hull, and what happened to prices on the occasions on which Mr. Hull was defeated—I went to Bob McNamara. I called him. I asked him to have lunch. During the three years I was at State, Bob McNamara gave me a lot of information, a lot of arguments, and a lot of lunches.

Now I could have gone to someone at the State Department. Jules Katz, who was assistant secretary for economics and business, would have been an obvious choice. But there were certain problems here, as I've explained. I was advisor to the secretary of state on consumer affairs, and since the chief consumer interest the State Department dealt with was trade, Jules felt quite naturally that I was interfering in his bailiwick.

And here was Robert McNamara, head of the World Bank, offering to advise me over lunch. The choice seemed obvious.

Anyhow, Bob McNamara treated me as a student who had

to learn a lot of things quickly. He brought a notebook to the lunch, which was always served in his private dining room at the World Bank, and always lasted precisely one hour. He used the notebook to jot down questions, dates, and names of people, and a note to question himself as to whether we were correct to impose higher tariffs on shoes. He knew the answers to most things. At the third or fourth lunch, as I was getting ready to leave, maybe as a way of ending the discussion, I remarked that he had eaten all the pickles.

It was true. The waiter in his private dining room had always set the pickles in the center of the table between us. Instead of a long table with many empty chairs lined up along both sides, as Kissinger had in the State Department dining room, Bob McNamara had a small private dining room with a table suitable for no more than four. Anyhow, he had taken the pickles from the center of the table and as lunch went on and the notes went down on the yellow pad, he ate them all.

"I like pickles too," I said. He looked at me with surprise and embarrassment. That was the first time I noticed through his glasses that his eyes were not at all the steely eyes which I had read about, but were in fact very large eyes, compassionate eyes, warm eyes and brown. And then he blushed. I think it was the first time he thought of me not merely as a recipient of information, as someone in the front seat of a lecture hall, but as a person, who might or might not like pickles. Obviously the thought occurred to him that he might have asked this person whether she liked pickles and he hadn't, and he was startled that he hadn't. Quite suddenly, he didn't seem square. We had been friends in a business sort of way. Now we were friends in a human way.

Friendship between a woman who is married and a man who is not involves problems, and the first of these is that some people look askance—in particular women look askance. I don't know why women disapprove, though I suppose if a man is single (Marg McNamara died in 1981), if he is intelligent, if he is versed in economics, arms control, population growth, underdeveloped countries, developed countries, banking, and business, and if he has enough money to travel widely and nearly all the time; if in addition he's physically fit (Bob McNamara runs a mile every morning and always takes the stairs two at a time), if he can ski, backpack, play tennis, swim, sail, owns a house in Aspen, Colorado, a house in Martha's Vineyard, and a house in Washington, D.C.—if, in addition to all these, he loves poetry and knows a lot of it by heart, he attracts the attention of a certain number of women who are divorced or whose husbands have died and who wouldn't mind going along.

And I'm the one who gets to go. Bob and I go to the Netherlands. We go to France. We go to Russia. We go to Greece. We go to Africa. We go to wherever he has board meetings or seminars or speeches that interest me.

In short, I have more fun with Bob McNamara than I do with anybody else in the world, sometimes but not always excepting my husband.

For there is a trouble with husbands, as every woman knows. Husbands tend to speak of mutual problems, family problems, children problems, financial problems, housekeeping problems. It is necessary to speak of these problems. It is also necessary to get away from them once in a while, and with Bob, I get away. There is another thing about husbands. I don't want to generalize from personal experience but I think that after a certain number of years, husbands tend to treat their wives as they treat their wallets or their easy chairs. Familiar objects. Always there. They wouldn't part with them for anything. But they don't notice them, don't pay particular attention to them, don't notice if the fabric in the easy chair is a little torn, don't even notice if the torn fabric has been repaired. Don't notice anything about the easy chair except if suddenly it should disappear, go, not be there at all.

It is my observation that when this occurs, there is consternation, sometimes grief, sometimes anger. Suddenly, everything is not in its place. Suddenly, there is a great and uncomfortable gap in the living room or by the fireside. Much attention is paid. Who removed the chair and why? And when the chair is returned to its customary place, there is a great sigh of relief. Life is restored; it is once again as it ought to be. The chair is, for a time at least, much noticed, much appreciated, much admired. It becomes once again as it was when first acquired, a beautiful object, extremely useful, even essential.

So it is, I think, with long-married husbands and their wives. But I am not married to Bob McNamara, so I am never cast in the role of the easy chair. He greets me with genuine pleasure; he holds my chair before the waiter can get to it when we sit down to dinner. He does not complain about the number of bags I carry with me when I go abroad. He never objects when I point out, as I once did during dinner with the Queen of the Netherlands, that he is in error on a particular point. And when, in conversation with some economist at a meeting on world economics, I get in deep and uncharted waters, he deftly rescues me without the slightest suggestion that I ought to have known better than to have said what I just said. Instead, he sees my point and then leads me along to where I am once again on firm ground, and aware of it. Moreover, when I have a new dress or a new sweater, he notices the dress or the sweater. I like this. I like all of this. And the best part is that when I get home, Tom greets me with genuine pleasure, takes me out to dinner, holds my chair before the waiters can get to it, notices what I am wearing, is attentive to what I have done, what I have learned, whom I have seen, what they said and what I think about it.

It is, I think, the best of all possible worlds. For me. I'm less sure about Tom. I say to Tom on a November morning, "Bob has a meeting in The Hague next May twenty-third and he's asked me to go. Do you mind?"

"I don't mind right now but I might mind next May twenty-third."

"If you mind, I won't go."

But he has never said not to go, either on May 23 or on any other date. He says, "Look, the conference in The Hague sounds fascinating for you because you are fascinated with economics. It wouldn't fascinate me, and moreover I can't go even if I were fascinated. I think you ought to learn and keep doing and going, and I think it would be selfish of me to say I minded. I do mind a little but not enough to keep you from doing something you want to do and learning something you want to learn. So go, and come back learned." He gave me just enough rope.

When I get back he's overjoyed.

Except once.

That was after a trip with Bob to Africa, when a reporter— who was and for all I know may still be preparing a biography of Bob—turned what had been up to then a private arrangement into a public affair. The consequences were probably predictable, and I should have known when the reporter called me that they would be dire.

"Mrs. Braden, I understand you've just come back from a trip to Africa with Mr. McNamara."

"That's true."

"Where did you go?"

"We went to South Africa and to Zimbabwe, where Mr.

McNamara made a speech, and then we went to Victoria Falls."

"Was it romantic?"

"Yes."

Now, unless her chief interest is in measuring the quantity of water passing a given point at a given time or the speed with which the water descends from the height of the precipice to the ground, I think any woman might say that Victoria Falls was romantic. "Spectacular," "thundering," "powerful," "magnificent"—she might use those words too. But I had answered a direct question. I am not a hydrographer. To me the trip to Victoria Falls was romantic. The reporter quoted me accurately.

And I now quote Tom accurately. He had just come home from work, and I had just arrived from abroad. It was the first time we had seen each other in ten days and he was standing by the fire in the living room, his eyes blazing.

"Goddamn it, Joannie, you've got everybody in town talking and how do you think I've come out of this? I look like a cuckold or a fool. You look like an adulteress, and the only guy who isn't embarrassed is Bob McNamara."

"I'm not an adulteress, which you know perfectly well if you trust me at all, and you're not whatever that word was, and Bob McNamara didn't intend any more than you or I did that this should get into the papers. You told me I could go—at least you didn't say I shouldn't, and I've done nothing wrong."

"But it is in the papers—all over the papers [a gross exaggeration] and how do you expect me to feel about it? Am I supposed to go to Bob and demand pistols at dawn or am I supposed to commit assault and battery on you? What am I supposed to do?"

"You're not supposed to do anything you don't want to do. It's all a question of whether you care most about what you think or whether you care most about what other people might think."

"The only way other people will stop thinking is for you to stop seeing Bob McNamara."

"If that's what you want, I will stop seeing Bob McNamara; but you're doing something to yourself and to your own integrity and you're also doing something to our integrity, and I don't think it can be good for you or for us."

Tom subsided. We were both tired and we ate dinner and went to bed and sometime during the night Tom put his arm around me. "I'm sorry, Joannie. I guess we have to decide whether we want to run our lives the way we want to run them or whether we're going to run them according to the way other people might say we should run them. I've decided."

So it was reaffirmed; the never-quite-spoken original compact of our marriage. It's been a great marriage. It still is.

As to whether I'm keeping Bob McNamara from getting married, it worries me. What would I do without him?

—•—

TWENTY FOUR

Guilt and the Balancing Act

Guilt is the constant companion of the working woman. Any woman who does not list herself after the word "occupation" as "housekeeper" must learn to live with it.

If she has children, she feels guilty the moment she gets a job because a job means she can't be at home to take care of them. If she doesn't have a job, she feels equally guilty because she won't be helping to pay the mortgage or she will be forcing her husband to buy her clothes. Besides, she will be "out of it."

I'm lucky. I've never felt jealousy, and people who feel jealousy tell me it's a most unlovely affliction. But I feel guilty nearly all the time; and my guilt, I suspect, is the guilt of most women—especially women who work. Some of the things I feel guilty about fall into the following categories.

Losses: I know this is childish. Why should I care about lost objects of chiefly or entirely sentimental value? Yet I do care. I feel as though I've lost a part of my life. Of these objects there are two that matter to me most. I care that I have lost the gift which Jackie sent me after the 1960 campaign, along with the letter with which it came. It was a beautiful gift, a small silver picture frame with a bowknot of stones at the top, and the letter was also beautiful. "I truly believe Jack would not have been president without your help." Untrue, of course, but how thrilling, how magnificently thrilling to be told by Jackie that she thought so. And with that thought came her hope that maybe Tommy, who was born right after the campaign, and John Kennedy, Jr., who was born right after the campaign, maybe one of them or both would grow up to be president. The dreams of a young woman whose husband had just become president and who has just had a son as sent to a young woman who helped her and who has also just had a son. Nice dreams. I care too much about losing the proof that they were once dreamed.

I've lost most of Nelson's letters, a whole cardboard box of Nelson's letters, which I'd kept in the basement of our Oceanside house. When we moved, Stewart Alsop was in Oceanside and he helped Tom carry out old rugs and old toys and old boxes of things. And Stewart and Tom examined the box full of Nelson's letters and threw them away. I couldn't believe they threw them away. Moreover, they both laughed at me, and Tom said, "We looked at some of them and they were about pink clouds. Is there any reason to preserve Nelson Rockefeller's thoughts on pink clouds?" I didn't answer. They were a part of me. I'm sorry they are gone.

Slips through the cracks: Women of my generation grew up

in the knowledge that it was their job to care about and to take care of the furniture, the silver—the lares and penates of the household. For their mothers, it was a full-time job. For me, as it turned out, it couldn't be. How could I hold down a full-time job and also make sure that the few pieces of good furniture we own were kept polished and without the rings that people make on table tops when they set a glass down? How can any working woman do the glassware, the furniture, the silver, the odd pieces of statuary, the tops of picture frames; how can any working woman keep her house in the same dustless order that her mother did? She can try as I have tried, but she will fail as I have failed.

I hit upon a solution for the guilt I felt when I looked around our rooms. The solution was plants; large plants, plants that grow tall and are lovely, or so I decided. Tom said I had overdone the solution because there were rings on the floors where the plants stood in pots for many years. And he complained that, as the plants have grown into virtual trees over the years, he couldn't get through to see whether he owned a book he'd been looking for or even what books there were.

But the plants served a purpose. They hid the unrepaired wear and tear that eight children and the animals they brought home had inflicted upon the house—its walls and its furniture. Therefore they kept me from feeling guilty.

That's also the reason I long ago took out the overhead lighting in all the downstairs rooms. Lamps don't reveal wear and tear as much as overhead lighting. Neither do candles. Tom and I always have dinner by candlelight whether we have guests or not. We have to use candles because I have removed all the lights in the dining room. We can't see with perfect clarity what's in the dishes before us, but at least we don't notice that some of the dishes are cracked.

It is my recommendation to every working woman that she use candles on the dinner table or if she must have electric light, use lamps, set very low to the floor. If she does this, the ravages of time will not be revealed clearly, either on the furniture, the dishes, or on herself.

Money: I'm an example of the American consumer whom economists say is at least partially responsible for the fact that the United States is now a debtor nation. I spend; I do not save. And I feel guilty, particularly when my habits are troublesome to Tom or to the children.

Or, I do good. I agree to take in six Cambodians. Tom pointed out that feeding six Cambodians, even though four of them were very young, would make the opening of the monthly grocery bill an experience in horror rather than a sad surprise.

"Six Cambodians, Joannie. What in the world ever possessed you? Cambodians eat and sleep just like we do. Where are you going to put them and how are you going to feed them, and why six?"

Well, it was a long explanation, and it was made during an airline trip between the Netherlands and the United States—and that was because I decided that now was the time to tell him because when we got home, they'd probably be there. You see, I had thought when the memorandum was circulated at the State Department that it would be only four Cambodians. I had, in fact, agreed to take in a Cambodian family and I had done so because Cambodian families were being butchered. Phnom Penh was being emptied, its people, if they could read and write, were being driven out of their homes and onto the road to die somewhere up that road. And what chance for escape would a Cambodian family have that had worked for the American embassy in Phnom Penh?

Son was a man who had waited on tables at the American

embassy. Son had a wife. I thought—and so did the State Department—that he had two children, but it turned out to be four. As I said to Tom, what difference did it make to us compared to the difference that escaping made to them?

They had escaped Pol Pot. They had gotten away to a strange land. Everybody at the State Department had been asked to do what he or she could, with private means, to help Cambodian refugees who had trusted us, worked for us, and faced death when we pulled out. We had a big house. There were unoccupied rooms on the top floor. I knew about the horror in Phnom Penh. Why shouldn't I help?

And so they came, tiny people. Son, the man, and Suwat, his wife, holding their hands before them as in prayer—the Oriental gesture of greeting and goodwill—and behind them four tiny children doing the same. It was early spring and Tom was picking up sticks from the yard to use for kindling. They observed him. The next evening when he got home, he went out back to find in every corner of the yard, pagodalike arrangements of sticks piled to a couple of feet. Son, Suwat, and the children were all busy gleaning, except that they were carrying not grain, but bundles of sticks on their heads, and making new pagoda piles.

They insisted on sleeping in one bedroom on the top floor, squeezed in, virtually on top of each other, and nothing I could say would get them to spread out and take advantage of another spare room. I put this peculiarity down to Cambodian custom. Afterward, when Tom and I took them all, along with our own children, to a Fourth of July festival, I was not so sure. We were all sitting on the grass, waiting for fireworks to begin and when the first boom broke the twilight air, the children scrambled for their mother and father in panic and Son and Suwat were scared too. Nothing, during the whole evening, pried their bodies apart from one another until the last shell had burst in a darkened sky and we rose to leave the grassy park. Tom and I had put them through the recall of terror that evening. They went to their room to huddle together in sleep.

Tom had made me feel guilty about taking in the Cambodians. They cost a lot of money. Today, he's very proud he spent the money. Once in a while we visit the Cambodians in their house and they visit us. The children are in college, one with a varsity letter, all with excellent grades, all hard workers, all as proud to be Americans as they were once afraid because they were Cambodians.

The clothes closet: I got caught somewhere in the generation gap between the time when my father said of my mother, "Mother needs a new dress," and the time when women really do need a new dress. To my mother, a new dress was a pleasure and a gift. To me, it's a necessity. I have to go to work in it. My mother never earned a penny in her life—nor my grandmother, nor very many of the mothers and grandmothers of my generation of middle-class Americans. So I grew up on the assumption that my husband would be, as my father and grandfather had been, a dress provider. He turned out to be no such thing.

As I recall, there was no ultimatum. No anger. He said he liked my new dress. He understood that a woman who goes to work each morning has to spend more on clothes than one who does not. And he acknowledged my contributions to the general welfare. "You're buying the Christmas presents for the kids. You're buying the plants and the flowers. But you're earning a lot of money. From now on, you ought to pay for your own clothes." I can't recall when Tom made this plea. It wasn't right after we were married. But it wasn't long after. And I don't recall that I protested. It must have seemed fair to me then, and it seems fair to me now. But partly as a result there is a room in our house which ought to have a sign hanging over the door, inscribed in large letters, "Joan's Guilt."

The room contains literally hundreds of dresses—old dresses, much-worn dresses, dresses that were mistakes and are hardly worn at all. They have accumulated over years and are stashed away on hangers, and the children go into the room from time to time to see whether they can find something useful, brilliant, or fitting. But I never do. It would remind me of guilt measured in hundreds of dollars which I once had and which I spent on clothes.

There is one more form of guilt and maybe I shouldn't mention it because it is a guilt known to many women and is seldom or never mentioned by them. But by not mentioning it, we run the risk of not counting it as among the trials of being a woman. I don't say it happens to every woman. But I doubt that it ever happens to a man. This is the way it happened to me.

It was almost midnight when we got home from the party and we sat for a while in the big, richly furnished living room in Connecticut, discussing what a beautiful party it had been. Shielded candles had been placed on each of the broad brick steps which curved downward toward the swimming pool and the greensward beyond. There must have been fifty steps in all, yet they were so wide that you didn't have to give a thought to the sweep of your dress as you went down those stairs.

And the tables beyond the pool had been exquisitely arranged. Each table of eight had seemed set apart in privacy as if you had been dining with seven good friends, though there must have been ten tables of eight along the line of big trees bordering the lawn and the pool.

It had been, the three of us decided, a perfect party. I went up to my room and to bed unaware that the perfect party was not to be the climax of the evening.

I awoke an hour or so later to a pleasantly pungent scent, faintly sweet, and strong in both nostrils. I opened my eyes, and there was a face leaning over mine. At first I started in fear; then when I saw the face, I started in a different kind of fear. It was the face of the man to whom I had just said good night. He was prone on the bed in white pajamas, his eyes looking directly into mine, both hands holding under my nose a small flask, source of the pungent odor. Then he whispered, a deep whisper, distinct but almost silent, "Try a little more of this. I've had some too."

It was my host, my friend, a man I've known and cared about for half my life. Also, the husband of one of my best friends, presumably asleep, down the hall.

I've been over that scene one hundred times in afterthought, and I don't see what I could have done. Screamed? Fought? At the cost of wrecking long friendships, maybe even a marriage? I summoned a hoarse whisper in return. "Get out of here. Get out of here right now."

Guilt is irrational. There is no reason why I should have felt guilt after that occasion, but I did and I told Mrs. Longworth that I did. She said, "You can waste a lot of time feeling guilty." I doubt that Mrs. Longworth ever felt guilty in her life.

But I think guilt is the price a working woman pays to keep her sense of balance. Her whole life is a balancing act. She has her husband, and he has to come first except when the job has to come first. And the job has to come first, except when the children have to come first—or friends or parents or relatives. Sometimes they have to come first.

All the while she has to keep her mind, or some part of her mind, touching the center, somewhere inside. As long as she knows she can feel that center and knows when she's straying from it, but knows that she's touching it, she's all right. If she strays too far from it or forgets where it is, she's all askew and doesn't feel right about herself. She's lost her balance. That's what I did, or almost did, when I met Kirk Douglas.

It was a dinner party in Beverly Hills at the home of Jules Stein, who used to be the head of MCA. I was seated next to Kirk Douglas. Shortly after I took my chair, I had what I can only describe as a chemical reaction.

Chemical reactions begin in the mind and move downward quite rapidly until you feel the tingling all the way to your toes.

Kirk Douglas introduced himself to me, and I introduced myself to him. He began asking me questions about whether I thought he should continue to make movies for a studio or whether he should make his own movies. "You see, I have this problem and I'm not sure what the answer is. Maybe you can help me."

I was fascinated by the reasons he found on both sides of the question, first arguing one side then posing arguments on the other, each counterargument blocking the effectiveness of the previous one.

So I asked questions intended to help him reach a conclusion because I didn't know enough about it to have a viewpoint. Suddenly, as I was asking him some trivial question, he turned to me, looked me full in the eyes and said, "I want to be your best friend."

That's when I had the chemical reaction. Maybe I'm wrong about the mind. Maybe chemical reactions begin in the eyes. Kirk Douglas is a very good-looking man. Anyhow, I resisted a strong inclination to reach down under the tablecloth and rub my toes because they were tingling. And I think I said thank you to his remark about being my best friend, but maybe I just said oh.

We were about to rise from the table, and I could still feel the tingling. And Kirk said, "Would you have lunch with me the next time you're in Los Angeles?" I said yes, and just then Kirk's wife, Anne, came up to us, glamorously beautiful in a white dress that made her blue eyes sparkle. "I see," she said to her husband, "that you've found your new best friend."

Balance. You have to keep your balance. I never knew any woman who balanced her responsibilities as gracefully and completely as Anne Douglas nor any who watched her husband try to balance his with more profound understanding, tolerance, and amusement.

She knew very well what she was doing. My guess is that she could have recited almost word for word the conversation that had taken place between her husband and me. My guess is that she knew all about chemical reactions and tingling in the toes.

And I also guess that she knew very well that there is a human tendency to confuse chemical reactions with love. I know that too. So I told myself to stop it, right now. Nevertheless, the thought of Kirk, his looks, the famous dimpled chin, the direct blue eyes, but more important the vitality and the enthusiasm, stayed with me. I fantasized. My husband didn't know I was fantasizing but I was, no matter how much I told myself to stop it right now.

And then I saw him again in New York. Roger Stevens and I had just been to a new Joseph Cotten play. We stopped in afterward at Sardi's and there he was at a long table in the back of the restaurant, a table filled with actors and writers and producers, all waiting for the reviews to come in. And there was Anne, also at the table. She rose and seized Kirk by the arm, "Aren't you going to say hello to your new best friend?"

Something happened at that moment. Happened in exactly the way Anne Douglas wanted it to happen and that in my better judgment I did too. The relationship was sealed. I don't say the chemistry disappeared. But the tingle faded, as tingles do between friends. Kirk Douglas is my friend. Anne Douglas is also my friend, one of my best friends. I got my balance. We're all three balanced. We manage the balance very well.

And wouldn't it have been ridiculous to have a secret affair with a man who can't walk down any street in any city in the world without instantly drawing a crowd? Or who can't escape recognition on any village lane?

We went ice skating one time when Kirk and Anne came to see us in Washington. In the car on the way to the rink, Kirk put on a ski mask. It was a small neighborhood rink, and I wondered about it. Was he being a little self-important? But after we had skated for an hour or more, Kirk sat down to take off his skates. Then he removed the mask. The entire crowd of skaters surrounded him, children pointing fingers. "You look like Kirk Douglas."

"Funny you should mention that." Kirk had his street shoes on and was eyeing a route of escape. "Other people have told me the same thing." The voice gave him away.

"You are Kirk Douglas. Hey, he's Kirk Douglas." Adults joined the crowd and teenagers skated up and thrust their arms out to touch him. Suddenly, I noticed that nobody was skating anymore; everybody on the rink was gathered around Kirk. Then he leapt over the wooden railing and was safely in the car by the time we made our way out. Tom retrieved his skates and took them to the rental desk. It was fun watching somebody get mobbed. I noticed that Kirk seemed to enjoy it too, but as he said later, "You have to get away because what are you going to do for an encore?"

Kirk Douglas helped me at a point in my life when his help counted a lot, and when, I think, his help counted to other people, not just me.

There came a time when the Kennedy Center, on which thousands of people had spent their labor and love, was built;

complete, finished. By that time, of course, Jackie had left Washington and I no longer carried her proxy as well as my own vote on the center's board of trustees. I had also by that time recovered my temper after a furious spat with Roger Stevens, the center's director.

But I wasn't at all sure that Roger Stevens had recovered from the fury I had directed at him. When you get angry and are rude to a friend, you think you're cutting him off. In fact, you are cutting yourself off. In time, you come to realize this, painfully.

My spat with Roger had occurred long before the center was completed. He had asked me to arrange a White House dinner party for a large group of contributors to the center. I had called Jackie, who had set a date. Roger then asked for a change in the date, and I called Jackie; she obliged. There followed a series of calls from me to Roger to get the guest list because no matter how much money you want to give or how much you care about the theater or the opera, you have to be cleared by the Secret Service in order to attend a dinner at the White House. Finally, the guest list was ready, and I, still in Oceanside, got a telephone call from Roger. I remember it was a Saturday because Tom was at home and in the bedroom when I took the call, and he couldn't help hearing my end of the conversation.

But Roger's end of the conversation was the reason for mine. He said, "I'm sorry, Joannie, but something has come up and we'll have to change that date for the White House dinner again."

"Roger, I changed the date once. That was because you didn't have the guest list ready. Now you say something has come up. You want me to call Jackie and ask her to change the date again. I won't, Roger. But I'll tell you what I will do. I'll resign." And then I hung up the telephone.

Tom, as I say, was standing in the bedroom. "Joannie, no

matter what, you must never hang up on anybody. It's more than rude. It's a declaration of war."

But I was still seething. I went out to the beach for a walk and took four or five children with me. To have to call Jackie again, ask her again to change the date, seemed to me embarrassing and unnecessary.

Was I to repeat Roger's excuse? Was I to say to Jackie that "something has come up"? It seemed to me that Roger was asking me to be rude to the wife of the president of the United States and that I was justified in being rude to him instead. All this I said to myself as I watched the children race each other and the fingers of water on the sand that waves make after breaking on the beach. We walked all the way to the pier and back, and when we all climbed the stairs to the house, it still seemed to me that I was right and Roger was wrong. Then a young lady from England who had come over for a year to help take care of the children said to me, "Mrs. Braden, the president called."

"What president? President of what?"

"I don't know. He said to call Washington and ask for the president."

It was *the* president. John Kennedy answered the telephone himself, and the conversation was brief. A cool deep voice, "Joannie, you're not really going to resign, are you?"

After the way I had behaved on the telephone, even months later, even after the death of John Kennedy and the half-conscious binding that his death imposed upon all who worked to build a monument in his name, I hesitated to go back to Roger Stevens and ask him for anything.

But Kirk Douglas said I had to. He got Rosalind Russell to back him up. He said that I had to go to Roger and tell him that the Kennedy Center wasn't finished, and that to build a cultural center in the nation's capital, place it right next to where the

Potomac sweeps south on its way to sea, spend millions of dollars on this center, count it among the capital's chief attractions right up there with the Lincoln Memorial, and then leave out one of the nation's principal achievements in culture, that is to say, the art of filmmaking, would be an error so noteworthy that future historians would not be the first to complain.

I thought Kirk was right. Rosalind Russell thought Kirk was right. Jackie thought Kirk was right. And so I went to Roger and told him what we all thought and what I knew he was unlikely to want to hear. (Mistakenly we all thought his love of the theater would prevent him being interested in movies.) Roger Stevens is a presence. His size (he is over six feet tall) ensures that he stands out in any room he enters. Maybe that fact has enabled him to go through life making millions in real estate and betting on Broadway plays without ever giving anybody any evidence that he dominates. He is affable, kindly, soft-spoken, and never loses his temper. He reveals distaste, strong disagreement, or anger only by an odd hardening of his usually bland, blue eyes. When Roger Stevens hears something he doesn't wish to hear and knows that a confrontation looms, the bland blue eyes darken, as with a storm at sea. You don't have to wait for him to speak as in time he will speak, and rather softly. You just watch his eyes.

So Roger Stevens listened while I spoke and I watched his eyes. When I finished, the eyes were a calm, bland blue.

"Let's go for a walk," he said, and we walked through the vastness of the Kennedy Center with its Eisenhower Theater, its Concert Hall, its Opera Hall, office, and foyer, and finally to a smaller space which Roger said had been set aside for storage. "Storage of what?"

"Anything and everything. Old furniture. Stage furniture, settings. How would it do if we placed a movie theater here and ran it out to an entrance in the foyer?"

And so it was done. The Kennedy Center had a movie theater, the American Film Institute headed by George Stevens (no relation to Roger) moved in, and now the Kennedy Center not only has a movie theater but a museum of the classics among all the pictures that have been made during America's long love with the screen.

The Kennedy Center holds an annual gala attended by people from all over the country, who are wined and dined in return for high-priced seats at an event staged by George Stevens.

It is a brilliant affair, attended by the president and his wife, who sit in their box, surrounded by the event's honorees: men and women who have achieved greatness in music and dance, on stage and in film. George Stevens prepares a film history of each artist's life and achievements and after it is shown, the honorees stand in the president's box and the president and first lady rise to applaud. The entire audience rises to applaud along with them. It's exciting. Tom and I go when we can afford it or when some friend invites us. We went one night when the honoree for the art of the motion picture was Jimmy Stewart.

The tribute to Stewart consisted of excerpts from his best films, *Mr. Smith Goes to Washington, Rear Window, Spirit of St. Louis, It's a Wonderful Life, Strategic Air Command;* and Stewart stood, handsome and tall, white-haired now. The audience thundered and then a strange thing happened, which caused a cheering crowd to cry. Air Force cadets were on stage in tribute to Stewart when suddenly a familiar figure strode out from the wings, took center stage, stood at attention, and gave Stewart a military salute. It was Chuck Yeager, saluting the man who had been his commanding officer during World War II.

That was pretty emotional. Everybody was wiping his eyes while applauding and Tom was too, and afterward he asked me about it.

"You were smiling, Joannie, when Yeager was saluting. Everybody else was crying."

"I was," I said, "thinking of something else." And it was true. It was great, stirring, fitting, and I was glad I was there to see it. But I was thinking of that walk I took with Roger Stevens and about the insistent advice of my "best friend."

Ancient Truths

I make no pretense of the discovery of deep philo-sophical truths. But I now know some things that I didn't know before and that I find some of my children didn't or don't know and that I should have known because people had told me. But what teachers, friends, or parents tell us we often ignore until we learn it from our own experience. I am old enough to have had experience, and experienced enough to have rediscovered many ancient truths.

Ancient truth number one: When men are younger, they're stronger and when they're older, they're better-looking. I said it was a man's world. Look around you at the way men age.

Here's Kirk Douglas, lean, muscular, a symbol of masculinity at seventy-one. What woman of any age could look at Kirk and not find herself attracted? Look back at white-haired Stuart Symington, the handsomest man on the beach or in the office. Look back at David Bruce, erect in posture, looking at sixty as I imagine his idol, George Washington, must have looked. At sixty, David worried about his age. I once made a promise to him that if he'd stop talking about it, I wouldn't have any more children. I didn't keep my promise, but he kept his. When he died at seventy-nine, he was as dashing, as exquisitely groomed, as sought after by women of all ages as any man I've ever known.

I know it's a generalization and that setting up Kirk Douglas, David Bruce, and Stuart Symington as examples of aging among American men would not meet George Gallup's standard for sampling. But if you count your aging friends on the fingers of one hand or even two, I think you will agree that your aging men friends are more attractive than your aging lady friends. It is unfair; but it is true.

Some men rub it in. Kirk Douglas, many years ago, opened an invitation from a lady who had once been "leading." "My God," he exclaimed to me, "she's inviting me to her fiftieth birthday party. I'll never dance with her again."

And Stewart Alsop, reflecting on the faded appearance of a woman whom he had once placed in the category of "those in whose company I must resist a powerful urge to try to leap into bed," remarked to me, "Women, unlike men, experience a *coup de vieux*." I'm glad he's not here to take secret assessment of whether I have or have not yet experienced that *coup de vieux*.

Which leads me to ancient truth number two: Lie about your age if you want to. Every woman does. Women know they don't age as well as men. They know it's a dirty trick God played upon them and, in a sometimes successful attempt to escape the dirty trick, they lie, not only to the world but to themselves. This lying has been going on for at least three hundred years, so eighteenth-century novelists confirm. I don't know when it started, but I suspect that while Ponce de León was slashing through jungles in search of the restorative fountain, Madame Ponce de León had already found a simpler remedy.

I know I have. We were seated at the table, all the children and their father and me in celebration of my birthday, an occasion which I have insisted upon over the years for no other reason than that it makes an occasion for celebration. I like celebrations. We have nine celebrations at our house every year. Tom won't celebrate his birthday, and I'm sorry he won't because then we could have ten.

Anyhow, we make a big occasion of my birthday, and I remind everybody in advance. Tom brings me roses and the children bring presents, and if they are away, they try to get back and if they can't get back, they call.

On this occasion, we were all at the table and Nicholas, who was then twelve years old, said offhandedly but quite seriously, "Mom, you're twenty-eight years old now, aren't you?"

His remark was greeted with such laughter and derision from all around the table that poor Nicholas blushed in embarrassment and I had to take his part. So I said quite firmly, that yes, I was indeed twenty-eight and on each succeeding birthday I have numbered my years according to the chronology established by Nicholas. He is twenty-three now, which means that on my next birthday, I shall be forty. I brook no argument to the contrary and when I say, as I shall, "This is my fortieth birthday party," everyone at the table will nod in solemn agreement.

It is my intention to keep this charade going for as long as I can, which may be for as long as I live; or if I should live as long as Mrs. Longworth lived, I may drift into the noncommittal status she always adopted for the intrusive at her annual birthday parties. "I have," she would say with a certain pride and a twinkle in her eyes, "reached the category of 'an ancient.'" When I get to be "an ancient," I shall say so. In the meantime, I shall lie.

Ancient truth number three: Never ever tell a white lie because you think that white lies give other people pleasure and don't matter very much. Eugene Black was president of the World Bank during the Eisenhower administration, a handsome and debonair Southerner as well as a distinguished one, and the only man I ever knew who wore his hats at such a rakish angle. When I first met him he was not wearing a hat but was lounging by a swimming pool, reading a book. I asked him what book it was. "*Titus Andronicus,*" he replied. "Have you read it?"

"No," I answered, and he said, "You should. I shall send you a copy."

Which he did, and a month or so later, he invited me to play golf with him. "Have you read *Titus Andronicus*?" he asked as we were strolling off the first tee. Why did I say yes? Because I wanted to please him? Because I wanted him to think I was flattered by his attention? One or the other, I suppose, but Eugene Black was a banker and bankers are blessed with suspicious minds. Eugene Black stopped walking toward his ball and looked at me directly. "What," he demanded, "happened to her tongue?"

How dared he do that to me? I blushed and stammered and confessed. He forgave me and we became fast friends, but he taught me a lesson I shall never forget.

Ancient truth number four: Never ever fail to check the address on the envelope with the letter you are putting into it. Once you have it in the envelope, take a peek. Make sure.

It was in 1960, just after the inauguration, that I wrote a long letter to Nelson Rockefeller, explaining why I hadn't taken a job in the Kennedy administration, embellishing a little bit on the jobs I had been offered. At the same time, I wrote a long letter to Bobby Kennedy, telling him that I wished I were in Washington and that I envied those who were.

I accidentally put the letter to Bobby in the envelope addressed to Nelson, and I put the letter to Nelson in the envelope addressed to Bobby.

Tom and I were playing golf on a subsequent Saturday afternoon when a messenger came out to get me in a golf cart. "Mrs. Braden, you have a phone call at the clubhouse from the attorney general of the United States."

"I have a letter," said the attorney general of the United States, "which begins 'Dear Nelson.' Do you want me to read it?"

I knew Bobby pretty well. "I know perfectly well," I said, "that you already have."

On Monday came a call from Nelson's office. There was a letter addressed to the governor, his secretary told me, that she thought was meant for someone else. Would I like it returned? When I got the letter back I sent it on to Bobby with a note: "This is the way a gentleman behaves when a lady makes a mistake."

Ancient truth number five: Always carry with you anything essential for the next day's meeting or pleasure. Never ever dress casually and for comfort on an airplane ride unless you can carry on the plane the dress or suit you intend to wear to the next day's meeting. Never ever put that bag in the trunk of the car in which you ride to the airport.

That lesson reminds me of Tom's 1967 four-door Lincoln Continental convertible that he still maintains, parked outside the house, sheltered in the winter, repainted every three or four years, and still roadworthy. I hate the car. It is that car from which Nicholas fell at age four when it was proceeding on a crowded highway at seventy miles an hour. (The rear doors open to the rear and, when the car is in motion, to the fullness of the wind. A child who plays with the door handle as Nicholas did can be caught by the wind as Nicholas was.) It is that car which I lent to Robert Kennedy in June 1968 for his last big rally, and which was bashed, dented, and all but stripped by a mob of enthusiasts. I was the one who had to tell Tom I had lent his now-ruined car to Bobby.

But those are not the memories the Lincoln evokes and which prove the wisdom of ancient truth number five. That was the car with the monsterlike folding trunk where I put my clothes and my broadcasting equipment—"Joan Braden will be reporting next from Venezuela," I had said on air the night before—when we departed the house in order to join the governor of New York on a three-week fact-finding mission for President Nixon to Latin America.

It was a cheerful trip as far as Andrews Air Force Base. All the children came and we sang all the old songs of Oceanside days. "It's a long long way from Richmond to Danville and it's marked by a mighty steep grade," Tom would begin in a deep voice and we all joined in.

We parked the car out on the tarmac where Nelson's big model of Air Force One was waiting, and Tom pressed the button for the trunk to open. It didn't open. It wouldn't open. It was unyielding, at first to the prying of a tire iron, then to a crowbar borrowed from some attendant Marines, then to four crowbars plied by four strong attendant Marines. Nelson sent a messenger out from his plane. He would wait. We drove a mile and a half to a service station and a twenty-dollar bill enlisted the immediate attention of the mechanic on duty. It still wouldn't open.

Without clothes, I might have gone. Without the camera and recording equipment essential to covering the story, there was no point in going. Sadly we all watched Nelson's plane take off. We didn't sing any songs at all on the way home.

Ancient truth number six: Never ever go to a dinner party when you're ill. Doctors will say this for the well-being of those whom your illness may infect. I say it for your own selfish sake. In the first place, you feel like hell. More important, you look like hell. The competition may finish you off. I learned the lesson at Bobby Kennedy's birthday party, which was given for him by his sister Pat and her husband, Peter Lawford. Despite a temperature of one hundred and four and despite the advice of my husband, I went. The room was crowded, and Bobby and I were sitting on the floor talking when I heard a voice from a corner of the room which without turning around I instantly recognized as that of my husband. "Good God, who is that?" And then Pat nudged Bobby, who was deep in conversation with me. She nudged him again, "Bobby, I'd like you to meet Marilyn Monroe."

Bobby turned and I turned and there she was—blond, beautiful, red lips at the ready, clad in a black-lace dress which barely concealed the tips of her perfectly formed breasts and tightly fitted every curve of the body unparalleled.

Bobby paid attention. He sat next to her at dinner; and around our table of eight were Kim Novak, Angie Dickinson, and me. Who the men between us were I can't remember. I can only remember the women and the dresses which showed off their bosoms. There I was in a high-necked dress. Tom always told me that my breasts did not reveal the ravages of eight suckling children, but I knew better. I was glad I'd worn a high-necked dress, sorry that I was sick, tried to make up for it by conversing as brightly as I knew how, and was suddenly silenced by the intervention of Miss Monroe.

From her tiny black purse, she extracted a folded piece of paper, and unfolded it to reveal, in bright lipstick, a list of questions which she proceeded to put to Bobby. The first was, What does an attorney general do?

There were some giggles from somewhere at the table and the man next to me whispered, "Don't. She's had a sad and lonely childhood and a sad and lonely life and she has no self-confidence at all."

Miss Monroe continued to read the large lipstick-written questions, and each was as innocent and childlike as the first, totally without guile or pretense except perhaps for the medium in which they were written, and Bobby was enthralled.

I've heard a lot about what happened after that first meeting between Bobby and Marilyn Monroe. I hope he helped her. I couldn't have rivaled Marilyn Monroe, Angie Dickinson, or Kim Novak at any time. But I'd have done better that night if I hadn't had a temperature of one hundred and four.

Ancient truth number seven: Never use age as an excuse. As Dorothy Parker declared in her poem "Little Old Lady in Lavender Silk" at the age of seventy-seven come August:

> *"When you come to this time of abatement*
> *To this passing from Summer to Fall*
> *It is manners to issue a statement*
> *As to what you got out of it all."*

Now I'm a great many years away from being entitled to issue a statement. But I'm far enough along the road to be able to say with some certainty that there are means other than lying by which you can stave off the day when you feel it mannerly to make one.

Don't use age as an excuse for not caring about how you

look, even if nobody is looking but you. How would you like to look in the mirror and not be able to say I'm fine or I will be fine in a minute? Don't let age make you decide to quit a job because you want some time to enjoy yourself. That's a trap. There is no enjoyment more profound than doing the best you can at whatever you're doing. And don't use your age as an excuse for slouching a little more than you used to or walking less briskly than you used to walk. Or changing from tennis to golf. Get out and play. You may not play as well as you used to, but you can play as briskly as you can.

Ancient truth number eight: There are changes ahead and you can't do anything about them, so welcome them if you can. I came home the other night from a week abroad and I stood in the eerie silence that only an empty house can invoke. There was no shouted greeting, "Hey, Mom, you're home." And then I remembered that during my absence the last child had left the house, and that meant that all of them were gone, not gone for a day or so but gone for good. Living elsewhere, working elsewhere, leaving Tom, who would be home soon, and me with eight empty bedrooms and a silent front hall.

The taxi driver set the bags down in the front hall while the dogs barked, and then closed the door. Suddenly there came from the room far back of the kitchen, the sound of a great many people in conversation—making declarations, asking questions, responding to each other in voices loud and soft, all mixed together and punctuated from time to time with a deep bass guffaw.

It was the bird, the parrot given to my daughter Nancy nearly twenty years ago, still in his cage in the far-off room back of the kitchen, running through his sequence of all of us assembled at dinner—laughing, questioning, asserting, and subject at intervals to Tom's deep bass guffaw.

I stood there and listened in amusement. Parrots live a long time, and it is quite possible that fifty years from now that parrot may be giving his imitation of our family at dinner to the consternation of browsers in a pet shop.

For a moment I was rather sad. Nobody here. Everybody gone, gone with the goats and the monkey and the lamb and the boa constrictor. Come to think of it, even Tom's great guffaw is mostly gone because I can't tell him as many funny stories as eight children once did.

But he would be home soon. He always looks more handsome to me when I've been away from him for a while, and he always asks a lot of questions and has almost as much to tell me as I have to tell him. Maybe he'd take me out to dinner, maybe we'd go to a movie. It was exciting to think about. So I left the bags for him to carry up (I still have that back) and I went upstairs to shower and put on a face.

I'm not nearly as old as Miss Parker's little old lady in lavender silk but I'm old enough to know that she is dead right about what you get out of it all:

> *"So I'll say though reflection unnerves me*
> *And pronouncements I dodge as I can*
> *That I think (if my memory serves me)*
> *There was nothing more fun than a man."*

ABOUT THE AUTHOR

———●———

Longtime aide to Nelson Rockefeller, Washington TV host, key Kennedy campaign worker, renowned hostess, public relations ace, wife of syndicated columnist and CNN's *Crossfire* combatant Tom Braden, and mother of the *Eight Is Enough* brood, JOAN BRADEN has long been a major player in the Washington power game. She currently lives with her husband in Chevy Chase, Maryland, where they are joined from time to time by some of their children.